Cucina & Famiglia

Cucina &

William Morrow and Company, Inc. New York

Famiglia

Two Italian Families Share Their Stories, Recipes, and Traditions

Joan Tropiano Tucci *and* Gianni Scappin

with Mimi Shanley Taft

Food styling by A. J. Battifarano
Prop styling by Barbara Fritz

It is the policy of William Morrow and Company, Inc., and its imprints and affiliates, recognizing the importance of preserving what has been written, to print the books we publish on acid-free paper, and we exert our best efforts to that end.

Library of Congress Cataloging-in-Publication Data

Tucci, Joan Tropiano
Cucina & famiglia : two Italian families share their stories, recipes, and traditions / Joan Tropiano Tucci and Gianni Scappin, with Mimi Shanley Taft.—1st ed.
p. cm.
ISBN 0-688-15902-8
1. Cookery, Italian. I. Scappin, Gianni. II. Taft, Mimi. III. Title.
TX723.T79 1999
641.5945—dc21 99-18805
CIP

Printed in the United States of America

First Edition

2 3 4 5 6 7 8 9 10

BOOK DESIGN BY LEAH CARLSON-STANISIC

www.williammorrow.com

Contents

Foreword

Throughout my childhood, almost every night in the middle of dinner, my father would shake his head and ask, "What does the rest of the world eat?" What he meant was that the food my mother had prepared was so good that it seemed inconceivable that anyone else could be eating as well as we were. I agreed with him every time.

Now, as an adult who has traveled, not extensively but I would say enough to have experienced a number of cultures and their cuisines, I think I still agree with my father. Not that I haven't discovered incredibly delicious dishes outside the old homestead, but for consistent ingenuity and excellence, my mother's cooking is hard to beat. I am all too aware of the cliché at work here: the eldest son of an Italian-American family saying, in essence, that no one cooks as well as his mother. But in this case it is not mere sentiment that leads me to this conclusion, but a sensitive and discerning palate.

Whether this palate is a God-given gift or something that has been honed over the years, I cannot say. I would think it is a little bit of both. Having grown up in a household that was "food obsessed," I cannot help but put a more than ordinary emphasis on what goes into my mouth and how it tastes. My family is one that spends hours deciding what will be made for a certain meal, days preparing that meal, and while that meal is being eaten, discussing not only its merits and its faults but what it tasted like when prepared at such and such a restaurant, or by this or that family member or friend, and what it really should be served with and when it was first eaten, which inevitably leads to a discussion of where it was first eaten and with what and how that dish was prepared and how one day wouldn't it really be nice to make that dish, which really is one of the best dishes ever eaten, though it could never compare to a dish once eaten in . . . etc., etc., etc. Food, above politics, art, or personal matters, is the subject to which we return over and over again. Possibly because we derive nourishment from it not only physically but also spiritually, the creation of a great meal is perhaps the ultimate artistic endeavor. Edible art.

My parents instilled in my sisters and me a great respect for our heritage and its traditions. Consequently, in my work I feel it is necessary to explore and celebrate from whom and where I come. The film *Big Night* was born partly from this need. In writing it with my cousin Joseph Tropiano, we hoped not only to offer a positive view of Italians (i.e., no gangsters) but also a more humanistic view, one that would show the complexity of this extraordinary people. Though the old adage "Most of the world eats to live, but Italians live to eat" is a bit heavy handed, it is somewhat based in truth. We had aimed to bring to the screen this truth and all the intricacies it involved.

During the final stages of writing the script, Isabella Rossellini was kind enough to make it possible for me to visit any of her friend Pino Luongo's six restaurants so that I might continue my research. I chose Le Madri, where I was introduced to the head chef, Gianni Scappin. For the next year and a half I would visit him and he would teach me whatever I asked to be taught. We would also spend hours just talking about food, restaurants, Italy versus America, my hopes for the film, and his hopes for his own restaurant. As I got to know Gianni better, I realized that not only was he an intelligent, witty, and generous person, but he was also an artist. Just to watch him create a meal is fascinating. He is a whirlwind of passion and professionalism and if you are ever fortunate enough to taste the results of his culinary expertise, you will understand what I mean when I use the word "artist."

Since the release of *Big Night,* people have always asked whether there would be an accompanying cookbook. Since the film has no real recipes to speak of save timpáno (which, for the first time ever, can be found in the following pages), no such book could be written. There is, however, a strong connection between the film and this book. I've always felt that *Big Night* was partly about respect for one's heritage and the pursuit of truth in one's art. To me this cookbook embodies those themes. It is a collection of recipes by people I love, who love to cook because they love their past and want to pass its truths on to the next generation. In each recipe my parents, Gianni, and Mimi have worked hard to document those often elusive touches and techniques that result in a great meal as opposed to an ordinary one. By worrying over each detail they have, for the first time in either the Tucci or Scappin family history, committed to paper the ingredients needed to create a collection of extraordinary meals. This cookbook will help you understand the root of our obsession with food and will, we hope, become a source for many of your own unforgettable meals.

Acknowledgments

JOAN

To Mom and Pop Tropiano and Nonna and Nonno Tucci—this book is a tribute to you from me and Stan. During our childhood and adult lives you taught us that growing, preserving, and preparing foods is truly a part of life. We have such marvelous happy memories. Thank you.

A special thank-you to our son, Stanley, without whom this book would not have been written, and his wife, Kate, for tasting many recipes and hosting the *timpáno* parties. Also to our grandchildren for their support and tasting of recipes.

To my husband, Stan, for his collaboration on the book, which includes his Italian translations of titles for each recipe, writing, proofreading, dishwashing, tasting, encouragement, and pride in his Italian heritage.

To our children, Stanley, Gina, and Christine, for their support and encouragement. We are especially thankful and pleased with their dedication to continuing the Italian cultural and culinary heritage.

To Mimi Taft, our writer, for her patience and friendship, and for keeping the testing as accurate as possible. Also for the friendship of her family and her parents, Isobel and Paul, in tasting the recipes.

To Gianni, who is now our adopted son, for his great sense of humor and patience with me during the testing of the recipes, and to his wife, Laura, who was our best audience during our cooking routine.

Stan and I are also eternally grateful to our grandparents and parents for the cultural and culinary heritage they have passed on to us. It is a wonderful feeling, knowing you possess something special with so much history.

Thanks also to the extended family of brothers, sisters, and relatives who have contributed in many ways to the making of this book.

To Marcy Posner of William Morris Agency, who guided us through our first cookbook effort.

To Pam Hoenig, associate publisher, and the cheerful staff of William Morrow & Company for believing in us and making the creation of our first book such a pleasure. And thanks to the designer, Leah Carlson-Stanisic; the photographer, Dennis Gottlieb; his assistant, Matt; the food stylist, A. J. Battifarano; and her assistant, Amy.

To George and Rita Vogliano and George and Helen Manizza, for their help in proofreading and their extensive knowledge of Italian food and language.

To all our friends who offered to taste and lend their support during this project.

Finally, we would like to thank Kristina Gorla of Filippo Berio Olive Oil, Aldo Rafanelli of Remy Amérique Incorporated for Antinori Wines, Julia Stamboulus of All-Clad Cookware, and Brian Maynard of KitchenAid mixer for their generous donation of products that greatly enhanced the process of creating this book.

GIANNI

First and foremost I would like to thank my wonderful and lovely wife, Laura, who has always believed in me, even when I didn't believe in myself. Her work as a nutritionist and cookbook author was a great help to me on this project.

I would like to thank my entire family, especially my mother, Maria-Bertilla, and my father, Luigi, whose examples have inspired me in life and in the kitchen. Thanks to my sisters, Livia, Catterina, and Bruna, and to my brother, Mario, their families, all my nieces and nephews, and my aunts and uncles for all the wonderful memories I have of growing up in Italy. And I especially want to thank my son, Christen.

Thanks to Laura's family, her father, Philip, and her mother, Jane, for their help and support both in Italy and in America.

I want to thank the entire Tucci family—really my second family—with special thanks to Stanley for the fun times we have had in the kitchen and for bringing me together with his mother, Joan, to create this book.

Thanks to my many friends in Italy, including Luigi Corra, Franco Pigato, Gianni Viero, Paolo Corrandin, and Attilio Nichele, whose honesty I have always been able to count on and with whom I have shared many food experiences. To Francesco, a great pastry chef who supported my restaurant in Italy, and to Daniela at the Ponticello bakery for the delicious bread she baked for my restaurant. Thanks to Sergio Guiotto and my other colleagues at the Recoaro Terme Culinary Institute, where my career began. To Ettore Alzetta, who opened the door for me to come to America, and to Ferdinando, who taught me how to organize a large kitchen while I was working with him at the Excelsior Hotel in Venice.

I want to thank Michele Castellano, who demonstrated his belief in me by giving me the opportunity to be creative at his restaurant in New York long before the new wave of Italian food had become popular. And thanks to the entire BICE organization, especially Roberto Ruggeri, who let me express myself in their kitchens. Thanks to Marta Pullini for her great support of my career and, above all, for her friendship. To Pino Luongo for giving me the chance to be a part of his company and to the crew at Le Madri, especially Alan, Gerardo, Sergio, Juan, Jose, and many others.

Thanks to my first American friend, Glenn Dopf, and to his warm and welcoming family. To Peter Reiss and his family for being there for me during the high and low points of my life. And to my newest friend, once lost but found again, Donato. Thanks to my coworker Dan Kish and his family and to Francesco Tonelli for their friendships. To the entire Culinary Institute of America and its numerous students who have been an inspiration to me.

Final thanks to Mimi Taft for her help with my English, her talent as a writer, and her work in finalizing the recipes in this book.

MIMI

I want to thank Stanley, Joan, Stan, and Gianni for giving me the opportunity to work with them on this project. I loved the whole process and learned so much as a writer, cook, and collaborator. Thank you all for your trust and for welcoming me into your families.

Thanks to my family and friends for sampling dishes, proofreading, and commenting on the book. Special thanks to my husband, Lloyd, a great cook in his own right, and my children, Daniel, Virginia, and Bennett—budding food critics all. I greatly appreciate the sound advice and support of my agent, Susan Ginsburg of Writers House. And particular thanks to Pam Hoenig at William Morrow for her discerning editorial guidance.

Introduction

JOAN

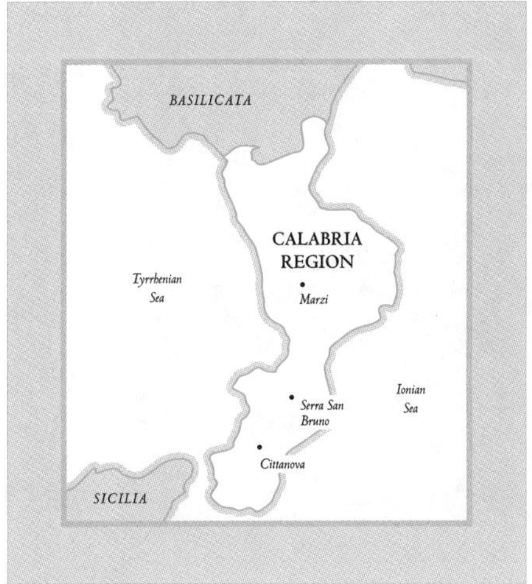

My father, Vincenzo Tropiano, was born in 1896 in Cittanova, Italy. He emigrated to the United States in 1917, after serving as a battlefield medic during World War I. He came looking for work, leaving behind his parents, four sisters, two brothers, and fiancée. He hoped they would all join him once he got settled.

My father had friends living in Verplanck, New York, near Peekskill, so he went there and quickly found work at the Trap Rock Corporation. As it turned out, only his sister Anna moved to America and settled nearby. His other three sisters, Carmela, Giovanna (for whom I was named), and Concetta, stayed in Calabria and married local boys while his brothers found work in France. Throughout his forty years at Trap Rock my father was the breadwinner for both the family he was raising and the one he left behind, regularly mailing money, clothing, and other items back to Italy.

Concetta Trimarchi, my mother, was born in 1908 and came to the United States with her family when she was six years old. Her family also had friends in Verplanck, so they settled there, opening a boardinghouse. My mother worked very hard as a young girl and completed school only to the sixth grade. She continued to teach herself at home, writing in Italian and English, reading avidly, and eventually taking care of all the household finances.

Young Vincenzo and Concetta Tropiano with a nephew.

Concetta Tropiano (left) with her sister Mary Curinga.

The Tropiano family's first home on Ninth Street in Verplanck, New York.

Even after she married, my mother continued to work hard—both at raising her five children and at her job on the assembly line at Standard Brands. In addition to her eight-hour workday, she pickled green tomatoes, canned pears and peaches, bottled eggplants, peppers, and tomatoes, made beer and root beer, baked her own bread, and, in her spare time, did the laundry, serving, cooking, and baking.

Verplanck had a large Italian population, so my parents were introduced to each other by mutual friends in that community. In 1926 they decided to marry, but first my father had to send a letter to his fiancée in Italy. She wasn't happy about the news, and when she wrote him back she enclosed a pair of scissors to symbolize the severing of their relationship. I don't know if it's an Italian tradition or not, but in my family whenever we give someone a knife or scissors, we always put a shiny new penny in with it so the person will know they are receiving a well-intentioned gift. Needless to say, there was no penny in the letter my father received. Years later, when he was able to return to Italy to visit his family, she still would not speak to him.

My parents had a long and happy marriage, celebrating more than sixty wedding anniversaries together and raising five children, Grace, Joseph, Angelina, Giovanna (me), and Vincent. Their first home was a two-family house set on a large piece of property on Verplanck's Point. Our family lived downstairs and my cousins lived with their family upstairs. My grandmother lived with us, and because my mother and father both worked, she helped to raise us.

This house on the Point was basically a mini-farm. Fruit trees were in abundance—cherry, mulberry, peach, plum, pear, and fig—and my father cultivated a wonderful grape arbor. We raised rabbits, pigs, turkeys, a cow, goats, and chickens. Everyone helped in the garden, tilling the soil and planting in the spring, harvesting and canning in the fall. My father worked a full day at Trap Rock and then, during the long days of the warmer months, he worked another half day in the garden. That was his health club.

We were surrounded by relatives and neighbors and shared in each other's happiness or grief. As children we felt safe and secure in this environment. As a result, I guess, I tended to wander quite a bit. My brother Joe and sister Grace like to remind me of how often they couldn't find me. One day, having hunted everywhere for me, they were on the verge of calling the police when they discovered me fast asleep behind the woodpile. My father's worry turned to anger pretty quickly when he realized I had slept through their frantic search.

Around 1958 my parents moved from the house on the Point into another two-family house on Broadway, closer to town. I lived there for two years before I married Stan. I thought my father was very brave to undertake building a house at the age of sixty. The garden was smaller but large enough for the two of them, and there was always extra if any of us needed vegetables. My father planted several fruit trees, including wonderful fig trees. All the animals were gone, except for a few rabbits, which he enjoyed raising. He built a big outdoor fireplace for grilling and for boiling the large vat of water they used to bottle tomatoes every fall. We have photographs of our son, Stanley, around age three, helping my father to build this fireplace.

My father brought cuttings from the original grape arbor on the Point to the new house, building a new arbor that expanded as our family grew. For large events he contrived an awning of sorts out of a blue

Me and my sisters, Grace and Angie. I'm on the left.

Three-year-old Stanley helping Pop Tropiano build an outdoor fireplace, 1964.

February 13, 1960, our wedding day. From left: *Pop Tropiano, Mom Concetta, Stan, me, Mom Teresa, and Pop Stanislao.*

Circa 1945, my sister Angie and me (right) capturing a runaway goat.

Mom and Pop Tropiano in their garden.

A younger Pop Tropiano (right) carrying the Madonna in the Our Lady of Mount Carmel festa parade.

tarp that extended the arbor. Tables arranged beneath the grapes and the tarp protected our family and friends from the hot sun or rain when we gathered to celebrate feasts or my parents' birthdays or anniversaries, or just to be together. Everyone brought food, and in most of the photographs of these gatherings you can see coolers lined up against the side of the house, filled with each family's contribution to the meal. Those coolers hardly ever went home empty. They were usually refilled with loads of freshly picked fruits and vegetables from my parents' garden.

One of our most important family gatherings was held every July for the Feast of Our Lady of Mount Carmel. My father was a charter member of the Our Lady of Mount Carmel Society and my brothers, Joe and Vinnie, are still members. The feast began on Thursday night and ended on Sunday evening with a tremendous fireworks display, attracting people from all over the area.

On Sunday there was a special mass, and my sister Angie, who has a beautiful operatic voice, sang at it. Members of the society, accompanied by visiting marching bands, then carried a statue of Our Lady of Mount Carmel through the village. My father had the honor of carrying the statue for many years. It was draped with a sash that people would pin money to as the parade passed by. This always brought tears

Circa 1961, a basement Thanksgiving at the Tropianos. Clockwise from left: *Pop Tropiano (standing); Concetta (seated); Stan, carving the turkey; Joe M.; Beth; Angie holding Connie; Kathy; Natalie; Joe T. holding son Michael; Grace; Donna; Toni Jean; Joseph; and Vincent.*

to the eyes of my family members, although I'm not sure why—emotional Italians, I guess!

Every year my sisters and I got a new dress to wear as we marched with the society members, carrying our flags and following the band. What I most looked forward to was the celebration after the parade. My parents would invite friends, neighbors, and visiting band members to share in the feast and help us celebrate this wonderful saint's day. Forty people were nothing to feed! We all helped with the cooking and cleaning and were happy to do it. In addition to eating, we had our traditional family bocce game. The competition was fierce—my sister Grace especially hated to lose. The family game always ended with cries of "Wait until next year!" and hugs all around. Then the game was turned over to the children and nonfamily members.

When Stan and I were first married, we lived in Peekskill, New York. Shortly after Stanley was born, we moved to an apartment in Mount Kisco, which was close to Stan's new job at Horace Greeley High School. We got to know our landlords, Mary and Angelo Cascioli, very well. Angelo enjoyed fishing in the nearby reservoirs. When he caught perch, Mary would flour and pan-fry the fillets. She always sent some upstairs for Stanley, who, at age two, greatly enjoyed them. Occasionally Mary and Angelo would invite us downstairs to join them, their granddaughters, Pam and Maria, son, Vincent, and daughter-in-law, Mary, for dinner. Mary would place a huge oval board in the center of the table, onto which she would pour cooked polenta. The polenta was then topped with a ragù sauce that included stewed meat and meatballs. Each person was given a fork and we ate toward the center, incorporating a little polenta in a little sauce for each bite. At the beginning of the meal one of the children would ask for a meatball, but Angelo would tell them they had to eat their way into the center before they could have one. Young Stanley and I enjoyed this fun and delicious meal, but Stan had a hard time sharing at the communal board and usually opted to eat something else.

Circa 1964, newly arrived Gina with me and big brother Stanley.

Our daughter Gina was born in 1964, and the following year we bought a house in Katonah, New York, where Christine was born in 1967 and where we still live today. Our lives were busy and full of family activities. As often as possible we got together with my family and Stan's, so this new generation of children got to know one another very well. In 1973 Stan had an opportunity to take a year's sabbatical in Florence, Italy. Little did we know what a lasting influence it would have on us and our three small children. Stan studied sculpture, the children attended school—becoming fluent in Italian—and I went to bookstores to learn about the wonderful northern Italian food. Although my Italian was limited, I knew enough to read recipes! Tortellini, *lasagne verdi,* rice salad—whatever the Florentines were eating, I wanted to do the same. Today I still make those recipes with great fondness.

Stanley at the age of three, in Depew Park, Peekskill, New York.

My parents came to Italy while we were there, and we all traveled to Calabria to visit relatives. My mother had returned to Italy only a few times before, but my father had gone back as often as he could, traveling by boat on a round-trip journey that took four weeks to complete. It was not easy for him to leave his wife and five children, and I always thought he was very brave. Our visit to Calabria to see my father's sisters and their families was quite an adventure. We slept on straw mattresses and were awakened by a donkey braying early in the morning, and Stan shaved looking into a broken mirror hanging in the chicken coop. The children were mesmerized by the photographs of relatives in their coffins that lined the bedroom dresser. We ate well—grilled rabbit, goat, homemade crêpes, bruschetta made with home-pressed olive oil as green as spring trees—and we laughed and would not have missed it for the world.

By the time we visited Italy, my father had retired after forty years of working for the Trap Rock Corporation. The company honored him for all his hard work by naming a barge the *Vincenzo Tropiano.* For several years we saw it on the Hudson River. Now my nephew Joseph sees it in Long Island Sound, near his home in Greenwich. Pop enjoyed his retirement and continued to work hard in his garden. He loved to experiment with grafting different fruit trees—splicing a branch of a peach tree onto a pear tree in an attempt to come up with some exotic fruit! After my father died in 1987 at the age of ninety-one, my mother continued to garden along with my brothers and to cook, but she complained about being lonely. This usually meant that only five people had come to visit instead of eight or ten. Her neighbor teased her, claiming my mother had so much company she needed valet parking!

The exterior of 9 via Crispi, our apartment house in Firenze, 1973–1974. Our apartment was on the third floor.

My mother had always been very independent. She had tried to teach my father to drive, but he almost hit the garage and that ended it! She continued to drive until her early eighties although her eyesight was failing, and eventually my brother Vince had to take her keys away. This cramped her style because when she baked something she wanted it delivered right away. My brothers and their wives lived nearby, and they helped Mom out during the week. On the weekends she would go to stay with her daughters. I always knew we would be cooking a lot when my mother came to visit.

My mother was a great storyteller. All the children came around when she was visiting, and my daughter Gina especially enjoyed spending time with her just to listen to her stories about growing up. My mother was proud of all her grandchildren and was anxious to share her words of wisdom with them. She never understood how we ended up with two actors in our family, and she often suggested to Stanley and Christine that they get regular office jobs. They laughed and told

Just returning from mass, Pop and Nonna Tropiano with Stanley in front of the house on Broadway in Verplanck, New York.

her not to worry. But how my mother bragged when Chris was on a soap opera or Stanley was in a movie—especially when they were on TV and all her friends could watch. She had to sit very close to the television, but just hearing their voices made her happy. It was especially thrilling for her to see her grandsons Stanley and Joseph sharing the limelight at a special viewing of the movie *Big Night* that was held in the Paramount Center for the Arts in Peekskill. The performance was sold out and the audience was full of family, friends, and neighbors from the community where we had all grown up.

When my mother died in 1997, at age eighty-eight, she had twenty-three grandchildren and twenty great-grandchildren. She and my father taught us the significance of family and we all understood that preparing and sharing food together would continue to be a central part of our family life. In 1997 Stan and I had the opportunity to return to Italy with his sister Rosalinda and her husband, Lee. We again traveled to Calabria to visit many of the same family members we had seen with Mom and Pop in 1973. My father's sisters, Carmella and Concetta, are still alive, maintaining the family traditions. Fig trees and homemade soppressata, salami, pasta, and wine are still a part of their lives, and our family still figures in the stories they tell. Because of our tight travel schedule we had set aside only one hour for our visit with

The Tropiano family with their spouses. Clockwise from top left: Tony Catalano, Joseph Tropiano, Grace Catalano, Vincent Tropiano, Joan and Stan, Angelina Manfredo, Joseph Manfredo, Concetta Tropiano, Natalie Tropiano, and Marilyn Tropiano.

them, but Carmella, Concetta, and their families were like drapes around us, smothering us with their love, and we ended up staying for five hours. As we tried to leave, they blocked the driveway, begging us to stay overnight. We all cried as we waved goodbye, promising to return soon.

From left: *Gina, Stanley, and Christine awaiting the rest of the family coming for Easter dinner. They are all dressed up, so why not take a photo?*

Now that Stanley, Gina, and Christine have grown up, it seems that we never have enough time together—soon Stan and I will be the ones blocking the driveway! But we do still get together for holidays and for dinners on most weekends. Our extended family has grown to such an extent that it is difficult to find a home where we all fit. My sister Grace and her husband, Tony, have a large enclosed, heated patio and we have held many a great Easter egg hunt there. The entertainment at these events was often provided by Stanley on drums, my nephew Joe (who cowrote the *Big Night* screenplay with Stanley) on keyboard, and occasionally my daughter Christine, who would sing for us—followed by tears from all the adults. But when they wanted to form a union and get paid, we fired them! I still keep a collection of instruments at the house so that during festive dinners we can take a break between courses, improvising while working up an appetite.

The Tucci and Tropiano children love to cook, and several of them are very inventive chefs. Food remains central in their lives as they establish their own families and households. When my children left home, the telephone calls requesting recipes began, and they continue to this day. So Stan and I decided to put together a book of the most frequently requested recipes—and that is how this book project began. We have included recipes from both our families, others we picked up during our year in Italy, and recipes we have created on our own.

Joan G. Tucci

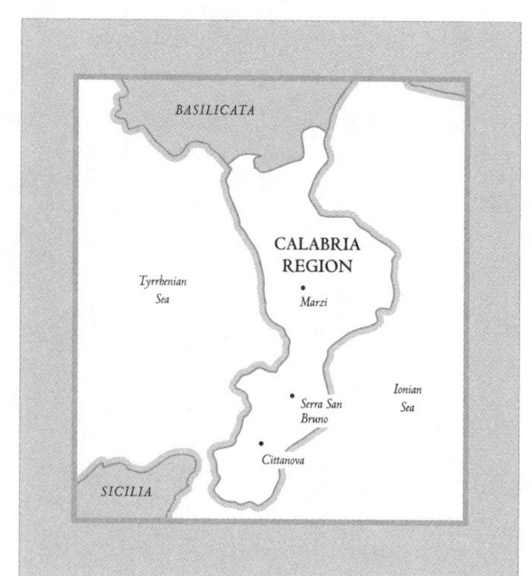

STAN

In 1904 my mother's parents, Domenico and Apollonia Pisani, left their mountaintop village of Serra San Bruno in Calabria, Italy, and traveled to Naples, where they planned to board a ship that would take them to America. They were accompanied by a relative and by their five children: my mother, Teresa, and her siblings, Ralph, Dominic, Henry, and Candida. When the family arrived in Naples, they detected that something was wrong with Henry's eyes. He returned to Serra San Bruno with the relative who had accompanied them to Naples and remained in Italy with his grandparents for two years until he was finally reunited with his family in America.

The Pisani family settled in Northfield, Vermont, joining Apollonia's brother, Emilio Politi, who was already established there. Northfield was one of several Vermont hill towns around Barre where work could be found cutting granite, marble, and slate. Drawn by the promise of work, hundreds of Italians journeyed there every year. The community my grandparents joined was so heavily populated by Italians that the area was nicknamed "Spaghetti Square" because of all the fresh pasta drying on outdoor racks.

In addition to the promise of work, my grandfather Domenico moved to America because he wanted to avoid Italy's mandatory military service for his sons. He had spent four unhappy years in the Italian cavalry. Ironically, time and circumstances conspired and his two oldest sons, Dominic and Ralph, served in the U.S. Army during World War I. Henry was too young for World War I and too old for World War II. However, Edwin, the youngest son, served in World War II, and three of Domenico's grandsons served in the armed forces during World War II or the Korean conflict.

Circa 1905, Stanislao (right) with brother Rosario (left) and their father, Francesco Tucci (center).

My father, Stanislao, was born in 1889 in the small town of Marzi in Consenza, Italy, the second son of Francesco and Rosa Tucci. My father had three brothers, Rosario, Angelo, and Vincenzo, and a sister, Marina. My grandfather Francesco was a stonecutter all his life. His search for work in the mid-nineteenth century took him to Egypt, India, and the United States. In 1904 my father, at age fourteen, sailed from Italy to the United States with a cousin and came to join his brother Rosario in Vermont. Upon his arrival, Stanislao lived for a short time in the crowded community of Little Italy in New York City. He was fond of telling us that the apartment he shared with other Italians was so crowded that there was no more sleeping space, even on the floor, so he slept on the fire escape. Stanislao soon left the city and headed to Northfield, Vermont, where he had heard that he could find stonecutting work.

Circa 1912, young Teresa Pisani (right) with two friends in Northfield, Vermont, before she married Stanislao.

In advance of his moving to Northfield, Stanislao arranged to take a room in a boardinghouse run by Emilio and Maria Politi. The Politi boardinghouse was located next door to that of my grandparents, the Pisanis. My mother, Teresa, heard a lot of gossip about the crazy Cosentino who was coming to board next door. When she first saw my father she thought the comments were true because he walked in the house carrying a rifle!

My father apprenticed as a stonecutter. Within a few years he had gained a reputation and respect among his peers as a master of carving and lettering in stone. When I was a young man we would travel together to New York City and my father would proudly point out the facades of various buildings that displayed his stone carving. Now I

Italian stone carvers and their families at a three-day picnic in Northfield, Vermont, circa 1910.

wish I had paid closer attention to the buildings he was pointing to because I cannot remember them all. However, I know that he carved some of the Corinthian column capitals on the Soldier's and Sailor's Monument on Riverside Drive and some of the window tracery on the Cathedral of Saint John the Divine.

Eventually Stanislao and my mother, Teresa, began a chaperoned courtship. Teresa was working in a clothing store in Northfield. Stanislao would visit her during his lunch break from his stonecutting job at Cross Brothers, which was located one block away. Stanislao tended to overextend these visits, which made him late getting back to work. He had a friend whose job it was to blow the factory horn, the signal that everyone should be back at work. He told Stanislao, "I'll blow the horn five minutes before the actual time and that will be a warning to you. This way you will not be late when the second and final horn blows." When I visited Northfield about thirty years later, the tradition of blowing two horns was still in practice—although no one seemed to know why.

Teresa and Stanislao were married in February 1914. My father recalled that it was so cold that day that the top hinge of the front door was frosted over. He used the frozen hinges as a type of thermometer. If the lowest hinge on the door was frozen, the temperature was 10 degrees below freezing; a frozen middle hinge meant 20 degrees below; a frozen top hinge indicated a temperature at least 30 degrees below freezing.

Teresa Tucci (center) *with* (from left) *her brother Henry, sister Emilia, son Frank, mother, Apollonia Pisani, and daughter Dora* (in front). *Check out Zio Henry's cool knickers!*

Shortly after my parents were married, they moved to Peekskill, and in 1915 my brother Frank was born. There were quarries in Peekskill where my father found work, and a few years later, Stanislao and his brother Rosario purchased a retail monument business in nearby Van Cortlandville, establishing the Tucci Brothers Monument Works. In 1936 the two brothers decided to go their separate ways. Rosario named his business "Tucci Memorials" and my father named his "Stanley Tucci and Son."

After a series of moves, the Tucci and Pisani families purchased a duplex home on Washington Street in Peekskill. This is the house I grew up in, along with my brother, Frank, and my two sisters, Dora and Rosalinda. My mother's parents lived in the other half of the house with my two unmarried uncles, Edwin and Henry, and my unmarried aunt, Emilia. Our extended family of uncles, aunts, and cousins lived within walking or short driving distance from this duplex. Our home served as the center for innumerable large family gatherings. Actually, most of the family stopped by every evening. I was nurtured by this intense family life throughout my elementary and high school years.

When I graduated from high school, I pursued a degree in art education at the State University of New York at Buffalo, and then

Down by the Hudson, 1932.
From left: *Me with my cousin Angela Russo, Zia Candida, my sister Dora, my mother, Teresa, holding my sister Rosalinda, and cousin Peter Russo.*

The Tucci family on the occasion of my First Communion, 1937. Back row, from left: *Stanislao, Teresa, my brother Frank;* front row, from left: *me and my sisters, Rosalinda and Dora.*

Me (right) *with my sister Rosalinda and Zio Eddie in the backyard of 347 Washington Street, Peekskill, New York, 1942.*

went on to receive a master's in art education from Columbia University. In 1953 I volunteered for the draft, requesting an August or September induction so that I could more easily apply for a teaching position after completing the two years of compulsory service in the army.

In 1955 I was living at home and began to teach art at the Drum Hill Junior High School in Peekskill. At the end of the school year I enrolled in a two-month art study tour that was part of Columbia University's summer program. We toured the ancient art centers of eight Western European countries, including Italy. This was my first trip to my parents' native land, and no city captivated me more than Florence. I knew that somehow I would return there to live. I continued to teach at the junior high for five more years. In an effort to return to Italy, I decided to apply for a teaching position at the United States military base in Naples.

Shortly before accepting the position I attended a local church picnic. I was alone, and Joan was there with a date who spent most of his time playing cards. Joan and I walked together to watch another picnic group that was dancing to the rhythm of empty beer cans knocked together. From that August day on, we spent some part of every day together. When we decided to marry, I discovered that the military could not guarantee that Joan would be allowed to join me in Naples. I was not as adventuresome as my Italian ancestors who had bravely left Italy and their families behind when they came to America, so I chose to stay in the United States with Joan and we were married six months after we met.

Eighteen years went by before I had another opportunity to return to Italy. In 1973, while teaching at Horace Greeley High School in Chappaqua, New York, I received a sabbatical to study figurative sculpture at the Academia di Belle Arti in Florence. Our year in Italy was probably the most important move I and our family ever made. The effects are evident in so much of our lives today—the language, culture, art, music, family, and food, food, food!

Our trip to Italy strongly influenced Joan's cooking. When Joan and I got married she did not have any cooking experience to speak of.

I don't know if this is universally true, but in the homes of the Italian-American families I knew, the girls never did any cooking prior to marriage. All the cooking was done by the mother, and often the father participated in the preparation of meals. Yet all these young girls, upon marriage, became wonderful cooks. My guess is that food, family, and tradition are such an integral part of the Italian heritage that there is a subconscious obligation, as well as a desire, to cook as well as their mothers did. Joan has an endless curiosity about food paired with a willingness to test new ideas, ingredients, and techniques that has resulted in her becoming an excellent, confident home cook.

Circa 1963, three-year-old Stanley joins me in playing the uke and singing.

Perhaps the most important consequence of our trip to Italy was that our children had the opportunity to understand that our family traditions extended beyond ourselves and connected to a complex, strong, and ancient culture. Stanley and Gina continue to speak Italian today. Gina went on to major in Italian at college, and she received a graduate degree in education from the State University of New York at Albany. She currently teaches English as a second language in New York State's Valley Central School District. Christine, who was only six the year we lived in Florence, was somewhat less influenced by the trip, but she did have the best Italian pronunciation of the three children. However, all three of the children remember our frequent visits to museums, churches, and galleries in Florence, Venice, and Rome. When we returned to America, I suggested going into New York City to visit a museum and they ran from the room shouting "*No!*" But their love of art and culture is strong today and surely must be rooted in our time in Italy.

Teresa and Stanislao Tucci with bouquets sent for their fiftieth wedding anniversary, 1964.

The influence of our trip is also, I believe, evident in Stanley's first directorial effort, *Big Night.* This story of two immigrant Italians running a restaurant in New Jersey in the 1950s uses food as a metaphor for the conflict between art and commerce. Stanley's preparation for *Big Night* led to our meeting Gianni Scappin. Stanley and his cousin Joseph Tropiano had completed the writing of the screenplay, and Stanley had spoken with Isabella Rossellini about her role in the film. He explained to her that he was interested in working in a professional restaurant kitchen to hone his skills for the role of Secondo and to accurately capture the atmosphere for the film. Isabella in turn spoke to her friend Pino Luongo, the owner of several New York City restaurants, including Le Madri. Stanley was granted permission to work under Executive Chef Gianni Scappin, and his "apprenticeship" lasted about eighteen months. He became even more enamored of food, its preparation, and its presentation while establishing a brotherly relationship with Gianni. With food as a central character in *Big Night,* Stanley began to think about the idea of putting together a cookbook. He spoke to us and to Gianni about collecting family recipes, and the idea for this book began.

Joan and Gianni have collaborated to create a cookbook that brings together wonderful examples of northern and southern Italian family cooking. Joan's recipes focus on vegetables and pasta. Their preparation always involves the use of olive oil, a reflection of the southern Italian agricultural tradition. Gianni's recipes include the use of dairy products, which are in abundance in the north of Italy. Joan and Gianni brought very different qualifications to the process of creating this book. Gianni is professionally trained and has had a wide range of experiences, while Joan's many years as a home cook were defined by her compulsive desire not only to learn but to create new recipes. They both have a wonderful sense of humor that is displayed when they are working together in the kitchen. Joan loves to tease Gianni about his English (which he speaks very well!) and Gianni loves to tease Joan about anything from our electric stove to the size of our frying pans. But when we are together we mostly enjoy discussing food. While we are in the midst of cooking a meal, we talk about variations on those recipes, critique other meals we have eaten, talk about meals we are looking forward to, wonder what we should eat the next time we are together. I think it is no exaggeration to say that when two Italians get together, within five minutes they will be discussing food. It is from this environment that Joan began her cooking journey, and this book is infused with that spirit.

Stanley V. Tucci

GIANNI

Halfway between Venice and Verona is the tiny village of Mason Vicentino, where I was raised. This area, known as the Veneto, is located in the northeast corner of Italy, very close to the Austrian border. Over the centuries, due to war and politics, the Veneto has alternated between Austrian and Italian rule, which has greatly influenced the local culture and cuisine. My mother, Maria-Bertilla, can trace her family back for at least five generations in Mason Vicentino. My father, Luigi, was raised eight miles away and his family has been living there for at least three generations, if not longer. When I was growing up, my family's frugal lifestyle was shared by most of our neighbors. Today there is a strong middle-class community in the towns of the Veneto, thanks to tourism and to the local artisans who create beautiful ceramics and jewelry.

In the decade before World War II my father operated a small candy factory, using old iron machines that are still stored in my family's barn. His business was quite successful, and he employed a number of local women to hand-wrap the candies in silver and gold foil. After the war, new automated machinery

My father's parents: my grandmother, or nonna, *Catterina, and my grandfather, or* nonno, *Giovanni Domenico.*

My parents on their wedding day, outside the only church in Mason Vicentino. The town is in the northeast corner of Italy, close to the Austrian border, in the region known as the Veneto.

changed the candy production business and my father, unable to profitably compete with larger companies, closed his business. He was a creative, artistic man, so for his next business he decided to make ceramic dishes, firing them in a kiln and painting them with his own designs. At this point in his career he met and fell in love with my mother.

Our home and bar, the Trattoria alla Pesa, during World War II. My mother worked there with her aunt, who was like a second mother to me.

When my parents met, my mother was helping her aunt to run the family's restaurant, Trattoria alla Pesa. My grandmother had left Mason Vicentino during the Depression to seek work in Switzerland, leaving her young daughter, Maria-Bertilla, in her sister's care.

My mother's aunt had inherited the Trattoria alla Pesa from a relative. It got its name, which roughly means "the place where you go to weigh," from the community scale that was located directly across the street. Local farmers who were waiting for their grain to be weighed would come into the trattoria for a glass of wine or grappa and a little something to eat.

During World War II German soldiers were stationed in Mason Vicentino. They commandeered the trattoria, and my mother's aunt was charged with cooking for them. She fell in love with a German lieutenant, and she was still in love with him when the German army left

Mason Vicentino. She never married but continued to run the trattoria, with my mother working at her side. When my parents began to date, the trattoria was doing well, while my father's ceramics business was struggling. They married and my father left his village to help run the trattoria with my mother and her aunt. This prompted a lot of talk among the neighbors, as it was considered more traditional for a wife to leave her family and support her husband's business.

My parents standing in back of my family's bar with my sister Catterina posed on top of the wall.

The first house my parents lived in needed to be restored. It was very old, unheated, and had a roof that leaked. I particularly remember the leaky roof because it was my duty, along with my brother and three sisters, to catch the rain in the enameled pans stored under the beds. At the time I didn't think this was unusual, and during thunderstorms it was actually sort of exciting. In the winter my brother and I used a bed warmer filled with coals from the wood-burning stove to heat the cold sheets. Then we piled so many heavy blankets on top of us that it was difficult to roll over. We clearly needed a new house, but my parents didn't have enough money to buy or build one. My father solved this problem in a creative and practical way.

Attached to our house was a rustic garage built out of brick. Every few days my father, assisted by my older sister, Catterina, would go there and gather some of the bricks. Together they cleaned them to remove the old mortar, and eventually they had enough to begin building us a new house. My father and Catterina did all of the work themselves, calling upon neighbors to help only when it was time to put on the roof. While Catterina helped my father, my sister Livia took his place in the restaurant, working alongside my mother as my mother had worked alongside her aunt. To further supplement the family's income, my father managed to buy a van from a local coffee company. Once a month he would drive to Emilia Romagna to purchase a few large wheels of Parmesan cheese, which he would cut and sell at a profit to the local restaurants and stores.

My father continued to work at the trattoria when there were special events, such as weddings, confirmations, and baptisms. My earliest memories of food are the love and preparation that my father put into

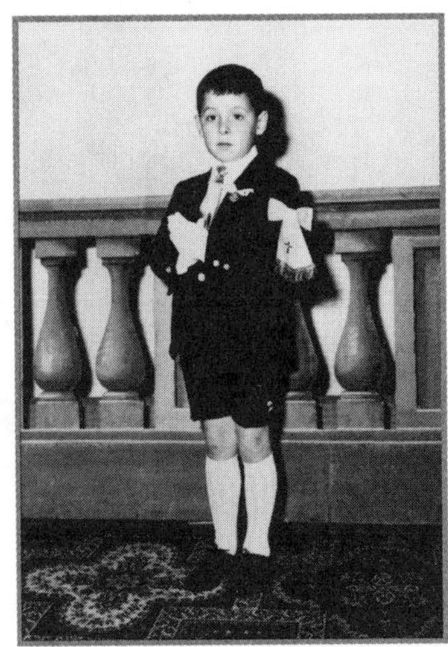

My First Holy Communion.

Here my parents are celebrating with friends at their bar. My father is holding a glass being filled with wine. My mother is to the left of the woman pouring the wine.

all of the dishes he made for these occasions. For example, he would spend days preparing seasonal dishes such as *lepre in salmi* (stewed hare) or *funghi trifolati con polenta* (wild sautéed mushrooms with polenta) *"nel modo giusto"* or "the right way." He never looked at running a restaurant as a business, but rather as a love, a duty to the community, and a means to support his family. It was the passion he had for cooking that made some of his dishes still the best versions that I've ever had.

With the other members of the family working so hard to provide for our welfare, I felt a lot of pressure to find a vocation and begin making a contribution myself. It was typical for children in our area to decide on a career at a very young age. At ten I felt my calling was to serve the church, so I decided to attend a type of pre-seminary school in anticipation of becoming a priest. My parents paid a very small fee for me to attend this school, which was located about an hour from Mason Vicentino. I received a good education, religious training, music lessons, sang in the choir, played sports, and, most important, was fed four meals a day. I slept in a room with thirty-nine other boys, and the priests kept us on a tight, almost military, schedule. At the same time they were sensitive to the needs of children. For example, I remember lying in bed each evening while a priest read us stories over the intercom system before going to sleep. However, I was not destined for the priesthood, and three years after starting that school I was kicked out for cheating on a test.

To their credit, the priests told my father that I had promise and should pursue a career. I didn't want to work at the trattoria and I was very interested in traveling, something no one in my family had done. I saw cooking as a way to make money, pursue a profession, and travel. So at fourteen, I began my pursuit of a culinary career. I attended Recoaro Terme Culinary Institute, where the four-year curriculum included an extensive externship program that took me to luxury hotels run by the CIGA (now Sheraton) chain and other kitchens throughout Italy. I worked in Piemonte, Emilia Romagna, Liguria, Lombardia, Trentino Alto Adige, and Sardegna. Having grown up with the regional foods of the Veneto, it was an extraordinary experience to cook and

My first restaurant job at the Ristorante Tre Venezie. I am on the right—the first person wearing a chef's toque. I was fourteen years old.

become familiar with the variety of ingredients used in these other regions of Italy.

At eighteen I traveled to England to learn English and work at the Dorset Hotel in Bournemouth. The restaurant menu was French-influenced, and this experience helped me to further develop my classic cooking skills. After one year I returned to Italy to fulfill my military obligations. I was very fortunate to be placed in the Alpini regiment, which is based in the awe-inspiring Dolomite Mountains near Cortina d'Ampezzo. After wonderful days of "military-related" skiing, I utilized the local mountain ingredients to prepare hearty meals for my commanding officers. When I completed my military duties, I joined the kitchen brigade of the Excelsior Hotel, located on the Lido in Venice. This experience provided me with the invaluable opportunity of working with large teams of other cooks. I acquired organizational skills and learned how to achieve finesse in large-volume food production.

I arrived in New York in 1983, and six months later became the executive chef of the highly successful restaurant Castellano. During my four years at Castellano I really developed as a chef, blending modern flair with traditional Italian cuisine. When I look back at that time I am astounded to realize that such words as "focaccia," "tiramisù," and "risotto" were unknown in the United States. As word got out that these dishes had been added to the menu, the popularity of Castellano exploded, and suddenly celebrities like Mick Jagger and Clint Eastwood were arriving in limousines to sample what I considered to be home-style dishes. Serious food lovers also flocked to Castellano, among them Glenn Dopf, a successful lawyer with a real passion for food. Glenn is not a shy person, and many nights I found him in my kitchen, asking me to teach him how to cook risotto or another favorite dish. As we stirred the rice our friendship grew, confirming my belief that food and friends go well together.

After Castellano my next adventure was as the executive chef for BICE Ristorante in New York, and later as the corporate chef for all of their operations. It was gratifying when the BICE that I helped launch in Washington, D.C., was rewarded with 3½ apples (the equivalent of 3½ stars) by *The Washington Post.*

In 1992 I returned to New York to head up the kitchen of Pino Luongo's Le Madri. I feel that I hit my stride creatively during my four years at Le Madri and really developed with regard to the management aspects of the restaurant business. It is my belief that the energy and open-minded nature of New Yorkers allowed me to explore Italian cooking beyond the flavors and tastes of my own experiences. It was at Le Madri, in fact, that I developed a balance between sophistication

Here is part of my excellent kitchen staff at Le Madri, in 1995. From left: *Victor, Ruben, Alberto, Raphael, Marlom, and Juan. The others, Geraldo and Sergio, are not pictured.*

and simplicity in cooking, often marrying compatible ingredients from the entire Mediterranean region while trying never to allow one ingredient to overwhelm the others.

It was also at Le Madri that I met Stanley Tucci. His passion for Italian cooking was apparent to me during his "apprenticeship" in my kitchen and in his dedication to the preparation for his cooking scenes in *Big Night.* Stanley and I had a lot of fun honing his (already good) skills, and we initiated an enduring friendship during the process. Through our friendship I've grown to know the immediate and extended members of Stanley's family. I have particularly enjoyed the company of his parents, Joan and Stan. Sharing our passion for Italian cooking in the development of this book has been too much fun to be called work. Joan and Stan are more youthful than many people my age, and have generously made me feel as though I have a second family here in America.

Here I am standing between my mother, Maria-Bertilla, and my father, Luigi, in 1989, two years before my father died.

During the creation of this book I have developed enormous respect for Mimi Shanley Taft. Mimi is not only a very knowledgeable culinarian and a gifted writer, but she is also patient and precise—not the easiest task when working with two "off the cuff," improvisational cooks like Joan and me. At times when other commitments prevented me from working with Mimi and Joan in person, I would regularly e-mail recipes that they would test together. I understand that recipes need to be exact for readers, but my cooking philosophy is very Italian—"*un po' di questo, un po' di quello,*" or "a little of this and a little of that." So my frequent use of the expression "*dipende,*" or "it depends," became an ongoing joke throughout this project.

At times during the last few years I have felt the pressure to "reinvent" Italian food to keep up with the trends and to break barriers. To me, however, it didn't feel right to re-create a cuisine that, in my mind, had not yet been fully explored or understood in this country. During the past year my wife, Laura, and I returned to Italy to reopen my father's trattoria, which had been closed since his death in 1991. During our exploration of the northeastern portion of Italy, it became clear to me just how many pockets of traditional cooking there are. In fact, Italian cuisine is not simply regional, it is provincial! Within a

Laura and I are cooking together at an event at New York's James Beard house.

thirty-mile radius the traditional dishes may be altogether different. During the time we operated the trattoria I prepared traditional gnocchi, *asparagi bianchi con uova* (white asparagus with hard-cooked eggs), and *baccalà mantecato* with my mother. I also introduced new flavors from other areas of Italy. In the rather sheltered confines of my hometown this was newsworthy, and we were very busy providing "*cucina diversa*," or different food.

My return to Italy marked the fulfillment of a longtime dream. For many years I had talked about and imagined going back to Mason Vicentino to reopen the family trattoria. I pictured sharing my cooking style, recipes, and culinary experiences with the community where my career began. After several months and much hard work, I discovered that in some ways there was no going back. I realized that my culinary style, while still pure in its Italian roots, had evolved much more than I could have measured.

Over the years I had developed dishes that interpret classic recipes from my region of Italy, which I was anxious to place on the trattoria's menu. However, only a few of the local customers were interested in trying something new. Most of the patrons requested traditional meals that I could easily prepare but which were not challenging for me as a chef. The longer I remained in Italy, the more I missed America's ever-dynamic culinary community. In the United States food is written and talked about by culinarians, foodies, and just about everyone else. Chefs are celebrated and people are curious and adventuresome about food.

So, although a large part of my heart will forever remain in Italy, in the spring of 1998 Laura and I returned to New York. Rather than return to work as a chef in a restaurant, I chose to join the faculty of the Culinary Institute of America in Hyde Park. I feel that there is a tremendous need to educate and expose future food professionals to what Italian cuisine is really about, especially as it becomes more and more popular among Americans. I have long held the conviction, although I was not certain, that a truly traditional Italian diet is also a healthy diet. My wife, Laura, a nutritionist and culinary professional, has confirmed my belief in the innate balance of Italian cuisine. Laura

Here I am with Laura on our honeymoon at a tapas bar in Barcelona.

believes, as I do, that the flavorful dishes of Italy, and the Mediterranean region in general, don't need to be "made healthy"—they simply are healthy. Through my teaching and with this book, I aim to share many of Italy's undiscovered recipes and traditions.

After a year of teaching at the Culinary Institute, I have returned to New York City, where I continue to provide culinary consultations through my company, Bigoli, named after a long tubular pasta from the Veneto region. Now my dream is to be able to experience the best of both Italy and America. I picture a life that includes spending part of each year absorbing the traditions and simplicities of Italy while devoting the other part of the year to continuing my culinary growth here in the United States.

Gianni Scappin

Antipasti ed Insalate

APPETIZERS AND SALADS

JOAN: The arrival of family and friends at our home is one of my favorite moments. I enjoy the enthusiasm of people coming through the door, embracing, talking, and greeting one another, and I take pleasure in introducing new visitors to longstanding friends and family members. As was the custom at my parents' house and at Stan's, we always have olives, salami, cheese, and *biscotto*—twice-baked bread—on hand to set out on the table for anyone who drops by. As our parents did, we offer drinks or demitasse, and with these few simple ingredients a guest feels warmly welcomed.

When we invite company for dinner, I round out these simple *antipasti* with dishes prepared from the recipes in this section. Many of these appetizers taste best if prepared several hours in advance, store well, and generally can be served at room temperature or reheated easily. The great thing about these recipes is that they can also be used to create a quick, casual lunch. A green salad and bread complete the meal. And don't forget the wine.

GIANNI: In my area of Italy, the Veneto, *cicchetti* is the dialect word for "little bite." These *antipasti*-type dishes are served everywhere, from little bars and trattorias to osterias. They are part of an everyday traditional way of socializing while playing cards or having a glass of wine. *Cicchetti* may be as simple as half a hard-boiled egg topped with a slice of anchovy and drizzled with olive oil or more complicated, like sliced frittata. My father prepared all types of *cicchetti* at our family-run trattoria, and several of the following dishes are based on his recipes.

STANLEY: Originally there were two appetizer sequences in *Big Night*. The first was at the beginning of the party scene and consisted of a series of tracking shots of a buffet table overflowing with culinary delights. The second, at the beginning of the meal, was a series of close overhead shots of artfully arranged vegetables. We cut both scenes because we felt they lessened the impact of the meal yet to come.

Luckily, when serving a meal in real life this need not be of concern! In fact, the appetizer recipes that follow *must* be served—they will help whet the appetite for the following meal or make a meal in themselves. Whichever you choose, I'm sure you will be satisfied.

BRUSCHETTA CLASSICA

Classic Bruschetta

MAKES 6 SERVINGS

GIANNI: Bruschetta is an example of *spuntini, cicchetti,* or *stuzzichini*—all Italian words for "little bites." My father, Luigi, was a very practical man who looked for inexpensive ways to concoct "little bites" for the cardplaying customers at our family bar. Whenever I prepare bruschetta I remember how he would grill slices of day-old bread, rub them with garlic, and top, with almost any mixture he had on hand—*baccalà,* tomatoes in the summer, pureed beans. He would bring a small tray of *spuntini* to the cardplayers, who of course would need to purchase a glass of wine to complete this small meal.

There are endless ways of making bruschetta, but this is my favorite. You can leave the skins on the tomatoes or peel them. To make peeling easier, blanch the tomatoes in boiling water for a couple of minutes, then cool them in cold water. This will loosen the skins. My only rule with bruschetta is to use the best olive oil you can find, preferably a cold-pressed variety.

1 pound ripe tomatoes, roughly chopped
1 tablespoon finely chopped fresh basil leaves
1 teaspoon dried oregano
½ cup extra virgin olive oil
Kosher salt and freshly ground black pepper
3 cloves garlic, finely chopped
Pinch of red pepper flakes (optional)
1 tablespoon diced onions (optional)
1 tablespoon balsamic vinegar (optional)
6 slices country-style bread
1 clove garlic, cut in half

Combine the tomatoes, basil, oregano, and olive oil in a bowl, season with salt and pepper. Stir in the chopped garlic and allow to marinate for half an hour. (Any of the optional ingredients may be mixed with these basic ingredients.) Toast or grill the bread, and rub with the garlic halves. Spoon generous portions of the tomato mixture onto the toast, and serve.

VARIATIONS: Grilled or toasted country bread that has been rubbed with garlic may be topped with:

- ½ head cauliflower florets boiled until tender, roughly chopped, tossed with 3 tablespoons olive oil and 1 tablespoon red wine vinegar, and seasoned with salt and pepper.

- ½ pound mushrooms, roughly chopped, 2 tablespoons chopped fresh parsley leaves, 2 teaspoons finely chopped garlic, and 2 tablespoons olive oil, cooked to soften over medium-high heat.
- *Caponata* (page 34)
- *Antipasto di Cannellini* (page 40)
- *Baccalà Mantecato* (page 31)
- A soft cheese such as Robiola topped with a thin slice of cured sausage, prosciutto, speck, or salami.

My father, Luigi, with his family. From left: *my father; his father, Giovanni Domenico (for whom I am named); his mother, Catterina; and my father's sisters, Maria, Esterina, Rosina, and Agnese.*

BRUSCHETTA CON POMODORO

Bruschetta with Tomato

MAKES 4 SERVINGS

STAN: In the late 1970s, Joan and I returned to Italy and ended our trip with a visit to Joan's cousin Tita. The moment we arrived, Tita insisted that we must stay not only for dinner but also for the night. Within moments she had lit a fire and was toasting slices of homemade bread. She rubbed each slice with garlic, drizzled olive oil on top, and spooned finely chopped tomatoes, basil, and parsley on each piece. This was our first experience with bruschetta, which soon after began to appear at Italian restaurants in America.

JOAN: My father built my mother an outdoor brick oven with a wooden roof over it so that she could bake in any weather. When the fire was almost out, my mother would slice and slowly toast homemade bread until it was golden and hard. We called it *biscotto,* and my mother would break it into small pieces and add it to her Fresh Tomato Salad (page 284).

STANLEY: Bruschetta is a terrific hors d'oeuvre but it doesn't lend itself to advance preparation—nothing is worse than soggy bruschetta. So I mix the tomatoes, garlic, and parsley together in a small serving bowl. I toast the bread, rub it with garlic, and place it on a platter with the bowl of tomatoes. I set this out along with other hors d'oeuvres—olives, soppressata, a hunk of Parmesan cheese—and allow guests to serve themselves while I pour the wine.

4 medium-size ripe tomatoes, roughly chopped
8 fresh basil leaves, chopped
1 tablespoon chopped fresh parsley leaves
3 cloves garlic, finely chopped
¼ cup olive oil
Kosher salt and freshly ground black pepper
4 slices Italian bread, toasted
1 clove garlic, cut in half
Extra virgin olive oil to drizzle on top (optional)

In a medium-size bowl, mix together the tomatoes, basil, parsley, chopped garlic, and olive oil, and season with salt and pepper. Rub the toasted bread with the garlic halves, then top with equal portions of the tomato mixture. Drizzle extra virgin olive oil on top if desired, and serve immediately.

BACCALÀ MANTECATO

Venetian Salted Cod Pâté

MAKES 6 TO 8 SERVINGS

GIANNI: One of the most ancient ways of preserving fish is by drying or salting. My family observed the Catholic tradition of abstaining from meat on Fridays, and so *baccalà*, or dried cod, was on the menu every week. As soon as I was old enough to drive, it became my job to go into Bassano del Grappa on Thursdays to purchase a whole dried cod. Although the drive was short, the pungent aroma of the fish permeated the car by the time I arrived home, and you could detect the smell of salted cod for several days afterward. Just about the time the odor disappeared, it would be time for me to go buy another fish. You don't know what a hard time I had trying to sell that car!

Don't be put off by the cod's aroma, because once the *baccalà* is soaked in liquid for a full day the smell disappears and its sweet taste is revived. (We selected salt cod for this recipe because it is widely available in American supermarkets.) I like to serve this dish while it is still warm on top of toasted bread that has been rubbed with garlic or on top of a slice of grilled polenta.

1 pound salt cod
2 cups milk or heavy cream
3 cloves garlic, peeled
1 Idaho potato (about 10 ounces), peeled, cut in half, and sliced
¾ cup extra virgin olive oil
2 tablespoons chopped fresh parsley leaves
2 tablespoons freshly grated Parmesan cheese
Freshly ground black pepper

Soak the cod in a large saucepan filled with cold water for 24 hours, changing the water three times during this period. Drain the cod and return it to the saucepan. Add the milk or heavy cream, which should cover the fish (add additional milk if necessary), two of the garlic cloves, and the potato. Bring to a boil, cover, and simmer until the potato is tender when pierced with a knife, 20 to 25 minutes.

Drain the fish, reserving ¼ cup of the soaking liquid, the potato, and the garlic. Remove and discard all bones from the cod.

Puree the cod in a food processor along with the reserved liquid, potato, garlic, and the remaining garlic clove. With the food processor running, add the olive oil in a steady stream and process until smooth. Stir in the parsley and cheese, season with pepper, and serve immediately.

VARIATIONS: Stir one of the following ingredients into the completed *baccalà*:

- ¼ cup seeded and diced red, yellow, or orange bell pepper
- ¼ cup pitted and diced Kalamata olives
- ½ cup small cubes peeled all-purpose potatoes that have been cooked in boiling salted water until tender, about 8 minutes

PÂTÉ DI FEGATINI DI POLLO

Chicken Liver Spread

MAKES ABOUT 1 CUP; 6 SERVINGS

GIANNI: Shopping for chicken in Italy is quite a different experience from shopping for it in the United States. When you unwrap your package from the butcher, you will find the whole chicken—head and claws intact and maybe even with some feathers left on. Italian cooks use every bit of a chicken, with the exception of the head. Often the livers are reserved for preparing a rich risotto dish. I like to use them to create a pâté of sorts, and this recipe is my favorite.

My sister Catterina and her husband, Piero, liked this spread the moment they first tasted it, and now she prepares it twice a week. Catterina particularly likes the fact that this pâté may be frozen for up to three months, guaranteeing that she will have something special on hand to serve at any spur-of-the-moment celebration. Serve it at room temperature on crackers, toasted bread, or grilled polenta.

2 teaspoons olive oil
½ cup finely chopped red or white onions
½ pound coarsely chopped chicken livers, trimmed of membranes
½ cup dry red wine, preferably Chianti
3 tablespoons capers, drained and rinsed
2 anchovy fillets
1½ teaspoons chopped fresh sage leaves
1 tablespoon extra virgin olive oil
Kosher salt and freshly ground black pepper

Warm the olive oil and onions in a medium-size sauté pan set over medium-low heat. When the oil begins to sizzle, add the chicken livers and wine. Cook gently, stirring occasionally, until the wine has evaporated, 20 to 25 minutes. Remove from the heat and stir in the capers, anchovies, and sage. Transfer to a food processor or blender, add the extra virgin olive oil, and process until finely chopped. Season with salt and pepper.

VARIATION: For a slightly sweeter version of this recipe, soak 2 tablespoons raisins in warm water for 15 minutes. Squeeze dry and process with the other ingredients.

CAPONATA

Eggplant Antipasto

MAKES 6 SERVINGS

JOAN: I served this traditional eggplant appetizer at Stanley and Kate's wedding reception. In keeping with Tucci tradition, it was spread on Italian country bread, although it is also delicious served on crackers or bruschetta. The guests enjoyed it immensely, and not a morsel remained at the end of the celebration.

Caponata should taste *algro dolce*, which means slightly sweet and slightly sour. It makes a delicious accompaniment to grilled meat or fish and may be prepared up to one week in advance. Cover and store it in the refrigerator, then return it to room temperature or reheat it before serving.

STANLEY: This was the dish that attracted Gianni to my mother. I remember him at the wedding, commenting over and over how delicious the caponata was. He kept asking me if my mother had in fact made it, and I assured him that she had. I think I watched him return to the hors d'oeuvre table at least half a dozen times.

½ cup plus 2 tablespoons olive oil
1 medium-size eggplant, cut into 1-inch cubes (about 5 cups)
1½ cups roughly chopped onions
1 cup roughly chopped celery
2½ cups canned whole plum tomatoes
1 tablespoon capers, drained, rinsed, and dried
1 tablespoon pine nuts
1 tablespoon plus 2 teaspoons sugar
3 tablespoons red wine vinegar
1 teaspoon kosher salt
Freshly ground black pepper

Warm ½ cup of the olive oil in a large skillet set over medium-high heat. Add the cubed eggplant and cook until lightly browned but still firm, about 5 minutes. Transfer to a wide, deep saucepan or flameproof casserole and set aside.

Warm the remaining 2 tablespoons olive oil in the skillet. Stir in the onions and cook until wilted, about 4 minutes. Stir in the celery and then the tomatoes, crushing them with your hands or the back of a slotted spoon as you add them to the pan. Simmer over medium-low heat until the tomatoes begin to sweeten but the celery is still crisp, about 15 minutes. Stir in the capers and pine nuts. Transfer this vegetable mixture to the casserole with the eggplant.

In a small saucepan set over low heat, stir together the sugar and vinegar. Warm until the sugar dissolves. Stir into the eggplant mixture in the casserole. Season with the salt and pepper.

Cover the casserole and simmer over low heat, stirring frequently, until the tomatoes are cooked and the vegetables are tender but not mushy, 15 to 20 minutes. Serve the caponata warm or at room temperature.

MOZZARELLA IN CARROZZA

Grilled Mozzarella Cheese

MAKES 4 SERVINGS

STAN: Tony Spaccarelli, of Spaccarelli's restaurant in Millwood, New York, introduced us to the procedure for making fresh mozzarella and *bocconcini,* or mozzarella balls. The delicate flavor and texture of fresh mozzarella are very different from the packaged variety found in most supermarkets. This simple dish will taste best if you use fresh mozzarella.

This recipe is my mother's variation on the classic Italian sandwich, which she prepared on slices of round or long Italian bread. Serve it for lunch with a light salad, or cut it into squares to serve with drinks before dinner. When properly cooked, the mozzarella will produce long strings when bitten into. Kids love this "Italian grilled cheese" and they will compete to see who can pull the longest strings. These sandwiches may be prepared one hour in advance. Before serving, reheat in an oven at 350 degrees F.

4 ounces fresh mozzarella cheese, cut into thin slices
4 slices bread
1 large egg
1 tablespoon water
Kosher salt
¼ cup olive oil

Divide the slices of mozzarella between two slices of the bread. Top with the remaining bread to make two sandwiches, and set aside. In a shallow bowl, beat together the egg, water, and a little salt. In a sauté pan large enough to hold both sandwiches, warm the olive oil over medium-high heat. Dip the sandwiches in the egg mixture, and when the oil is hot but not smoking, add them to the pan. Cook until golden brown on both sides, about 3 minutes per side.

Remove from the pan, slice in half, and serve.

MOZZARELLA CON POMODORO

Mozzarella with Tomato

MAKES 4 SERVINGS

JOAN: Mozzarella cheese is used in a lot of the recipes in this book, but here it is the main ingredient. Fresh handmade mozzarella—which is widely available at gourmet stores—bears no resemblance to the commercial type. For the best fresh mozzarella, we shop at Joe's Deli on 187th Street near Arthur Avenue in the Bronx, one of the last old Italian neighborhoods in New York City.

This simple dish heightens the flavor of ripe summer tomatoes and may be served as a first course or as part of a buffet. During the winter I use thin slices of sun-dried tomatoes packed in olive oil in place of fresh tomatoes.

1 whole fresh mozzarella cheese (about 1 pound)
2 large ripe tomatoes
5 fresh basil leaves
3 tablespoons extra virgin olive oil
Kosher salt and freshly ground black pepper

Cut the mozzarella and tomatoes into ½-inch-thick slices. Arrange on a serving platter, alternating slices of mozzarella and tomatoes. Place the basil leaves between a few of the mozzarella and tomato slices. When ready to serve, pour the olive oil over all of the ingredients and season with salt and pepper.

PASTA FRITTA

Fried Pasta

MAKES 6 SERVINGS

JOAN: Most people have never heard of fried pasta, but once you've tasted it, you'll be addicted. It's usually made with leftover plain pasta, but it may be prepared with freshly boiled pasta. Stan's family traditionally fried linguine until his sister Rosalinda experimented with frying penne and ditalini and found that they were equally delicious. This liberated us, and our new favorite pasta for frying is orecchiette. Fried pasta may be prepared as a lunch dish, served with a tossed green salad, or as an irresistible appetizer before dinner, accompanied by a glass of wine.

1 pound linguine
½ cup plus 1 tablespoon olive oil
Kosher salt

Bring a pot of salted water to a rapid boil and add the linguine. Cook according to the package instructions. Drain and toss with 1 tablespoon of the olive oil.

Warm the remaining ½ cup olive oil in a large frying pan set over medium heat. When the oil is hot but not smoking, add the pasta, spreading it out to fill the pan. Cook the pasta until it is evenly browned and sticking together as a solid piece, about 6 minutes. Turn the pasta and continue cooking to evenly brown the other side, about 6 minutes. Remove from the heat and transfer to a serving dish. Season with salt. Cut the pasta into wedges with a pizza cutter or a sharp knife. Serve immediately.

VARIATIONS: Smaller pastas, such as penne, ditalini, or fusilli, will not stick together but will still fry nicely and may be eaten as individual pieces.

- When frying smaller quantities of pasta, reduce the amount of oil proportionately.

TORTA SALATA

Delicious Vegetable Tart

MAKES 8 MAIN-COURSE SERVINGS; 10 FIRST-COURSE SERVINGS

GIANNI: When I had completed my training as a chef and was still living in Italy, I would get together with my good friend and fellow chef Alberto Vanoli. We would cook up a storm, often experimenting with unusual combinations of ingredients just for the fun of it. We'd end up with much more food than the two of us could possibly eat, but it was a great learning experience. After trying several dough recipes, we agreed that this one was the finest. It makes a wonderful tart that may be filled with an infinite variety of cooked vegetable combinations. Serve it as a first course before roasted chicken or fish, or as the main dish of a light meal accompanied by a green salad.

I recommend baking this tart in a springform pan. You can also roll the dough to fit a 9 × 15-inch baking sheet with a 1-inch rim; cut the baked tart into small cubes and serve it as an appetizer, hot or at room temperature.

FOR THE PASTRY:

2½ cups all-purpose flour
2 teaspoons kosher salt
Freshly ground black pepper
15 tablespoons cold butter, cut into small pieces
1 large egg yolk
½ cup water
¼ cup dry white wine

FOR THE FILLING:

2 tablespoons olive oil
2 cups thinly sliced onions
3 tablespoons chopped fresh parsley leaves
2 pounds Swiss chard, leaves and stems roughly chopped
2½ cups fresh or frozen artichoke hearts cut into 1-inch pieces
Kosher salt and freshly ground black pepper
¼ cup freshly grated Parmesan cheese
¼ cup freshly grated pecorino Romano cheese
1 large egg, beaten
¼ cup light cream or milk
1 large egg yolk
2 tablespoons water

To prepare the pastry, combine the flour with the salt and pepper to taste in a large bowl or on a marble surface. Use your fingers or a pastry blender to cut the butter into the flour until it resembles coarse meal. Mound the flour mixture up and make a well in the center of it. Pour the remaining ingredients into the well. Slowly incorporate the liquid ingredients by working the flour into them a little at a time. When the dough comes together, compact it into a large disk, wrap it in plastic wrap, and refrigerate it for at least 30 minutes or up to 1 day.

To make the filling, warm the oil in a large skillet set over medium-high heat. Add the onions and cook, stirring occasionally, until soft but not brown, about 5 minutes. Stir in the parsley. Reduce the heat to medium and add the Swiss chard and artichoke hearts; season with salt and pepper. Stir to combine, and cook until the vegetables have softened and most of the liquid has evaporated, about 20 minutes. Remove from the heat and cool completely. (This filling may be prepared 1 day in advance. Cover and refrigerate. Return to room temperature before proceeding with the recipe.)

Stir the cheeses, the beaten egg, and the cream into the vegetable mixture. Set aside.

Preheat the oven to 375 degrees F. Lightly grease a 10-inch springform pan with butter and set aside.

Cut a quarter of the dough away from the disk and reserve in the refrigerator. On a lightly floured surface, roll the remaining three quarters of the dough into a ⅛-inch-thick circle that will cover the bottom of the springform pan and come three quarters of the way up the sides. Line the pan with the dough.

Fill the shell with the vegetable mixture, patting it down with the back of a spoon so it is compact. Roll the remaining one quarter of dough into a circle slightly larger than the pan. Place it on top of the filling. Use your fingers to crimp together the sides and top of the dough. Pierce the top of the tart with a fork to make tiny air vents.

Whisk together the egg yolk and water. Brush this egg wash on the top and edges of the pastry. Bake until golden brown, about 1 hour. Allow to rest for 10 minutes before serving.

VARIATIONS:

- Ricotta salata cheese may be used in place of the pecorino Romano.
- Canned artichoke bottoms may be used in place of fresh or frozen artichoke hearts.
- In place of Swiss chard and artichokes, 1 medium-size head cauliflower, cut into small florets, may be added to the cooked onions along with 4 chopped anchovy fillets and 2 large potatoes, peeled, quartered, and thinly sliced. Cook until the cauliflower has softened, about 20 minutes, then proceed with the basic recipe.
- In place of the Swiss chard and artichokes, 3 cups quartered mushrooms (such as cremini or portobello), 2 large potatoes, peeled, quartered, and thinly sliced, and ⅓ cup julienned pancetta may be added to the cooked onions. Cook until the potatoes have softened, about 10 minutes, then proceed with the basic recipe.
- To prepare an all-onion version of this tart, increase the onions to a total of 7 cups and cook until softened. Increase the pecorino Romano cheese to 1 cup, and stir it into the onions along with the Parmesan, beaten egg, and cream. Proceed with the basic recipe.

ANTIPASTO DI CANNELLINI

Cannellini Bean Antipasto

MAKES 6 SERVINGS

JOAN: I serve this dish along with several others as an antipasto, or as a lunch dish accompanied by a tossed green salad. When I prepare *Antipasto di Cannellini* for lunch, I always include the shrimp called for in one of the variations, and present it on a bed of lettuce accompanied by focaccia. For hors d'oeuvres I would serve this dish with a selection of olives, roasted peppers, soppressata, and Parmesan, or goat's or sheep's milk cheese.

One cup of dried beans will produce the two cups called for in this recipe after they have been soaked and cooked. Canned beans should be drained and rinsed. Allow the completed bean dish to sit for at least half an hour at room temperature before serving.

2 cups cooked (or drained and rinsed canned) cannellini beans
½ cup extra virgin olive oil
¼ cup chopped red onions
Two 5-inch sprigs fresh rosemary
½ teaspoon balsamic vinegar
Kosher salt and freshly ground black pepper
1 tablespoon chopped fresh basil leaves

In a serving bowl, toss the beans with the olive oil and red onions. Remove the rosemary leaves from the stems and add to the beans. Toss, then add the vinegar and season with salt and pepper. Toss again before adding the basil. Just before serving, toss the beans once more and test for seasoning. Add more oil, salt, pepper, and balsamic vinegar as desired.

VARIATIONS:

- Add 1 tablespoon freshly squeezed lemon juice to the basic recipe.
- Add 1 medium-size ripe tomato cut into ½-inch pieces to the basic recipe.
- Shrimp make a delicious addition to this dish. Shell and devein ½ pound medium-size shrimp. Warm 1 tablespoon olive oil and 1 clove garlic, quartered, together in a sauté pan set over medium-high heat. When the oil is hot but not smoking, add the shrimp and cook, stirring frequently, until they turn pink, about 4 minutes. Remove the shrimp from the pan, reserving the garlic and oil. Chop the shrimp into pieces slightly larger than the beans. Toss the shrimp with the beans, adding the reserved oil and garlic. Then proceed with the basic recipe.

PEPERONI ARROSTITI

Roasted Red Peppers

MAKES 10 SERVINGS

JOAN: Roasted peppers remind me of bottling tomatoes in the late summer. My mother, father, and whichever children were at home would gather to pick the tomatoes. The tomatoes were placed on a large table to be checked over to make sure they were ripe, and then put in a large tub filled with water. We sat around the tub with an apron over our laps, picking out tomatoes, coring, and cutting them. They were placed in a strainer to drain into a pail. (If you picked out a nice small ripe tomato, you'd pop it into your mouth as a reward for working hard.)

When the strainer was full, the tomatoes were dumped into a pillowcase that was tied to a tree limb. Salt was added (always by an adult—but I don't know why, since they never measured). We would rub the pillowcase with our hands to extract the water. When all the water had been extracted from the tomatoes, the tomatoes left in the pillowcase were placed in a machine that reduced the pulp to a thick seedless, skinless liquid.

All of the rich tomato liquid we had gathered was then funneled into 8-ounce soda bottles and a fresh basil leaf was added to each one. Not everyone was allowed to cap the bottles. You had to be strong enough to make the indentation on the top of the cap so the juice wouldn't leak out in the boiling process. I couldn't wait to be old enough to cap. Fortunately my children had the chance to bottle and cap tomatoes with us before my father died.

Finally, the filled and capped bottles were placed in a 55-gallon drum half filled with water that was set over an outdoor open fireplace. The water would boil, sealing the bottles and preserving the fresh summer tomatoes, which my mother cooked with all winter long. While the fire was warming and we were squeezing liquid from the tomatoes, my mother would roast fresh peppers over the coals. We ate those roasted peppers served on toasted slices of my mother's homemade bread or tossed them with quartered boiled potatoes drizzled with olive oil.

STANLEY: Roasted peppers are a great complement to almost any sandwich. If I have leftover pasta and not enough sauce, I will sauté garlic in some olive oil, add these peppers to heat them through, and toss this simple sauce over the pasta for a quick lunch dish.

10 red bell peppers
½ cup olive oil
2 cloves garlic, quartered
Kosher salt
1 tablespoon chopped fresh parsley leaves

continued

Preheat the oven broiler. Place a brown paper bag inside a plastic shopping bag and set aside.

Lay the peppers on their sides on an oven rack. Place a cookie sheet below the peppers to catch any juices. Broil the peppers, turning occasionally, until the skins are charred on all sides, including the tops and bottoms. Remove the peppers from the oven and immediately place them in the paper bag. Close the paper bag and the plastic bag around it, and allow the peppers to cool slightly, about 5 minutes.

Remove one of the peppers from the paper bag. Peel away and discard the charred skin, stem, and seeds. Tear the pepper lengthwise into ½-inch-wide strips, and place the strips in a bowl. Continue with this procedure until all of the peppers have been peeled. Set the bowl aside for 10 minutes.

Drain off all but ¼ cup of any liquid that may have accumulated in the bowl. Add the olive oil, garlic, salt to taste, and parsley to the bowl and toss to coat the peppers.

NOTE: If you do not plan to serve these roasted peppers immediately, place them in a jar and cover with the olive oil. The peppers may then be stored in the refrigerator for up to 1 week. Bring to room temperature and add the remaining ingredients before serving.

Roasted peppers may also be frozen. Divide the peppers into two batches. Place in airtight containers along with 2 tablespoons of the olive oil (or enough to cover) in each one. Freeze for up to 3 months. Thaw the peppers and then combine with the remaining ¼ cup olive oil and the other ingredients before serving.

OLIVE MARINATE

Marinated Olives

MAKES 6 TO 8 SERVINGS

GIANNI: The town of Marostica, Italy, is very near Mason Vicentino, where I grew up. Every other year in Marostica a game of living chess is played in the piazza of a medieval castle. Local townspeople dressed as chess pieces position themselves on an ancient red-and-white marble chessboard. As the game is played, spectators may gaze up at the olive tree–covered hills surrounding Marostica.

In October, when it is time to harvest the olives, people gather in groups around the trunks of the trees. As they shake the trees, ripe olives rain down on tarps that have been spread on the ground below. The olives are gathered up and taken to the community olive press, where they are made into oil. These small pressings of olive oil vary in flavor and color from town to town and are rarely tasted outside their own communities.

This recipe is for spicy marinated olives. Serve them as part of an antipasto or to accompany a simple lunch. They also make a nice gift.

¼ cup fennel seeds
1 tablespoon cumin seeds
⅛ teaspoon ground cardamom
1 cup Picholine olives (mild, green)
1 cup Sicilian olives (small, green, oval)
1 cup Kalamata olives (black)
1 cup extra virgin olive oil, plus more for covering
2 tablespoons loosely packed long thin strips orange zest (from about 1 orange)
5 cloves garlic, peeled
⅛ teaspoon red pepper flakes

Place the fennel seeds, cumin seeds, and ground cardamom in a small sauté pan set over low heat. Toast the spices, stirring frequently, until they begin to release their aroma, about 5 minutes. Remove from the heat and set aside.

Place the olives, olive oil, orange zest, garlic, and red pepper flakes in a large bowl. Add the toasted spices and stir with a large spoon to evenly coat the olives. Allow to marinate at room temperature for 24 hours. Discard the garlic and transfer the olives to a large jar. Add enough olive oil to cover, seal with a lid, and store in the refrigerator for up to 5 days. Serve at room temperature.

FUNGHI RIPIENI

Stuffed Mushrooms

MAKES 6 SERVINGS

STAN: During late August and early September my family would visit Zio Emilio and Zia Maria Politi at their summer camp in Roxbury, Vermont. The entire family would venture out to the pine forests to gather wild mushrooms. My task was to stay in a given place to receive and clean the treasures they found in the woods. The mushrooms were then brought to the Politi camp, where they were put on large screens, exposed to the sun, and air-dried. They were used in *giardiniera* (homemade pickled garden vegetables) and in *Risotto alla Milanese* (page 184), a northern Italian dish that Zia Maria introduced to our southern Italian family.

JOAN: I serve these with drinks before dinner or as part of a buffet. The filling may be prepared and the mushrooms stuffed several hours in advance. Drizzle with the oil just before baking.

STANLEY: Always make more of these than you think you may need as they seem to be addictive. Though most children despise mushrooms, they can't seem to get enough of these. Watch them argue over the last one.

10 ounces medium-size white mushrooms
½ cup plus 1 tablespoon olive oil
¾ cup plain dried bread crumbs, or more as needed
½ cup finely grated pecorino Romano cheese
1 teaspoon finely chopped garlic (about 2 small cloves)
2 tablespoons finely chopped fresh parsley leaves
Kosher salt and freshly ground black pepper
1 tablespoon extra virgin olive oil

Preheat the oven to 375 degrees F.

Remove the stems from the mushroom caps and set the caps aside.

Finely chop half the mushroom stems (discard the other half). Warm 1 tablespoon of the olive oil in a small sauté pan set over medium heat. Add the mushroom stems and cook, stirring, until they have softened and are lightly browned, about 5 minutes.

In a medium-size bowl, mix together the cooked mushroom stems, bread crumbs, cheese, garlic, and parsley, and season with salt and pepper. Slowly stir in the remaining ½ cup olive oil to form a moist dough. (If the dough is too oily, add more bread crumbs.)

Divide the dough equally among the mushroom caps. Place the filled caps on a baking sheet. Drizzle the olive oil over the mushrooms, and bake until the mushrooms are browned but still firm, about 8 minutes. Remove from the oven and serve warm. (If the tops of the mushrooms have not browned, place them under the broiler for 1 minute.)

VARIATIONS:

- The mushroom stems may be sautéed in butter rather than olive oil.
- The chopped mushroom stems may be cooked in a microwave. Place them in a small dish and toss with the olive oil or melted butter. Cook on high power until firm but cooked through, about 2 minutes. Proceed with the recipe.
- This same recipe may be prepared using large stuffing mushrooms. Chop half of the mushroom stems and double the remaining filling ingredients. These mushrooms will take longer to brown, about 12 minutes.

CROCCHETTE DI PATATE

Potato Croquettes

MAKES 6 SERVINGS

STANLEY: Taken with a stomach flu the year we were living in Italy, I was instructed to eat only crackers, bananas, water, and ginger ale. By what seemed a fortnight of eating this bland diet (probably only two or three days), I began to yearn for many of my mother's and grandmother's dishes. I remember lying on the couch and rattling off some of my favorites. My mother looked at me sadly and told me, "All in good time." But what I wanted most of all were my grandmother's potato croquettes. I could see, smell, and taste them so clearly. I would try to rid my mind of them and concentrate on something else, but it was no use. The potato croquettes haunted me. They gnawed at my stomach, my senses, my soul. I swore I could see them dancing, spinning mockingly around my head, their delicate aroma taunting my nostrils. I pleaded with my mother, telling her I was desperate to partake of the potato croquettes. "Soon," she said, "soon." If memory serves me, she did indeed make the croquettes within the week. But it's strange how one remembers the longing more than the eating.

4 medium-size all-purpose potatoes, peeled and quartered
2 large eggs, beaten
½ cup plain dried bread crumbs
2 tablespoons all-purpose flour
3 tablespoons finely grated pecorino Romano cheese
1 tablespoon chopped fresh parsley leaves
Kosher salt
¼ cup olive oil, plus more as needed

Place the potatoes in a large saucepan and fill with enough water to cover. Bring to a boil and cook until the potatoes are tender when pierced with a fork, 15 to 20 minutes. Drain the potatoes and mash them in a bowl with a potato masher. Add the eggs, bread crumbs, flour, cheese, parsley, and salt to taste. Mix with your hands to make a firm, dry dough, adding more bread crumbs or flour as necessary.

Heat the oil in a small frying pan (about 8 inches in diameter) set over medium heat. Roll tablespoons of the dough between the palms of your hands to form 3- to 4-inch-long logs. When the oil is hot but not smoking, add a few croquettes to the pan and fry until lightly browned on all sides, about 6 minutes. Transfer the cooked croquettes to a plate lined with paper towels to drain before serving. Continue to cook the croquettes in small batches. Add more oil to the pan if necessary, being sure to allow it to heat up before adding the croquettes. The croquettes are best if served immediately, but they can be made ahead and reheated in the oven if necessary.

VARIATION: The potatoes may be cooked whole. Peel and quarter them when cool to the touch and then proceed with the recipe.

FRITTELLE DI ZUCCHINE

Fried Zucchini Fritters

MAKES 6 SERVINGS

JOAN: My mother cooked these in a very well seasoned enameled pan. Today I use a nonstick pan for guaranteed best results. A nonstick pan also means that the fritters may be fried in less oil. These are best served warm immediately after frying; however, they may be made ahead and reheated in an oven at 350 degrees F.

We grew our own zucchini, and they seemed to have less water in them than those I purchase at the grocery store. That is why, although my mother did not use this method, I recommend salting and draining the zucchini before proceeding with the recipe.

3 cups grated zucchini (about 2 medium-size zucchini)
2 teaspoons kosher salt
1 large egg
¼ cup finely grated pecorino Romano cheese
3 to 5 tablespoons all-purpose flour, as needed
¼ cup olive oil

Place the grated zucchini in a colander. Toss with the salt. Place the colander over a bowl to catch any water, and let stand for 30 minutes.

Press all of the water out of the zucchini by squeezing small portions of it in your hand or by pressing on the zucchini in the colander with the back of a wooden spoon. Transfer the drained zucchini to a bowl. Add the egg, cheese, and 3 tablespoons of the flour to the bowl. Stir with a fork, adding more flour as necessary to create a batter that holds together.

Warm the olive oil in a small sauté pan (about 8 inches in diameter) set over medium-high heat. When the oil is hot but not smoking, scoop out rounded tablespoons of the zucchini batter and add to the pan. Flatten the fritters slightly with a spatula. (It is best to cook only two or three fritters at a time to maintain the oil at an even heat.) Fry the fritters until they are golden brown on each side, about 3 minutes per side. Transfer to a paper-towel-lined plate to drain before serving.

VARIATION: Chopped zucchini blossoms may be prepared following this same recipe. Be sure to remove the blossoms' pistils first.

VEGETALI CROCCANTI

Crispy Vegetables

MAKES 8 TO 10 SERVINGS

GIANNI: I like to serve an assortment of fried vegetables in a basket as an appetizer or as a side dish with grilled meat or fish.

1¼ cups sifted all-purpose flour
¼ cup plus 1 tablespoon cornstarch
1 teaspoon kosher salt
½ cup plus 2 tablespoons cold water
¼ cup olive oil
¼ cup cold beer
3 large egg whites
2 medium-size carrots, peeled and cut on the bias into ¼-inch-thick slices
Canola oil for frying
2 medium-size zucchini, cut on the bias into ¼-inch-thick slices
1 small red onion, cut into ½-inch-thick slices and separated into rings
12 tender green beans or haricorts verts, ends trimmed
1 small head broccoli, tough stems discarded and florets cut into bite-size pieces
1 portobello mushroom, stem discarded, bottom gills trimmed off until smooth, cut into ¼-inch-thick slices
3 small fresh artichokes, tough outer leaves discarded, cut into long ¼-inch-thick slices, and choke removed and discarded

In a medium-size bowl, whisk together the flour, cornstarch, and salt. Whisk in the water, oil, and beer to form a smooth, stiff batter. In a separate bowl, beat the egg whites until stiff but not dry peaks form. Fold the egg whites into the batter. Fill a large bowl halfway with equal parts ice and water. Place the batter bowl into this ice bath and set aside.

Bring a small pot of water to a boil. Add the carrots and blanch until slightly softened, about 1 minute. Remove, pat dry, and set aside with the other vegetables.

Fill a medium-size frying pan with canola oil to a depth of 1 inch. Set over medium-high heat and warm until hot but not smoking. Dip the vegetables, one at a time, into the batter to lightly coat, shaking off any excess. Add a few vegetables at a time to the oil in the pan. If the oil is hot enough, the vegetables will float on the surface. Cook the vegetables, turning frequently, until lightly browned on both sides, about 1 minute. Remove to a paper-towel-lined surface to drain before serving. Continue frying the vegetables in small batches until done. Serve immediately.

VARIATION: This batter may also be used to fry shrimp, calamari, or scallops.

PROSCIUTTO CON FICHI

Prosciutto with Figs

MAKES 6 SERVINGS

JOAN: This simple variation on the traditional prosciutto-with-melon appetizer is infused with memories for me. My father planted fig trees in his yard, and for several decades these trees produced abundant quantities of delicious purple figs. In early autumn the trees were tightly wrapped in oilcloth, bent over, staked, and buried under dirt and leaves to protect them from the bitter winter weather. Each spring the fig trees were righted and unwrapped in time to bloom and bear fruit for another season.

This dish may be served on individual plates to guests seated at the table or presented on a platter as part of a buffet.

STANLEY: This is a simple, elegant, and profoundly sexual appetizer. I won't elaborate but leave it up to you.

6 ripe figs	*8 very thin slices prosciutto*

Quarter each fig. Slice each piece of prosciutto lengthwise into thirds. Drape a slice of prosciutto over each fig quarter so that the prosciutto covers most of the fig. When serving buffet style, secure the prosciutto to the fig with a toothpick.

VARIATIONS: Sections of peeled cantaloupe or honeydew melon, or sliced pears, persimmons, or peaches may be substituted for the fresh figs.

COSTICINE DI MAIALE

Spareribs

MAKES 6 SERVINGS

JOAN: Stan's sister Dora and his sister-in-law, Teddy, often cook together, particularly when preparing for a holiday or other family gathering. They share recipes back and forth, so I'm not sure who originated this dish—they both serve these spareribs as appetizers. Since we all greatly enjoy them, these quickly became a summer staple especially when the children were growing up. That is why I have chosen to include this recipe, even though it isn't classically Italian.

½ cup soy sauce
½ cup dry white wine
½ cup water
⅓ cup sugar
1 teaspoon kosher salt
2 cloves garlic, crushed
18 individual spareribs (about 3 pounds)

In a 2-cup measuring cup, whisk together the soy sauce, wine, water, sugar, salt, and garlic. Place the spareribs in a single layer in a baking dish. Pour the sauce over the ribs, turning to coat them with the marinade. Cover and allow to marinate for at least 1 hour and up to 1 day in the refrigerator.

Prepare a charcoal or gas grill. Cook the ribs, turning frequently, until the meat easily pulls away from the bone, 15 to 20 minutes. Serve immediately or at room temperature.

VARIATION: This marinade may also be used on chicken wings or pork tenderloin for grilling.

Instead of grilling, the spareribs or chicken wings may be cooked in the oven under the broiler, turning frequently.

COZZE, PATATE, E ZUCCHINE

Mussels, Potatoes, and Zucchini

MAKES 6 SERVINGS

GIANNI: One summer I visited friends in Rimini, which is in the Emilia Romagna region of Italy. They prepared this dish, and the memory of its sweet fresh taste and delicate flavor has stayed with me. The best mussels to use when preparing this recipe are from Prince Edward Island or New Zealand when they are in season. Leave the mussels in their shells, making for a less formal, hands-on presentation, or remove the mussels from their shells before serving, return them to the pot to warm through, and then ladle them out with the vegetables and broth. Either way, this is a delicious warm appetizer or light luncheon dish. It may also be tossed with cooked short-cut pasta such as penne or ziti.

4 tablespoons extra virgin olive oil
2 tablespoons thinly sliced shallots
½ pound all-purpose potatoes, peeled and cut into ⅛-inch-thick slices
½ pound zucchini, cut into ⅛-inch-thick slices
1 clove garlic, thinly sliced
¼ cup dry white wine
3 tablespoons water
Kosher salt and freshly ground black pepper
48 mussels (about 4 pounds), scrubbed and debearded
½ cup cubed ripe tomatoes (about 2 plum tomatoes)
2 teaspoons chopped fresh parsley leaves
6 slices country-style bread, toasted or grilled
1 clove garlic, cut in half

In a flameproof casserole set over medium-high heat, warm 2 tablespoons of the olive oil with the shallots, potatoes, zucchini, sliced garlic, wine, water, and salt and pepper to taste. Cook, stirring a few times, until the potatoes have softened, about 6 minutes. Place the mussels on top of the vegetables and sprinkle the tomatoes on top of the mussels. Cover and cook until the mussel shells have opened, about 5 minutes. Remove from the heat and discard any unopened mussels.

Remove the vegetables with a slotted spoon and distribute them evenly among six plates or shallow soup bowls. Top with equal portions of mussels. Add the remaining 2 tablespoons olive oil and the parsley to the liquid remaining in the casserole. Set the casserole over high heat and whisk the broth to combine the ingredients, adding more water if necessary. Cook just to warm through, about 1 minute, and pour on top of the mussels. Serve immediately, accompanied by toasted bread rubbed with the garlic halves.

VONGOLE GRATINATE AL FORNO

Baked Clams on the Half Shell

MAKES 4 TO 6 SERVINGS

JOAN: When we were testing this recipe for the book, I wanted to be sure to purchase the correct size clams. I told Ben Conti, our local fishmonger, that I wanted either big littleneck clams or small cherrystone clams. He said, "What you want are top neck clams." I had never heard of them, but they proved to be the perfect size. Be sure to ask for them by name.

The topping may be prepared several hours in advance. Spoon it onto the clams just before broiling. Stan opens the clams over a big bowl so that he can collect the juice, which we strain and reserve in the refrigerator or freezer to use when we prepare *Linguine con Vongole* (Linguine with Clam Sauce) on page 158.

12 top neck clams
1 cup plain dried bread crumbs
¼ cup chopped fresh parsley leaves
1 tablespoon finely chopped garlic
½ cup olive oil

Scrub the clams under cold running water. Pry them open and gently remove any sand or grit. Gently separate the top and bottom shells, loosening and allowing the clam to divide, with some remaining on the top shell and some remaining on the bottom shell. Use a knife to loosen the clam in the shell, removing any sand or grit that may have been under the clam. All of the clams may not divide evenly between the top and bottom shell. Cut these clams into small pieces and distribute among the other shells. You should have at least 16 clamshell halves to fill and bake. Arrange the clam-filled shells on a baking sheet and set aside.

In a small bowl, toss together the bread crumbs, parsley, and garlic. Use a fork to stir the olive oil into this mixture. It should be moist but not oily. Set aside.

Preheat the oven to 350 degrees F.

Fill each clam with a portion of the topping mixture, spreading it evenly over the clam and to the edge of the shell. The filling should be about ⅛ inch thick. Bake until the topping begins to brown slightly, about 5 minutes. Remove from the oven and adjust the oven temperature to broil. Place the clams under the broiler and cook until golden brown, about 2 minutes. Serve immediately.

CALAMARI AFFOGATI IN BRODETTO

Pan-Seared Calamari in Its Own Broth

MAKES 4 SERVINGS

GIANNI: This is a quick summer dish that was very popular when I was working as an apprentice chef in Venice. Calamari can be tricky to cook because they become tough and rubbery if they are under- or overcooked. To ensure perfection, I slice the calamari into rings, sauté for no more than two minutes, and then reheat in broth. Prepared this way it may be served as a first course with grilled or fresh polenta or accompanied by toasted bread rubbed with fresh garlic.

3 tablespoons extra virgin olive oil
2 cloves garlic, thinly sliced
½ teaspoon red pepper flakes or 2 teaspoons seeded and chopped jalapeño peppers
1 tablespoon minced shallots
2 tablespoons chopped fresh parsley leaves
1 pound cleaned calamari, cut into bite-size rings
Kosher salt and freshly ground black pepper
¼ cup dry white wine
1½ cups diced ripe plum tomatoes (about 3 large tomatoes)
2 teaspoons chopped fresh basil leaves
2 tablespoons butter or extra virgin olive oil (optional)

Warm the olive oil in a large skillet set over high heat. When the oil is hot but not smoking, add the garlic and red pepper flakes. Cook until the garlic just begins to color, about 30 seconds (do not let it brown). Stir in the shallots and 1 tablespoon of the parsley. Cook until the shallots begin to color, about 10 seconds. Add the calamari and cook over high heat, stirring frequently, until it begins to soften, about 1 minute. Season with salt and generous grindings of black pepper. Add the wine and cook until the calamari absorbs the flavor of the wine, about 1 minute.

Remove the calamari from the pan with a slotted spoon and set aside. Stir the tomatoes into the skillet and continue boiling until slightly thickened, 2 to 3 minutes. Stir in the remaining 1 tablespoon parsley and the basil. Return the calamari to the skillet and adjust the seasoning with salt and pepper. For a slightly richer sauce, stir the butter into the calamari just before serving, or drizzle with the extra virgin olive oil just before serving. Serve immediately.

VARIATIONS:

- 1 cup cooked or canned white beans (drained and rinsed), such as cannellini, may be added to the sauce along with the tomatoes.
- A pinch of ground cumin or paprika may be added in place of the red pepper flakes.

STUFATINO DI CRESCIONE CON PESCE E FUNGHI

Watercress, Seafood, and Mushroom Casserole

MAKES 4 SERVINGS

GIANNI: The idea of wilting bitter greens—such as escarole, spinach, and broccoli di rape—has long been a part of Italian cooking. One day I decided to try using watercress, a salad green I like for its appearance but not for its too-tart taste. I experimented with various taste combinations and created this recipe, which reduces the bitter taste of the watercress and shows off the sweet flavor of the shrimp.

1 tablespoon extra virgin olive oil, plus more for drizzling if desired
1 tablespoon chopped fresh parsley leaves
¼ cup chopped shallots
½ pound medium-size shrimp, shelled, deveined, and cut in half lengthwise
1½ cups thinly sliced white mushroom caps
Kosher salt and freshly ground black pepper
⅓ cup dry white wine
½ cup chicken broth
4 ounces watercress (about 2 bunches), tough stems removed
1 ripe plum tomato, diced
1 tablespoon butter

Warm the olive oil in a skillet set over high heat. Add the parsley and shallots and cook, stirring constantly, to wilt the shallots, about 2 minutes. Add the shrimp and cook, stirring frequently, until the shrimp just begin to turn pink, about 2 minutes. Stir in the mushrooms, and season with salt and pepper. Cook until the shrimp are cooked through, 3 to 5 minutes. Add the wine, broth, and watercress. Cook, tossing the watercress until wilted, about half a minute. Remove from the heat.

Use tongs to remove the watercress from the skillet and distribute it evenly among four shallow bowls. Top with the shrimp. Return the skillet to the heat, and stir the tomato and butter into the remaining liquid. Cook, stirring frequently, to melt the butter and slightly thicken the sauce, about 2 minutes. Distribute the sauce evenly among the serving bowls. Serve immediately, drizzled with additional extra virgin olive oil if you like.

VARIATION: Whole bay scallops or quartered sea scallops may be used in place of shrimp.

INSALATA DI FRUTTI DI MARE VENEZIANA

Venetian Seafood Salad

MAKES 6 TO 8 SERVINGS

GIANNI: My wife, Laura, and I had a memorable version of this salad at a trattoria near my hometown of Mason Vicentino. It was served with a chilled Novello, a young red wine that is made from the first pressing of the grapes and is available only three months out of the year. A chilled Prosecco wine also pairs well with this dish.

The seafood for this recipe may be prepared one day in advance. Toss it with the remaining ingredients one or two hours before serving. If your fishmonger cannot get fresh octopus, simply increase the amounts of calamari and shrimp.

FOR THE SEAFOOD AND POACHING LIQUID:

1 celery stalk
1 medium-size carrot
1 small onion, cut in half
1 bay leaf
3 tablespoons freshly squeezed lemon juice (from about 1 lemon)
1 teaspoon kosher salt
2 quarts water
1 pound cleaned calamari, cut into 1-inch-thick rings
½ pound sea or bay scallops, tough part removed
1 pound medium-size or large shrimp
1 pound octopus

FOR THE SALAD:

1 cup julienned tender celery
1 cup julienned carrots
½ cup seeded and julienned red bell pepper
½ cup seeded and julienned yellow bell pepper
1 scallion (white part only), julienned
2 tablespoons chopped fresh parsley leaves
2 tablespoons chopped fresh basil leaves
2 large cloves garlic, finely chopped
6 tablespoons freshly squeezed lemon juice (from about 2 lemons) or lime juice (from about 3 limes)
1 tablespoon white wine vinegar
½ cup extra virgin olive oil
½ teaspoon kosher salt
Freshly ground black pepper
6 to 8 cups baby lettuce

To poach the seafood, you will need a large saucepan fitted with a colander insert. In the bottom of the pan, combine the celery, carrot, onion, bay leaf, lemon juice, salt, and water. Bring to a boil.

Place the calamari in the colander and cook in the boiling water for 2 minutes. Remove from the water, transfer to a large bowl, and set aside. Place the scallops in the colander and cook in the boiling water for 3 to 4 minutes. Remove from the water and transfer to the bowl with the calamari (large sea scallops may be cut in half horizontally after cooking; bay scallops may be left whole). Place the shrimp in the colander and cook in the boiling water until pink, about 3 minutes. Remove from the water. Peel, devein, and cut in half horizontally, adding them to the bowl with the calamari and scallops.

Remove the colander from the pan and place the octopus directly in the saucepan, adding more water if necessary to completely cover. Bring to a boil. Reduce the heat and gently simmer until you can easily push your finger through one of the thickest portions of the tentacles, 40 to 50 minutes. Transfer the octopus to a bowl and place under cold running water until cooled, about 5 minutes. Use your fingers and a small paring knife to remove the outer skin. Discard the hard mouth and head sac. Cut the tentacles on the bias into 1-inch pieces and add to the bowl with the other fish.

To prepare the salad, toss the julienned celery, carrots, bell peppers, scallion, parsley, basil, and garlic together in a serving bowl. Add the seafood and toss. Add the lemon juice, vinegar, and olive oil, and toss well. Season with the salt and generous grindings of pepper. Arrange 1 cup of lettuce on each serving plate. Top with equal portions of the seafood-and-vegetable mixture, and serve immediately.

VARIATIONS:

- 6 to 8 steamed mussels may be added to the basic recipe and tossed with the other seafood.
- To extend the recipe and add a new texture dimension, ½ cup cubed, peeled, cooked Idaho potatoes and/or ½ cup cooked or canned (drained and rinsed) cannellini beans may be added to the basic recipe.
- Although it isn't traditional, I like this salad with a hint of cilantro—2 teaspoons chopped should do it.

INSALATA DI FUNGHI E ASPARAGI BIANCHI

Mushroom and White Asparagus Salad

MAKES 4 SERVINGS

GIANNI: Bassano del Grappa, located in northeastern Italy just above Venice and near my hometown of Mason Vicentino, is renowned for its white asparagus, the best in the world. They are abundant from the end of April through the end of May. During that season every restaurant, trattoria, and even osteria serves boiled white asparagus with hard-boiled eggs. The procedure for eating this local dish is almost like a religious ceremony. Each person is served a plate on which are placed several very soft, warm asparagus, a hard-boiled egg, and some good olive oil. The egg is crushed with the back of a fork and mixed with the oil and some salt and pepper to make a dressing. The asparagus (which is always eaten by hand) is dipped into the egg dressing and then consumed in one long bite. If you have never eaten asparagus this way, you must.

My version of this local dish includes mushrooms and a delicate salad. It may be prepared with white or green asparagus. Pencil-thin asparagus do not need to be peeled.

16 white asparagus
3 medium-size cremini or porcini mushrooms
¾ pound purslane, mâche, or a mixture of lettuce greens
1 tablespoon balsamic vinegar
Kosher salt and freshly ground black pepper
1 teaspoon Dijon mustard
2 tablespoons olive oil
2 tablespoons hot water
¼ cup roughly chopped toasted (see Note) hazelnuts

Bring a large pot of salted water to a boil.

Cut 1 inch of tough stalk off the bottom of each asparagus spear. Use a vegetable peeler to remove a thin layer of tough outer stalk from the lower third of the asparagus. Blanch the asparagus in the water until slightly tender, about 1 minute. Drain and run under very cold water to cool. Cut the asparagus on a sharp bias into 4-inch lengths and set aside.

Remove and discard the mushroom stems. Trim away and discard the soft brown gills on the undersides of the mushroom caps. Cut the mushroom caps into very thin slices. Set aside.

Place the salad greens in a large bowl along with half the sliced mushrooms.

In a bowl, whisk together the vinegar and salt and pepper to taste. Add the mustard and whisk until smooth. Whisk in the olive oil and the water, 1 tablespoon at a time, beating to produce a smooth, emulsified dressing.

Pour the dressing over the salad and toss to coat evenly. Distribute the salad among four serving plates. Arrange the remaining mushrooms on top of each portion. Top with the asparagus. Sprinkle with the hazelnuts and serve.

NOTE: To toast hazelnuts, preheat the oven to 300 degrees F. Spread the nuts evenly in a small baking sheet or cake pan. Toast in the oven, stirring once or twice, until the nuts turn light gold and release their aroma, about 5 minutes. Allow to cool before chopping and sprinkling on the salad.

VARIATIONS:

- As an addition to the basic recipe, 1 large portobello mushroom, with the stem removed, may be very thinly sliced, dusted in flour, and fried in 2 cups of hot but not smoking peanut or canola oil. Drain on paper towels before serving as a garnish on top of the salad.
- In place of the hazelnuts, long, thin slices of aged ricotta salata or aged goat's cheese may be arranged on top of the salad. I recommend using a vegetable peeler to create these slices. (Or you can simply grate the cheese.)

INSALATA DI FUNGHI ARROSTITI

Roasted Mushroom Salad with Lettuces, Balsamic Vinaigrette, and Parmesan Shavings

MAKES 4 SERVINGS

GIANNI: Asiago is a beautiful hill town in the northeastern section of the Veneto region of Italy. In the late autumn, before the hard frost of winter, people go to Asiago and the surrounding area to gather the wild mushrooms that grow there in abundance. At the same time the menus of every local restaurant and trattoria feature a wide assortment of mushroom-based *antipasti,* soups, *risotti,* and pastas.

I was inspired by that tradition to create this simple salad, which relies on only a few ingredients for its rich flavor. The mushrooms may be prepared several hours ahead and set aside until you are ready to toss the salad. I recommend using a vegetable peeler to create the Parmesan shavings.

¾ pound any single variety of mushroom or a combination (shiitake, oyster, cremini, portobello, porcini, chanterelle, cinnamon caps), cut into wedges
5 tablespoons plus 2 teaspoons extra virgin olive oil
1 shallot, thinly sliced
1 tablespoon chopped fresh parsley leaves
Kosher salt and freshly ground black pepper
2 tablespoons balsamic vinegar
¾ pound mixed tender lettuces
16 large shavings Parmesan cheese (about 2 ounces)

Preheat the oven to 450 degrees F.

Toss the mushrooms in a baking dish along with 3 tablespoons of the olive oil, the sliced shallot, and the parsley, and season with salt and pepper. Roast in the oven until the mushrooms are browned but still firm and the shallots have wilted, 6 to 8 minutes. Set aside.

In a large bowl, whisk together the remaining 2 tablespoons plus 2 teaspoons olive oil, salt and pepper to taste, and the vinegar. Add the lettuce and toss thoroughly. Distribute the lettuce evenly among four salad plates. Top with the roasted mushrooms and Parmesan shavings. Serve immediately.

CARCIOFINIE RUCOLA CON PARMIGIANO

Baby Artichokes and Arugula with Parmesan Cheese

MAKES 4 SERVINGS

GIANNI: During a vacation in Rome, I stopped into a small bar to have a little something to eat. I was served the house salad, which was made with shaved uncooked artichokes. I thought this was odd, but when I tasted the salad I found the artichokes were crunchy yet easy to chew, with a different but familiar flavor. When I returned home I created my own version of this Roman recipe, using tender artichokes, about 2½ inches tall, shaved very thin, ⅛ inch or less. Then I added the arugula and Parmesan cheese to accent the flavor of the artichokes. Use a vegetable peeler to create large, thin shavings of Parmesan cheese to garnish the salad.

1 lemon
10 baby artichokes (about 1 pound)
1 tablespoon finely grated Parmesan cheese
3 tablespoons freshly squeezed lemon juice (from about 1 lemon)
5 tablespoons extra virgin olive oil
Kosher salt and freshly ground black pepper
2 tablespoons balsamic vinegar
¾ pound arugula, washed and stemmed
16 large shavings Parmesan cheese (about 2 ounces)

Fill a large bowl with cold water. Cut the lemon in half and squeeze the juice into the water. Place the lemon halves in the water and set aside.

Cut away and discard the artichoke stems. Peel off and discard several layers of tough outer leaves until you reach a layer where the artichoke leaves are half pale green and half pale yellow in color. Trim off the top pale green portion of the artichokes and discard. Slice the artichokes in half lengthwise, and remove any of the fine choke from the center. Place in the lemon water, rubbing each half with a bit of the lemon, and set aside.

In a large bowl, whisk together the grated cheese, lemon juice, and 2 tablespoons of the olive oil. Season with salt and pepper, and set the dressing aside.

Remove the artichokes from the water and pat dry. Slice the artichokes lengthwise into very thin strips—⅛ inch or less—and add the slices to the bowl with the dressing. Toss to coat evenly with the dressing and set aside for at least 15 minutes or for up to 2 hours.

In a large bowl, whisk the vinegar with salt and pepper to taste. Whisk in the remaining 3 tablespoons olive oil. Add the arugula and toss to evenly coat with this dressing. Distribute evenly among four salad plates. Top the arugula with equal portions of artichokes. Garnish each portion with 4 long strips of Parmesan cheese just before serving.

VARIATION: Celery root or jícama may be used in place of the artichokes. Peel the celery root or jícama, then cut into julienne strips using a food processor or knife. Toss with the dressing and proceed with the basic recipe. One quarter teaspoon red pepper flakes or ¼ fresh jalapeño pepper, seeded and finely chopped, may be added to the celery root or jícama just before tossing with the dressing.

A very early picture of me with my mother, Maria-Bertilla, outside our house/bar.

INSALATA DI RUCOLA, PROSCIUTTO, PERA, E PARMIGIANO

Arugula with Prosciutto, Pears, and Parmesan

MAKES 4 SERVINGS

GIANNI: In Italy only baby arugula is served in salads. The longer, more mature arugula is fed to cows to flavor the milk for certain cheeses. When I came to the United States I saw that the long leaves were served in salads and were quite delicious. So I created this salad to prove to my Italian friends that they could eat the longer leaves. This recipe is based on the Italian tradition of serving seasonal fruits—such as pears, apples, grapes, or figs—with Parmesan cheese at the end of the meal. The sweet pears perfectly complement the tangy arugula and salty prosciutto. This refreshing, easy-to-assemble salad may be served either before or after a main course.

¾ pound arugula, washed and stemmed
½ recipe Sherry Shallot Vinaigrette (page 323)
8 thin slices prosciutto
2 firm ripe pears, peeled, cored, and thinly sliced
16 large shavings Parmesan cheese (about 2 ounces)

Toss the arugula with the vinaigrette in a large bowl. Distribute evenly among four plates. Garnish each plate with two slices of the prosciutto and equal portions of pear. Use a vegetable peeler to shave portions of the Parmesan on top.

VARIATIONS:

- Arugula tossed with shallot sherry vinaigrette is also delicious served with sliced figs and crumbled goat's cheese.
- Toss the arugula with a balsamic vinaigrette and top with strawberries or orange sections and thin slices of fennel bulb and red onion.
- Top arugula tossed with balsamic vinaigrette with thin slices of Granny Smith apples, coarsely chopped walnuts, and crumbled Gorgonzola or blue cheese. If you like, the walnuts may be toasted: Preheat the oven to 350 degrees F. Place the chopped walnuts on a small baking sheet, and cook until they release their aroma and have browned slightly, about 5 minutes. Allow to cool before adding to the salad.

Uova

EGGS

JOAN: Stan and I don't usually eat eggs for breakfast—we like these egg-based dishes for lunch and light suppers. Both our families typically prepared these recipes on Friday evenings, following the Catholic tradition of abstaining from meat. Because we raised chickens, we always had fresh eggs on hand. Every time my mother sent me out to the coop, I was afraid to stick my hand under the chickens and take their eggs. But knowing my mother would make something delicious like a frittata was incentive enough.

GIANNI: To prepare for his movie *Big Night,* Stanley worked with me in the kitchen at Le Madri. The first thing he asked to be taught was how to cook a frittata. After flipping half a dozen eggs on the floor, he started to get the hang of it. Stanley now claims he can accomplish this culinary feat only when the camera is rolling!

STANLEY: This is true. I've seldom been able to cook a frittata with such ease in my daily life. The scene was shot completely in a master (no cutaways) 5½ minutes long, so I knew I must perform this task effortlessly. At the last minute, knowing that the prop pan wasn't right, I borrowed an 8-inch All-Clad pan from the food stylist. Along with having the right pan, I had found that a very high heat was the key to success with a frittata. We did seven takes, two of which were aborted halfway through—but not because of the cooking, which was successful every time. It is because of this scene that people believe I can really cook. If they only knew!

CROSTONE DI PANE "ALL'OCCHIO DI BUE"

Poached Eggs on Country Bread with Pecorino Toscano

MAKES 4 SERVINGS

GIANNI: *All'occhio di bue* means "the eyes of the bull," which is a colorful way of describing what poached eggs look like. In this recipe, simple poached eggs are taken to a higher level with the addition of fresh herbs and pecorino Toscano cheese. Pecorino Toscano is a soft, mild sheep's milk cheese that I love. Unfortunately, it is very difficult to find in the United States, so instead I substitute Asiago, Fontina, Emmenthaler, or even an extra-sharp cheddar.

I love pecorino Toscano cheese so much that I use it in desserts. I slice a pear, drizzle it with honey, sprinkle it with chopped walnuts, and top it with a slice of cheese. For these recipes I use a vegetable peeler to shave paper-thin slices. Any of the substitute cheeses mentioned above may also be served this way.

4 slices country-style bread
1 clove garlic, peeled and cut in half
1 tablespoon chopped fresh herbs (rosemary, sage, parsley, oregano, marjoram, tarragon, or chives)
1 quart water
3 tablespoons white or cider vinegar
Kosher salt
4 large eggs
½ teaspoon white truffle oil (available in specialty food stores)
½ teaspoon extra virgin olive oil
Freshly ground black pepper
16 large shavings pecorino Toscano cheese (about 3 ounces)

Toast the bread. Rub with the garlic and sprinkle the herbs over the toast. Set aside.

Place the water, vinegar, and some salt in a 2-quart saucepan and bring to a boil. Reduce the heat to a simmer. Break 1 egg into a small bowl and gently slide it into the water. Do the same with the other 3 eggs. Cook until the whites of the eggs are solid but the yolks are still runny, 3 to 5 minutes. Remove with a slotted spatula and place one egg on top of each slice of bread.

In a small dish, whisk together the truffle oil and olive oil. Drizzle over the eggs. Season with salt and pepper, and top with the cheese shavings. Serve immediately.

VARIATION: More extra virgin olive oil may be used in place of the truffle oil.

FRITTATA CON PEPERONI

Eggs with Peppers

MAKES 4 SERVINGS

JOAN: Before my mother went to work, she would make a frittata and take some with her to eat for lunch. She filled them with different vegetables—my favorite was made with fresh wild asparagus that we picked along the roadsides in the spring. I serve frittata for a light lunch or supper accompanied by focaccia and a green salad.

STANLEY: Frittata was a staple for lunch when I was growing up. Though I loved it, I must confess that at times I traded it for a sandwich of peanut butter and Fluff.

¼ cup olive oil
2 red or green frying or bell peppers, seeded and cut into ½-inch-wide strips
4 large eggs
Kosher salt and freshly ground black pepper

Warm the olive oil in a medium-size nonstick or regular frying pan set over medium heat. Add the peppers, cover, and cook until softened, about 20 minutes. In a small bowl, beat together the eggs and salt and pepper to taste. Add the eggs to the softened peppers in the pan. Allow the eggs to set, about 2 minutes, then turn over and continue cooking on the other side until firm, about 2 minutes more.

VARIATIONS:

- Here is how my mother prepared asparagus frittata: Cut about ½ pound asparagus on the bias into 1-inch pieces. Blanch in boiling water for about 1 minute. Drain, pat dry, and cook in the oil to soften, about 5 minutes. Proceed with the basic recipe, adding 2 tablespoons finely grated pecorino Romano cheese to the egg mixture.
- 1 small all-purpose potato, peeled, or 1 small zucchini, cut into ⅛-inch-thick slices (about ½ cup each) may be used instead of the peppers.
- 1 small onion, roughly chopped (about ½ cup), may be sautéed with the peppers or other vegetables.
- 1 tablespoon finely grated pecorino Romano cheese may be added to the eggs before frying.
- If you are really hungry, *all* of the above ingredients may be added to the frittata.

UOVA AL POMODORO

Eggs with Tomato

MAKES 2 SERVINGS

JOAN: My mother often served this dish, made with her own bottled tomatoes, on Fridays. This recipe uses a simple method of poaching the eggs in tomato sauce. It makes a terrific lunch dish, served with slices of bread for dipping in the sauce and accompanied by a tossed salad.

STANLEY: As a kid I looked forward to this Friday night meal. Not only was it unusually beautiful but its sweet flavor, thanks to the onions, would linger long after the last bite.

¼ cup olive oil
1 small onion, thinly sliced
1 cup canned whole plum tomatoes
4 large eggs
Kosher salt and freshly ground black pepper

Warm the olive oil in a medium-size nonstick or regular frying pan set over medium heat. Add the onion and cook until soft, about 3 minutes. Stir in the tomatoes, crushing them with your hand or the back of a slotted spoon as you add them to the pan. Cook until the tomatoes have sweetened, about 20 minutes, stirring occasionally. Gently break the eggs into the pan and cover. Cook until the whites are opaque and the yolks are moderately firm, about 5 minutes. Serve immediately, seasoned with salt and pepper to taste.

VARIATIONS:

- 1 cup Basic Tomato Sauce or *Salsa Marinara* (page 123, 124, or 125) may be substituted for the olive oil, onion, and canned tomatoes. Warm the sauce over medium heat for 5 to 7 minutes before adding the eggs.
- **STAN:** I love eggs cooked this way, but for health reasons I now avoid egg yolks. To make a heart-healthy and tasty version of this dish, I follow the basic recipe but use 6 egg whites.

TORTINO DI UOVA PATATE E SPINACI AL FORNO

Egg Tart with Spinach and Potatoes

MAKES 4 SERVINGS

GIANNI: This recipe is a variation on one that my father used to make. He would prepare a similar tart in the late afternoon to serve to the patrons of our family-run bar. The *tortino* was cut into small squares and placed on top of the counter to be eaten as a snack with a glass of wine. At home this type of *merenda,* or little dish, was served to the children after school along with a slice of bread. It is delicious eaten warm from the oven, at room temperature, or even cold.

1 large Yukon Gold potato, peeled
8 large eggs
½ pound fresh spinach, stems removed, leaves washed well, roughly chopped, and blanched in boiling water for 1 minute
Kosher salt and freshly ground black pepper
2 teaspoons chopped fresh parsley leaves
1 tablespoon butter
1 tablespoon canola or vegetable oil

Preheat the oven to 375 degrees F.

Place the potato in a pot filled with cold salted water. Bring to a boil and cook the potato until just tender when pierced with a fork, 20 to 25 minutes. Cut the potato in half lengthwise and then into thin half-moon-shaped slices. Set aside.

In a medium-size bowl, whisk the eggs until frothy. Squeeze all of the water out of the spinach and add to the eggs along with the potato slices, salt and pepper to taste, and the parsley. Stir briskly to incorporate all the ingredients.

Heat a 10- to 12-inch nonstick ovenproof frying pan or well-seasoned cast-iron skillet over medium-high heat. Add the butter and oil. When the butter has melted and is foaming, pour the egg mixture into the pan, stirring well. Continue to cook and stir until the eggs become slightly scrambled, about 2 minutes. Transfer the pan to the oven and bake until the eggs are firm but still moist, about 6 minutes. Remove from the oven and flip the egg tart over onto a serving plate. Slice and serve immediately.

UOVA, INSALATA, E SOPPRESSA

Eggs with Salad and Soppressata

MAKES 4 SERVINGS

GIANNI: I grew up in a large family in Mason Vicentino, Italy. My mother and father ran a *bottega di alimentari,* a sort of small grocery store, where they sold many locally produced goods, including soppressata. This hard salami was handmade each year by Piero Perin, my brother-in-law, who was renowned for his recipe. In this dish the soppressata and eggs are cooked together and tossed with a lightly dressed salad. It makes a simple meal that may be served for lunch or for a casual Sunday supper. Pancetta, other hard salamis, or bacon may be substituted for soppressata.

4 tablespoons olive oil
1 tablespoon balsamic or red wine vinegar
Kosher salt and freshly ground black pepper
¾ pound mixed bitter salad greens, washed, patted dry, and roughly chopped (see Note)
¼ pound soppressata, sliced, or lean pancetta or bacon, cut into strips
1 tablespoon chopped fresh herbs (see Note)
2 tablespoons roughly chopped scallions (white part only)
8 large eggs, lightly beaten

In a salad bowl, whisk 3 tablespoons of the olive oil with the vinegar and salt and pepper to taste. Add the salad greens and toss to coat evenly with the dressing.

In a large nonstick sauté pan or a well-seasoned cast-iron skillet set over medium heat, cook the soppressata, pancetta, or bacon in the remaining 1 tablespoon olive oil. When it is crisp, add the herbs, scallions, and eggs. Cook, stirring the eggs to scramble. When the eggs are firm but not dry, spoon them over the salad. Toss quickly but gently. Serve immediately.

NOTE: Any of the following fresh herbs may be used individually or in combination when preparing this dish: chives, basil, parsley, oregano, or majoram. Some of the bitter salad greens I recommend using include frisée, radicchio, dandelion greens, endive, and Romaine.

PASTINA CON UOVA

Pastina with Eggs

MAKES 2 SERVINGS

STAN: My mother would prepare this simple, quick warm dish for our lunch or if we weren't feeling too well. (My favorite morning egg dish was prepared by my father—eggs to dunk. He would bake whole eggs in their shells in the oven, watching them carefully. The eggs would sweat once and dry off, and when they broke into a sweat the second time they were done. My father would cut off the top of the shell and use a shot glass as an egg cup. He served this with "Italian toast," which is Italian bread cut, buttered, and then placed under the broiler. After toasting it, my father cut the bread into half-inch strips for dunking into the egg.)

JOAN: In Italy *pastina* is any of the little pastas given to babies and small children, such as orzo or small star shapes. I usually use a bead- or couscous-shaped pasta when preparing this dish. My grandmother, whom we called Momma Grande, lived with us and helped to prepare the daily meals while my mother and father worked. We came home from school at lunchtime, and I remember her serving us dishes of plain warm pastina drizzled with olive oil. Delicious. So try this dish the Tucci way, with eggs, or the Tropiano way, without eggs.

½ cup pastina pasta
Kosher salt
2 large eggs (optional)
1 teaspoon butter or olive oil

Fill a small saucepan with salted water and bring to a boil over medium-high heat. Add the pastina and cook according to the package instructions.

Reserve 1 cup of the cooking water before draining the pastina. Return the cup of hot water and the drained pastina to the saucepan over medium-high heat. Break the eggs directly into the saucepan. Whisk together and simmer to cook the eggs, about 1 minute. Divide between two plates, and top with equal portions of the butter or oil. Serve immediately.

Zuppe

SOUPS

JOAN: My mother loved soup, and she prepared a fresh batch once or twice a week year-round. Chicken soup was her favorite. She used every part of the chicken—even scraping and scrubbing the feet before adding them to the pot. Sometimes the fresh chickens would have a small unformed egg inside them. When this tiny egg was hard-boiled, my mother would remove it from the soup and serve it to us in a little dish as a special treat. We ate soup for lunch, or it was served as a first course followed by a meat dish.

STAN: On the evening we arrived in Rome to begin our yearlong sabbatical, Joan's cousin Tita prepared a memorable chicken soup. Tita miraculously picked Joan out of a huge crowd at the Rome airport and whisked us to her home. As we recovered from our jet lag, it seemed to take Tita no time at all to select a chicken from their coop and create a rich and comforting soup. We discovered later it was an old-fashioned pressure cooker that allowed her to do so. That was the first of many delicious meals.

GIANNI: My father enjoyed soup most evenings as a first course, so my mother prepared it almost every day, using leftover meat or chicken in combination with fresh vegetables. She made each soup two ways—thin for my father and thickened with grated potato for us children. I think the trick to making a good soup is to be patient and allow it to cook slowly, the way my mother did on the back of our wood-burning stove.

STANLEY: Ever since childhood I've loved soup, and I still find myself making it—even on the hottest of summer days. Struggling in New York after college, I found that making a large pot of chicken soup or buying a bowl of split pea soup from a coffee shop provided a nutritious, filling, and inexpensive meal. It was a comfort to know that a little soup could go a long way. Whether budget is a concern for you or not, I'm sure you will find the following soups to be varied and delicious.

BRODO DI GALLINA CON POLPETTINE DI POLLO

Chicken Soup with Tiny Chicken Meatballs

MAKES 8 SERVINGS

JOAN: My father never learned to speak English properly, primarily because he was surrounded by Italians. As my children grew up, they loved to hear him speak English because his thick accent made everyday phrases comical. For instance "vegetable soup" became "dirigible soup." Knowing it was funny, he laughed as hard as the children.

This is my mother's basic chicken soup recipe, which is made special by adding her tiny, delicious chicken meatballs. She always had extra meatballs on hand for her grandchildren because they were not patient enough to wait and enjoy them in their soup. Whether served for lunch or as a casual Sunday supper, this healthy soup will be loved by all.

One 3-pound free-range chicken, quartered
4 quarts water
2 large celery stalks, cut into thirds
2 medium-size carrots, cut into thirds
4 sprigs fresh parsley
1 large onion, peeled
Kosher salt
2 very ripe or canned plum tomatoes, quartered

FOR THE MEATBALLS:
½ boneless, skinless chicken breast
1 large egg, lightly beaten
¼ cup plain dried bread crumbs
2 tablespoons freshly grated pecorino Romano cheese
Freshly grated Parmesan or pecorino Romano cheese for garnish (optional)

Place the quartered chicken in a large pot and cover with the water. Set the pot over medium-low heat and slowly bring the water to a simmer, skimming off any foam that accumulates on top. Add the celery, carrots, parsley, onion, and salt to taste. Simmer, uncovered, to soften the vegetables, about 10 minutes. Add the tomatoes and continue to simmer, with the lid slightly askew, to sweeten the tomatoes and make a flavorful broth, about 30 minutes.

Remove the chicken, carrots, and onion to a platter and set aside. Strain the broth through a fine-mesh sieve, discarding the celery, parsley, and tomatoes. Transfer 1 cup of the broth to a small pot. Return the rest of the broth to the large pot. Shred the cooked chicken, discarding bones and skin, and add to the large batch of broth. Dice the cooked carrots and onion. Add them to the large batch of broth. Cover the pot and keep the broth warm while you cook the meatballs.

continued

In a food processor, finely chop the chicken breast. Transfer to a small bowl and add the egg, stirring with a fork to combine. Mix in the bread crumbs and Romano cheese. Season with salt to taste.

Use a ½-teaspoon measuring spoon to shape the mixture into small balls. Bring the small pot containing the 1 cup broth to a gentle boil and cook the meatballs, 8 to 10 at a time, in the broth until they are cooked through, about 5 minutes. As they finish cooking, transfer them with a slotted spoon to the large pot of broth.

When all the meatballs have been cooked and added to the broth, strain the broth the meatballs cooked in through a fine-mesh strainer and add it to the soup. Serve immediately, or set the soup aside at this point and reheat it a few hours later.

Serve with grated Parmesan or Romano cheese if desired.

VARIATIONS: The beauty of soup is that it can be varied to accommodate ingredients you have (or don't have) on hand. Here are a few suggestions:

- The cooked chicken may be served separately, rather then shredding it and adding it to the soup. Serve the soup, containing the vegetables and the chicken meatballs, as a first course.
- 2 cups cooked pasta, such as orzo, or 2 cups cooked rice may be added to the strained broth and warmed through just before serving.
- 2 medium-size all-purpose potatoes, peeled and quartered, may be added to the soup with the tomatoes. Return to the pot with the carrots and onion, and serve with the soup.
- This soup may be prepared using a fowl. Allow an additional 30 minutes of cooking time to tenderize the meat.

NOTE: This rich broth may be strained and frozen for up to 3 months and used in recipes that call for chicken broth.

ZUPPA DI POLLO CON MOZZARELLA ALLA GRAZIA

Grace's Chicken Soup with Mozzarella

MAKES 6 SERVINGS

JOAN: Chicken soup reminds me of my godfather, Compare Pullano, who lived near us in Verplanck, New York. He and my father shared many interests, including gardening, raising animals, and making wine. They were very competitive and rarely acknowledged each other's successes. One afternoon Compare arrived at our house carrying a shopping bag with a dishcloth draped over it. He sat down at the kitchen table, placing the bag alongside his chair. Pop offered Compare a glass of homemade wine and they talked for about twenty minutes. Neither of them mentioned the bag. Now the wineglasses were empty and Compare, who was slightly deaf, was talking even louder than before. As Pop poured them each another glass of wine, Compare, with sleight of hand, removed the dish towel from the shopping bag and revealed a beautiful, very much alive, chicken. Pop didn't even blink in surprise or remark on how healthy the chicken was. He just gave it to Mom who, I'm sure, used it to prepare soup.

This dish is a delicious variation on our mother's recipe, created by my sister Grace. It is a meal in itself when served with a slice of crusty bread. Begin with the recipe for Chicken Soup with Tiny Chicken Meatballs on page 71, or use your own favorite chicken broth.

2 small heads escarole, chopped
7 cups chicken broth
1 whole chicken breast, bone in, skin removed
20 small chicken meatballs (page 71)
1 cup grated mozzarella cheese
4 tablespoons finely grated pecorino Romano cheese
1 large egg, lightly beaten

Bring a large pot of salted water to a gentle boil. Blanch the escarole until tender, about 5 minutes. Drain and set aside.

Bring 3 cups of the chicken broth to a gentle boil in a large saucepan. Add the chicken breast, cover, and poach until cooked through, about 12 minutes. Skim off and discard any foam that rises to the surface. Remove the chicken with a slotted spoon and set aside to cool.

Add the meatballs to the chicken broth and poach until cooked through, about 1 minute. Remove with a slotted spoon and set aside.

Strain the chicken broth through a fine-mesh strainer into a large saucepan or mixing bowl, add the remaining 4 cups broth, and set aside.

continued

Shred the chicken meat into bite-size pieces and set aside, discarding the bone.

Preheat the oven to 350 degrees F.

Pour ½ cup of the chicken broth into a small casserole or soufflé dish. Layer one quarter of the escarole over the broth. Add one quarter of the meatballs, one quarter of the shredded chicken, 1 cup of the broth, one quarter of the mozzarella, and 1 tablespoon of the Romano cheese. Top with another quarter of the escarole and continue to layer the ingredients, ending with mozzarella and Romano cheese. Pour the beaten egg over the top. Bake until the cheese has melted and the broth is heated through, about 20 minutes. Serve immediately.

VARIATION: This is also wonderful prepared without the meatballs.

Nonno and Nonna Tucci with me holding six-month-old Stanley at the house on Ringgold Street, Peekskill, New York.

MINESTRA ESTIVA

Summer Vegetable Soup

MAKES 6 TO 8 SERVINGS

GIANNI: During the hot summer months my mother would prepare a big batch of this soup. She stored it in the refrigerator, where it would keep for three or four days. In this way my mother avoided heating up the whole house with the wood-burning stove while providing us with a refreshing lunchtime meal accompanied by bread, cheeses, and olives. Usually I drizzle a tiny bit of olive oil over each portion. This soup may also be served hot if you prefer.

2 tablespoons extra virgin olive oil
¾ cup ¼-inch onion cubes (about 1 medium-size onion)
½ cup ¼-inch carrot cubes (about 1 medium-size carrot)
1½ cups ¼-inch celery cubes (about 2 stalks)
¾ cup ¼-inch all-purpose potato cubes (about 1 medium-size potato)
2 tablespoons chopped fresh parsley leaves
1 tablespoon chopped fresh basil leaves
¾ cup ¼-inch ripe tomato cubes (about 1 medium-size tomato)
6 cups vegetable broth (see Note) or water
3 cups ¼-inch zucchini cubes (about 2 medium-size zucchini)
¼ cup fresh peas
1 cup ¼-inch tender asparagus cubes (about 6 spears)
Kosher salt and freshly ground black pepper

Place a large flameproof casserole over medium-high heat. Add the oil and the onion, carrot, and celery cubes. Cook, stirring occasionally, until the vegetables soften, about 7 minutes. Stir in the potato cubes, parsley, and basil and cook, stirring occasionally, to season the vegetables with these herbs, about 2 minutes. Add the tomato cubes and 3 cups of the stock or water. Bring to a boil, reduce the heat to medium-low, and simmer to warm through, about 5 minutes. Add the zucchini cubes, peas, and asparagus cubes along with the remaining 3 cups stock or water. Season with salt and pepper. Cover with the lid slightly askew and return to a boil. Reduce the heat to medium-low and simmer to heat through and soften the vegetables, about 10 minutes. Remove from the heat. Allow to cool and serve at room temperature, or keep in the refrigerator for the next day.

NOTE: Homemade vegetable stock for this soup may be prepared while you are cooking the soup. Place 10 cups water in a stockpot. Add the peelings from the carrot and potato. Add the tops and bottoms of the zucchini, along with the tough asparagus bottoms. Then add:

1 carrot, broken in half
1 small potato, quartered
½ small onion, peeled
5 sprigs fresh parsley
4 small celery stalks with their leaves
5 black peppercorns
½ teaspoon kosher salt

Bring to a boil, then reduce the heat to medium-low and simmer, with the lid slightly askew, while you chop the vegetables and prepare the soup. By the time it is called for in the recipe, the stock will be done. Strain, measure, and add it to the soup.

*My brother Mario (*left*) and me on our sister Bruna's wedding day.*

PATATE E CAVOLI

Potatoes and Cabbage

MAKES 4 SERVINGS

JOAN: This was another typical meal served on Fridays, when we abstained from eating meat. It usually wasn't filling enough for my father, so he would follow it with homemade bread, olives, and cheese. I serve this as a lunch dish or as a vegetable course before a main meal.

1 small head Savoy or green cabbage, trimmed, cored, and quartered
1 clove garlic, cut in half
2 tablespoons chopped fresh or canned plum tomatoes
2 tablespoons olive oil
Kosher salt and freshly ground black pepper
2 small all-purpose potatoes, quartered

Place the cabbage in a medium-size saucepan. Add the garlic, tomatoes, olive oil, and salt and pepper to taste. Pour in enough water so that three quarters of the cabbage is immersed in water. Cover and bring to a boil. Reduce the heat to medium-low and simmer for 5 minutes. Add the potatoes, pushing them down into the water. Cover and continue to simmer until the cabbage and potatoes are just tender, about 25 minutes. Distribute the vegetables and broth among four shallow soup bowls and serve.

VARIATION: *Canederli* dough (page 80) may be shaped into teaspoon-size balls and added to the broth during the last 5 minutes of cooking.

ZUPPETTA DI FUNGHI E FAGIOLI

Cremini Mushroom and White Bean Soup

MAKES 8 SERVINGS

GIANNI: When you are obsessed with food, fresh ingredients are a must and you will go to absurd lengths to get them. That is why when I am in Italy in the late summer, I drive an hour from my home to Lamon, a village known for wonderful fresh and dried beans. Along the streets and roadsides old men sit beneath market umbrellas selling beans and potatoes on stands they construct from upturned vegetable crates. Between selecting beans at two or three different stands and talking with the old men, a simple task becomes an all-day excursion.

I like to cook the beans separately from the vegetables in this soup so that the beans do not become overcooked and muddy the crisp flavors of the vegetables. I prefer to use fresh beans I have shelled myself, both for their flavor and because they take less time to cook. However, I have used dried beans in this recipe because they may be purchased anywhere at any time of the year. *Zuppetta di funghi e fagioli* may be prepared several hours in advance. Combine and heat through just before serving.

1½ cups dried borlotti (cranberry or pinto) or white beans such as cannellini
12 cups chicken broth or water
1 clove garlic, lightly crushed
1 tablespoon finely chopped fresh sage leaves
½ cup thinly sliced celery
½ cup thinly sliced onions
2 tablespoons olive oil
1 tablespoon finely chopped fresh rosemary leaves
1 tablespoon finely chopped fresh parsley leaves
1 pound cremini mushrooms, cut into ¼-inch-thick slices
¾ cup canned whole plum tomatoes
2 cups ½-inch all-purpose potato cubes
Kosher salt and freshly ground black pepper

Rinse the beans, removing any stones or grit, and place them in a bowl or saucepan. Fill the pan with water to a level 2 inches above the beans, and allow them to soak for 6 to 8 hours. Drain and proceed with the recipe. (A quick method for soaking beans is to place them in a pot of cold water, cover the pot, bring the water to a boil, and allow the beans to boil for 2 minutes. Remove from the heat and let the beans stand, covered, for 1 hour before draining and proceeding with the recipe.)

Combine the beans, 8 cups of the broth or water, the garlic, and the sage in a large pot. Bring to a boil, reduce the heat to medium-low, cover, and simmer until the beans are soft, about 50 minutes. Up to 1 cup of the remaining broth may be added to the beans, ½ cup at a time, to maintain a constant level during cooking.

Meanwhile, in a wide sauté pan set over medium heat, cook the celery and onions in the olive oil until soft, about 7 minutes. Add the rosemary, parsley, and mushrooms, and cook, stirring, to soften the mushrooms, about 10 minutes. Stir in the tomatoes, crushing them with your hands or the back of a slotted spoon as you add them to the pan. Add the potato cubes and cover the vegetables with the remaining 3 to 4 cups chicken broth or water. Bring to a boil, reduce the heat to medium-low, and simmer until the potatoes are soft when pierced with a fork, about 10 minutes.

Stir the mushroom mixture into the beans, season with salt and pepper, warm through, and serve immediately.

CANEDERLI ZUPPA

Italian Bread Dumpling Soup

MAKES 4 SERVINGS

GIANNI: This is a very traditional soup from my region of northern Italy, which is close to the Austrian border. It is very practical, relying principally on stale bread, and is often served as a pasta course. This same spiced bread may be rolled into a 3-inch-thick log, wrapped in a clean dish towel, and boiled. When cooked through, it is then sliced and served with a meat-based pasta sauce, such as ragù.

6 cups chicken broth
2½ cups diced stale bread (about 4 ounces)
1 cup all-purpose flour
½ cup thinly sliced, then finely chopped pancetta (about 2 ounces)
⅓ cup thinly sliced, then finely chopped hard salami (about 1 ounce)
1 large egg, lightly beaten
1 cup milk
1 tablespoon chopped fresh chives
2 tablespoons chopped fresh parsley leaves
Pinch of ground nutmeg
½ teaspoon kosher salt

Place the chicken broth in a medium-size saucepan set over medium-high heat. Cover with the lid askew and bring to a boil, then reduce the heat to a simmer.

Meanwhile, in a medium-size bowl, combine the bread with the flour, pancetta, salami, egg, milk, chives, parsley, nutmeg, and salt. Mix well, using your hands if necessary to evenly incorporate the ingredients. The dough should be moist and malleable. Scoop out rounded tablespoons of the dough and roll into balls.

Add the dough to the simmering chicken broth. Cook until all the balls are floating on the surface of the broth and are cooked through, about 8 minutes. Do not stir.

Remove the dumplings from the broth with a slotted spoon, and distribute them equally among four soup bowls. Ladle the broth into the bowls and serve immediately.

VARIATIONS:

- Other fresh herbs, such as thyme or sage, may be substituted or added to the dough.
- *Canederli* dough may be shaped into teaspoon-size balls and added to Joan's *Patate e Cavoli* (Potatoes and Cabbage) recipe on page 77.

RIBOLLITA REVISIONATA

Peasant Soup

MAKES 8 SERVINGS

GIANNI: *Ribollita* means "reboiled" and describes a hearty traditional soup that is usually cooked over two or three days. In this recipe I have devised a short cooking method that still achieves the rich flavor attained by many hours of simmering. Recipes for preparing *ribollita* vary from region to region in Italy, so there are no steadfast rules about what can be tossed into the pot. (For example, I always add a chunk of Parmesan cheese rind to flavor the broth.) Once the basic recipe has been mastered, it may be altered to accommodate any vegetables you have on hand.

When it is in season, I prefer to prepare this soup using black cabbage, which is shaped like Romaine lettuce. Black cabbage may not be as widely available in America as it is in Italy, so in this recipe I recommend Savoy cabbage, which has a short growing season but can be found in supermarkets here. If you cannot find either of these, use very thinly sliced tender green cabbage. (I do not like using red cabbage, which has a strong flavor that tends to overpower the other vegetables in this soup.)

In Italy *ribollita* has a thick consistency closely resembling a vegetable stew. If you prefer a soupier dish, add more broth as desired. Top each serving with a wedge of sweet red onion.

¼ pound stale bread, crusts cut off, cut into ½-inch cubes
1 cup roughly chopped celery (about 2 stalks)
1 cup diced carrots (about 2 medium-size carrots)
1 cup diced red onions (about 1 medium-size onion)
3 cloves garlic, chopped
2 tablespoons olive oil
1 tablespoon coarsely chopped fresh parsley leaves
2 teaspoons coarsely chopped fresh sage leaves
½ teaspoon chopped fresh thyme leaves
One 3-ounce rind Parmesan cheese (optional)
1½ cups canned whole plum tomatoes
6 cups chicken broth or water
1½ cups cooked cannellini or great Northern beans (½ cup dried; see Note)

1½ pounds Swiss chard, leaves and stems roughly chopped
¾ pound Savoy or black cabbage, trimmed, cored, and roughly chopped
Extra virgin olive oil to drizzle on servings

continued

Air-dry the bread cubes overnight, or place them on a baking sheet and bake in an oven preheated to 300 degrees F, stirring occasionally, until dry but not brown, about 20 minutes. Set aside.

Place the celery, carrots, onions, garlic, and olive oil in a large, heavy-bottomed soup pot set over medium heat. Cook the vegetables until softened but not browned, about 15 minutes. Stir in the Swiss chard and cabbage, and cook to wilt slightly, about 1 minute. Add the parsley, sage, thyme, cheese rind, and tomatoes. Simmer gently until the Swiss chard leaves have completely wilted, about 10 minutes. Add the chicken broth or water and the beans. Cover the pot, with the lid slightly askew. Slowly bring the soup to a boil and then simmer gently until the cabbage and chard are tender, about 20 minutes. The soup may be prepared up to this point and allowed to cool to room temperature for a few hours before reheating and serving.

Just before serving, add the bread cubes. Simmer for 5 minutes. Remove the cheese rind. Spoon the soup into bowls, and drizzle some extra virgin olive oil on top of each bowl. Serve immediately.

NOTE: Canned beans that have been drained and rinsed may be substituted for cooked beans in this recipe.

ZUPPA DI PESCE ALLA VENETA

Venetian-Style Fish Soup

MAKES 6 SERVINGS

GIANNI: I was always taught that "the uglier the fish, the better the soup." In my opinion this is true. The fish that live close to rocks are the tastiest and also the ugliest. So I begin my fish soup recipe by selecting a good, fresh, ugly fish. The type I use determines how the recipe will proceed, so there isn't really a set recipe to follow. The basic idea is to cook the firmest fish first, adding the more delicate fish and seafood later on to produce a soup with great flavor and texture.

It also helps to purchase the smallest, sweetest clams available. Littlenecks are a good choice. Some specialty fish markets may be able to supply Manila clams, which are ideal. This simple soup is delicious served with grilled or toasted bread that has been rubbed with garlic. *Zuppa di pesce alla Veneta* may be prepared several hours in advance. Store it at room temperature and slowly reheat it before serving.

¼ cup extra virgin olive oil, plus more to drizzle over each serving
5 cloves garlic, lightly crushed
2 tablespoons chopped fresh parsley leaves
1 small jalapeño pepper, seeded and diced, or ½ teaspoon red pepper flakes
2 lobster tails (1 pound each), each cut into 3 pieces with shell
12 littleneck clams, scrubbed
½ cup dry white wine
2½ cups peeled and chopped fresh or canned tomatoes
18 ounces white-fleshed fish fillets (see Note), such as scrod, cut into 1-inch cubes
12 mussels, scrubbed and debearded
6 jumbo shrimp, shelled and deveined
6 large sea scallops
½ teaspoon chopped fresh oregano leaves
½ teaspoon chopped fresh marjoram leaves
1 tablespoon chopped fresh basil leaves
Kosher salt and freshly ground black pepper

Heat the oil and garlic together in a large flameproof casserole set over medium-high heat. When the oil is warm, add the parsley and jalapeño or red pepper flakes. When the garlic begins to brown lightly, add the lobster and clams. Stir and begin to warm the clams, about 2 minutes. Stir in the wine and cook, allowing the lobster to absorb the flavor, about 2 minutes. Add the tomatoes. When they begin to simmer, add the fish. Cover and simmer until the fish is no longer translucent, about 5 minutes.

continued

Add the mussels, shrimp, and scallops along with the oregano, marjoram, and basil. Gently push this new layer of seafood down into the broth. Cook until the mussel shells have opened and the shrimp are pink, about 5 more minutes. Season with salt and pepper to taste, discard any clams and mussels that haven't opened, and serve immediately.

NOTE: Halibut, bass, or red snapper may be used. Monkfish is also a good substitute, but it will require more cooking time. Add it to the casserole along with the lobster.

BRODETTO DI PESCE ALLA MARCHIGIANA

Fish Stew in the Style of the Marche Region

MAKES 6 TO 8 SERVINGS

GIANNI: My friend Francesco Tonelli's mother is a wonderful, hardworking woman who spends most of her time in the kitchen. She often says that if someone paid her one cent for every animal she has slaughtered for food she would be a millionaire. She makes this quick, flavorful sauce in the winter when there are no fresh tomatoes available. It is essentially a "poor man's" tomato sauce made with onions, garlic, and tomato paste, and it may be used in a variety of recipes for lunch dishes. The sauce may be prepared one day ahead of time. Refrigerate it and reheat before proceeding with the recipe.

I like to use an assortment of fish and seafood in this stew, but it may also be prepared using just one type of fish. Select any you like—although I would not recommend oily fish, such as salmon, tuna, or bluefish. Serve it as a main course over boiled rice or pasta or over slices of toasted bread that have been drizzled with olive oil.

¼ cup extra virgin olive oil
1 cup finely chopped onions
2 bay leaves
2 cloves garlic, thinly sliced
¼ cup tomato paste
Freshly ground black pepper
3 cups water
Kosher salt
1 pound rockfish, halibut, or striped bass steaks, bone in, skin removed, cut into 6 to 8 portions
1¼ pounds scrod, snapper, or cod fillets, cut into 3-inch chunks
½ pound cleaned calamari, cut into 2-inch chunks
6 to 8 jumbo shrimp, shelled and deveined
3 tablespoons torn fresh basil leaves

Warm the olive oil in a large wide saucepan set over medium-low heat. Stir in the onions, bay leaves, and garlic and cook until the onions soften and are golden yellow, about 8 minutes. Stir in the tomato paste and generous grindings of pepper. Cook, stirring constantly, to sweeten the paste with the onions, about 2 minutes. Stir in the water and season the sauce with salt. Bring to a slow simmer over low heat. Cook to thicken and reduce the sauce, about 20 minutes.

Add the rockfish (or other fish), cover the pan, and cook over low heat to soften slightly, about

5 minutes. Add the scrod (or other fish) and the calamari. Do not stir the fish, as it may break. Instead, shake the pan back and forth to incorporate the new fish and coat it with some of the sauce. Cover and cook to soften slightly, about 7 minutes. Add the shrimp, cover, and cook until they just begin to turn pink, about 3 minutes. Remove from the heat and set aside, allowing the fish to finish cooking off the heat, about 5 minutes more. Season with salt and garnish with the basil leaves. Serve immediately.

VARIATION: This dish may be served as a hearty soup appetizer. Reduce the amount of fish by half. Slice the shrimp in half lengthwise. Proceed with the recipe as written, serving the finished, slightly soupier stew in shallow bowls.

Pane e Pizza

BREAD AND PIZZA

JOAN: Homemade bread and pizza were staples in our household. My mother worked during the week, so on the weekends she would bake several loaves at once. We ate this bread throughout the week—topped with jellies made from fruit my father grew or generously spread with ricotta cheese that my grandmother prepared from fresh goat's milk. Fresh ricotta cheese is set in a basket to cure slightly, and although I don't make cheese, I have kept my grandmother's basket all these years.

When she was done baking, my mother would put aside one or two loaves of bread for slicing. She would return these slices to the oven to be baked a second time. We called this bread *biscotto.* It was excellent eaten like a cracker with soup or topped with chopped fresh tomatoes and olive oil. I ate *biscotto* as a snack. To me it tasted better than a cookie.

There is such good bread available from Terranova on Arthur Avenue in the Bronx that I don't bake bread as often as my mother did. I do bake focaccia and pizza all the time, however, using the recipes and techniques my mother taught me. To make a dough as soft and light as hers, I prefer to use solid fresh yeast. I buy it in a half-pound block from a local bakery and cut it into 1-inch-square, ½-inch-thick cubes. I wrap them individually in plastic wrap before storing them in the freezer. (One cube of fresh yeast is equal to the package of dry yeast called for in the following recipes.) There is no need to defrost the yeast before mixing the dough. Just place one cube in a measuring cup and cover with cool water (about ½ cup). Stir it with a fork occasionally, and it will dissolve in about 5 minutes. Then you can proceed with the recipes as written.

GIANNI: I will never forget the aroma of the bread baking in the early morning. My mother baked sliced bread in the oven to create what we called *pane biscottato.* She used it to create a hearty warm dish that she brought to us every morning while we were still lying under the covers in bed: crumbled portions of *pane biscottato* in deep soup bowls with warmed milk and a little bit of coffee poured into each bowl. It was a wonderful way to wake up. Although we were very thankful, my brother and I insisted on having our bread crumbled differently. I liked mine very finely ground, so my mother would place the *pane biscottato* in a bag and flatten it with a wine bottle. My brother liked his *pane biscottato* chunky, so my mother broke it into small pieces with her hands. I can't believe that she went to the trouble of preparing two different versions of this special dish.

STANLEY: "Man cannot live on bread alone." I wonder if this is true, because sometimes I think I might be able to, I love it so much. Its pure simplicity is its attraction. Bread is a before, an in-between, and an after. It is the first food that most of us turn to when hunger begins to gnaw. The baguettes of France, the flatbreads of the Middle East, the soda breads of Ireland, and the countless Italian breads: focaccia, schiacciata, pizza, the bland saltless bread of Florence (made this way so as not to interfere with the flavor of the sauce when used for dipping)—the varieties are endless. But what is constant is that we all find comfort in this most basic and spiritual of foods.

GRISSINI

Bread Sticks

MAKES 8 SERVINGS

GIANNI: I like to make these bread sticks in a pasta machine. It makes quick work of rolling them out and guarantees they will be of uniform width. Of course they may also be made by rolling sections of the dough on a floured surface and then cutting them into long, thin strips. Bread sticks that are twisted into shapes or that are more than ¼ inch wide will take slightly longer to bake.

1 package dry yeast
1 tablespoon sugar
1⅓ cups warm water
3 cups all-purpose flour
½ cup semolina flour, plus extra for dusting
1 tablespoon kosher salt
1 tablespoon chopped fresh rosemary leaves
¼ cup extra virgin olive oil
2 teaspoons grappa or vodka

Stir the yeast and sugar together in a 2-cup measuring cup. Stir in the warm water and set aside for 5 minutes.

In a large bowl or on a clean work surface, mix together the all-purpose flour, semolina flour, salt, and rosemary. Mound the mixture, and make a well in the center. Add the yeast mixture, olive oil, and grappa to the well. Using a fork at first and then your hands, gradually blend the flour mixture into the wet ingredients. Turn the dough out onto a lightly floured work surface and knead until it is smooth and not sticky. Place in a clean bowl. Cover with plastic wrap and a clean dish towel. Set aside in a warm place to rise until doubled in size, about 1 hour.

Preheat the oven to 350 degrees F. Dust several baking sheets with semolina flour and set them aside.

Turn the dough out onto a lightly floured surface. Cut the dough into six equal pieces. Flatten one piece to the width of the pasta machine opening. Lightly flour the dough and pass it through the widest opening of the machine to produce a flat 12-inch-long piece of dough. Lightly flour the dough again and pass it through the wide noodle setting to create individual strands of dough. Arrange them ½ inch apart on a prepared baking sheet. Repeat this procedure with the remaining pieces of dough. Bake until golden brown on the bottom, about 5 minutes. Turn and continue baking until evenly brown, about 5 minutes more. Allow to cool on wire racks before serving or storing in an airtight container.

continued

VARIATIONS: Sometimes I like to serve an assortment of flavored bread sticks. Divide the risen dough into quarters, setting one quarter aside to be baked as in the basic recipe. To one of the remaining quarters add ¼ cup finely grated Parmesan or cheddar cheese. To another quarter add 1 teaspoon chopped fresh herbs such as sage, thyme, oregano, or marjoram. To the last quarter add 1 teaspoon olive paste. Knead each quarter well to incorporate these ingredients. Allow to rest for 10 minutes before passing through the pasta machine.

That's me, Gianni, in between my sisters Livia (left) *and Catterina.*

FOCACCIA AL ROSMARINO

Rosemary Focaccia

MAKES 10 SERVINGS

GIANNI: The bakeries in Italy are open Monday through Saturday. If my family forgot to buy a double order of bread on Saturday—which happened quite often—my father would bake focaccia on Sunday. This basic recipe can be changed by adding different herbs or toppings, sometimes becoming a meal in itself (see the Variations below).

1 package dry yeast
2¼ teaspoons sugar
½ cup warm water
2 cups all-purpose flour
2 cups bread flour
4 teaspoons kosher salt
1 cup milk
5 tablespoons olive oil, plus more for oiling the bowl
Leaves from one 5-inch sprig fresh rosemary

In a measuring cup, stir together the yeast, sugar, and warm water. Set aside for 5 minutes.

In the bowl of an electric mixer fitted with a dough hook, mix the all-purpose and bread flours with 2 teaspoons of the salt. Stir in the yeast mixture. Gradually stir in the milk and 3 tablespoons of the olive oil. Mix at low speed until the dough has come together and is smooth, about 5 minutes.

(To mix by hand: Combine the all-purpose flour, bread flour, and 2 teaspoons of the salt in a large bowl. Make a well in the center of these dry ingredients and add the yeast mixture. Mix with a fork while adding the milk and 3 tablespoons of the olive oil to form a soft, dry dough. Turn the dough out onto a lightly floured surface and continue mixing it with your hands. Knead until the dough has come together and is smooth, about 8 minutes.)

Lightly grease a bowl with olive oil. Place the dough in the bowl, cover tightly with plastic wrap, and drape a dish towel over the bowl. Set aside in a warm place and allow to double in size, about 2 hours.

Lightly grease a large baking sheet (about 9 × 15 inches). Gently punch down the dough. Place it on the baking sheet and roll it out to fit evenly on the sheet. Cover with a dish towel and allow the dough to rise for 20 minutes.

Preheat the oven to 375 degrees F.

Use your fingertips to make random indentations in the dough. Drizzle the top with the remaining 2 tablespoons olive oil. Sprinkle with the remaining 2 teaspoons salt and the rosemary leaves. Bake until golden brown, about 30 minutes. Allow to cool slightly before slicing and serving warm.

VARIATIONS:

- Before baking, top the focaccia with any combination of the following ingredients: ¼-inch-thick slices ripe plum tomatoes; 24 pitted Kalamata olives; ¼ cup very thinly sliced red onions; ⅓ cup crumbled goat's cheese; ¼-inch-thick slices peeled eggplant; ¼-inch-thick slices zucchini; ¼-inch-thick slices bell peppers; ⅓ cup pesto.
- For a sweet variation on this recipe, gently press 1 cup dried fruit such as raisins, cherries, or blueberries, or 1 cup chocolate chips, into the rolled and risen focaccia. Brush with 3 tablespoons melted butter and bake.

FOCACCIA TUCCI

Tucci Family Focaccia

MAKES 12 SERVINGS

JOAN: My mother baked every weekend, filling our home with the wonderful aroma of fresh breads and pizzas, which were prized by our family and throughout the community. This recipe makes two medium-size focaccias, which may be served with lunch, as an appetizer, or with dinner. For variety, fresh herbs such as rosemary, sage, marjoram, or basil may be added to the dough when the focaccia is first kneaded, or combined with the olive oil that is drizzled on top just before baking.

I enjoy mixing this dough by hand. However, it may also be prepared in a stand mixer fitted with a dough hook.

STANLEY: During our year in Italy it seems to me that I lived on focaccia. I would buy a piece after school every day. Though mass-produced and sold from a cart, this hearty oiled and salted bread was the perfect treat.

1 package dry yeast or 1 cake fresh yeast
2 cups warm water
4 cups all-purpose flour
1 tablespoon kosher salt, plus more for sprinkling
4 tablespoons cornmeal
4 tablespoons olive oil

In a measuring cup, combine the yeast with ½ cup of the warm water. Stir until the yeast dissolves.

In a large bowl, combine the flour and salt. Make a well in the center and add the yeast mixture. Mix with a fork while adding enough of the remaining 1½ cups water to form a soft, dry dough.

Turn the dough out onto a lightly floured surface and continue mixing it with your hands. Add more water or flour as necessary to keep the dough from being too sticky. Knead it ten to twelve times. Form the dough into a ball and place in a bowl. Cover loosely with a clean dish towel. Set aside in a warm place and allow to rise until it has doubled in size, about 2 hours.

Preheat the oven to 400 degrees F.

Divide the risen dough in half. Roll one half of the dough on a lightly floured surface to a size that will roughly fit a baking sheet, about 9 × 13 inches. Sprinkle the baking sheet with 2 tablespoons of the cornmeal. Place the dough on the baking sheet and cover with plastic wrap or a clean dish towel. Allow to rise for 30 minutes. Proceed in the same fashion with the other half of the dough.

Use your fingertips to make random indentations in the risen dough. Drizzle 2 tablespoons of the olive oil over each piece of dough, and sprinkle with additional salt. Bake on the bottom rack of the oven until golden brown, about 15 minutes.

Serve sliced, warm or at room temperature.

NOTE: Dough that has risen once may be wrapped in plastic and stored in the refrigerator for up to 3 days, or frozen for up to 1 month. Allow the dough to come to room temperature before rolling it out to fit on a baking sheet. Then set it aside to rise for half an hour before proceeding with the recipe.

PANE DI SEMOLINA

Semolina Bread

MAKES 2 LOAVES

GIANNI: Several years ago I worked as a chef in Washington, D.C. Finding good bread to serve in the restaurant was a tremendous problem at that time, so we decided it would be best to bake our own. After trying different recipes, we settled on this baguette-shaped semolina loaf as a simple and reliable bread. We created a customer-pleasing bread basket that included this bread, *grissini* (bread sticks), and focaccia.

1 tablespoon dry yeast (about 2 packages)
1 teaspoon sugar
⅓ cup warm water
3 cups semolina flour
1 cup all-purpose flour
2½ teaspoons kosher salt
1 tablespoon olive oil
1¼ cups cool water, plus more as needed

In a small bowl, stir together the yeast, sugar, and warm water. Set aside for 5 minutes.

In a large bowl, combine the semolina flour, all-purpose flour, and salt. Make a well in the center and add the yeast mixture and the olive oil. Using a fork at first and then your hands, gradually blend together the wet and dry ingredients. Slowly add the cool water to the flour and continue blending until the dough comes together.

Turn the dough out onto a lightly floured surface and knead for 5 minutes. If the dough becomes stiff or dry, add 1 to 2 additional tablespoons of water. Do not add any extra flour.

Place the kneaded dough in a bowl that has been lightly dusted with flour. Cover the dough with an oiled piece of plastic wrap, then with a clean dish towel. Set aside in a warm place and allow to rise until doubled in size, about 2 hours.

Preheat the oven to 400 degrees F.

Turn the risen dough out onto a lightly floured work surface. Divide the dough in half and shape each half into a long loaf, measuring about 12 inches long and 3 inches wide. Place on a baking sheet, seam side down, and cover with an oiled piece of plastic wrap. Cover the baking sheet with a dish towel. Set aside and allow to rise until just under double in volume, about 30 minutes.

Score the loaves with a sharp knife or razor blade. Mist with water. Bake until the bread is lightly browned and sounds hollow when gently tapped, 20 to 25 minutes.

PANE DI NOCI

Walnut Bread

MAKES 2 LOAVES

GIANNI: As an Italian, I find that bread is a huge part of my culture. On a trip to France as a young chef, I tasted a sweet and salty walnut bread, the special flavor of which stayed with me for years. I have experimented with different recipes to recapture that memory, and this is as close as I have gotten. The dry milk produces a light, airy loaf and the walnuts release a rich aroma while the bread is baking. It is excellent served with assorted cheeses and a tossed salad, or dipped in a flavorful olive oil. Save some to toast in the morning, and top with marmalade or your favorite jam.

2½ cups warm water
1 package dry yeast
6 cups whole wheat flour, or more as needed
1 teaspoon kosher salt
⅓ cup whole milk powder
3 tablespoons honey
¼ cup olive oil
½ cup walnut oil
1½ cups roughly chopped walnuts

In a small bowl, stir together ¼ cup of the warm water and the yeast. Set aside for 5 minutes.

In a large bowl, toss together 3 cups of the flour, the salt, and the milk powder. Stir in the yeast mixture along with the remaining 2¼ cups warm water, the honey, olive oil, and walnut oil. Mix with a fork or the dough hook of a stand mixer until well combined. Add the walnuts and 1 cup of the remaining flour to the mixture, kneading to combine. Continue adding the remaining 2 cups flour, ¼ cup at a time, until the dough is moist and slightly sticky. Set aside to rest for 5 minutes.

Turn the dough out onto a lightly floured work surface. Knead until the dough is soft and elastic, about 8 minutes. If the dough is very sticky, add more flour, ¼ cup at a time, while kneading.

Place the dough in a clean bowl and cover with plastic wrap and a clean dish towel. Set aside in a warm place and allow to rise for 1 hour.

Preheat the oven to 375 degrees F. Line two baking sheets with parchment paper and set them aside.

Divide the risen dough in half and shape each half into a round loaf. Place on the baking sheets and cover with a dish towel. Set aside and allow to double in size, about 40 minutes.

Bake the loaves until they are deep golden brown and firm, 40 to 45 minutes.

VARIATIONS:

- A delicious bread may be made by eliminating the walnuts and replacing them with an equal amount of roughly chopped fennel leaves and 2 tablespoons fennel seeds.
- The walnuts may be replaced by an equal amount of coarsely chopped sun-dried tomatoes or chopped pitted mixed olives. With either of these variations, regular olive oil may be used in place of the walnut oil. Any variation of this bread freezes well.

ANELLO DI PASQUA DI MARIA PIA

Maria Pia's Easter Bread

MAKES 10 SERVINGS

STAN: My mother baked this cakelike bread, decorated with eggs, every Easter. I believe the recipe originated with my grandmother, who lived next door. The flavor reminds me of her home, where I ate cookies that she baked from this same dough. Now my sister Dora's daughter, Maria Pia, prepares this bread each year. She knows just how soft and sticky the dough should feel to create a light, not too sweet, bread. She serves it along with other desserts and coffee. Leftovers are great for breakfast.

JOAN: When I bake at Eastertime, I always save the eggshells. I wash and pat them dry and then Stan paints each family member's name on the outside of the shells. I fill them with jelly beans and we use them as place cards at the table.

STANLEY: At Easter my grandmother Tropiano or my aunt Angie would give us each one of these breads as a gift. We would carry them around, munching on the sweet dough for hours.

9 large eggs, at room temperature
½ cup granulated sugar
1 teaspoon pure vanilla extract
4 cups all-purpose flour
½ teaspoon kosher salt
4 teaspoons baking powder
12 tablespoons (1½ sticks) butter, softened
1½ cups confectioners' sugar
2 tablespoons milk or water
½ teaspoon pure lemon extract

Preheat the oven to 350 degrees F.

Beat 6 of the eggs, the granulated sugar, and the vanilla together in a medium-size bowl until pale yellow and frothy. Set aside.

In a large bowl, stir together 3 cups of the flour, the salt, and the baking powder. Add the butter and blend with an electric mixer to form a crumbly mixture. Gradually beat in the egg mixture. Add up to ½ cup of the remaining flour to form a soft dough that can be easily removed from the bowl. Turn the dough out onto a lightly floured work surface. Gently knead the dough, adding enough of the remaining ½ cup flour to form a soft dough that is dry on the outside but still sticky on the inside.

Gently roll the dough into a log about 15 inches long and 2 inches in diameter. Cut off a 1-inch-long piece of the dough and set aside. Place the log on a baking sheet. Bring the ends of the log together to form a circle, pinching the dough together to seal the ends. Press 1 of the remaining eggs into the dough at this joint. Place the other 2 eggs an even distance apart on either side of the joint, gently pressing them into the dough.

Roll the reserved dough into six ropes about ½ inch wide and 4 inches long. Place two ropes over each egg to form an X or cross, pinching gently to seal the ends of the ropes to the bread dough. Bake until the bread is light golden brown and a skewer inserted in the center comes out clean, about 30 minutes. Remove from the oven and allow to cool completely.

In a small bowl mix together the confectioners' sugar, milk or water, and lemon extract until smooth. Drizzle this icing back and forth over the bread to create a decorative topping. Allow the icing to set for 30 minutes before slicing and serving.

VARIATIONS: Stan's mother made several different types of confections from this same dough.

- *Cicirata,* also known as *struffoli,* are deep-fried teaspoon-size balls of this dough that are dipped in honey and mounded together to create an Italian version of a croquembouche. This dough should not be sticky in the center; an additional ½ cup of flour may need to be kneaded into the dough before rolling small sections into ½-inch-thick ropes. Cut the ropes into ½-inch sections. Fill a small frying pan with vegetable oil to a depth of 1 inch. Warm over medium-low heat until the oil is hot but not smoking. Fry batches of the cookies in the oil until golden. While the oil is warming and before frying the cookies, place 1 cup honey, 1 cup granulated sugar, and 1 cup water in a medium-size saucepan and slowly bring it to a boil. Boil to dissolve the sugar and thicken the mixture slightly, about 20 minutes. Use a fork or tongs to dip the fried cookies into the honey syrup. Shape the cookies into a mound on a serving plate. Decorate with sprinkles and serve in the middle of table.

- *Anellini* are small ring-shaped cookies. Preheat the oven to 350 degrees F. Roll small sections of this dough into ½-inch-thick ropes. Cut the ropes into 2-inch lengths. Wrap each length around the ends of your two middle fingers and pinch together to form a small ring. Place the cookies on a baking sheet and bake until lightly browned, about 12 minutes. Allow to cool completely before drizzling with the same icing mixture used on the bread. Garnish with sprinkles if you like.

- *Fiocchi* are a fried cookie similar to Regina cookies (page 298). Use a rolling pin or a pasta machine to roll small sections of this dough until very thin. Cut the dough into 4-inch-long strips. The strips may be fried individually or a few may be shaped together to form bows or wreaths. Fill a small frying pan with vegetable oil to a depth of 1 inch. Warm over medium-low heat until the oil is hot but not smoking. Fry the cookies in the oil, a few at a time, until golden brown on all sides. Transfer to a paper towel-lined plate to drain before dusting with sifted confectioners' sugar.

- *Regina* are baked cookies made from this dough—they're delicious with coffee. Pinch off tablespoon-size pieces of dough. Roll into 2-inch-long ropes, and roll to coat in sesame seeds. (You will need about 1 cup of sesame seeds.) Arrange 1 inch apart on a baking sheet and bake in a preheated oven at 350 degrees F until golden brown, about 10 minutes. Store in an airtight container for up to 1 week.

ZEPPOLE

Fried Dough

MAKES 10 SERVINGS

JOAN: In all modesty, my mother's *zeppole* were the best I've ever tasted. Even fellow Italians agreed. They were lighter than all others and not laden with oil. She prepared them for holidays and special occasions such as Christmas Eve and St. Joseph's Day, my brother's name day. *Zeppole* taste best if you eat them right after they've been fried. But sometimes my mother fried them earlier in the day and reheated them in the oven. Either way, we ate *zeppole* in my mother's kitchen, talking and keeping her company while she prepared the rest of the meal, always eating more *zeppole* than we should.

STAN: Joan's family ate *zeppole* plain, but my family dusted them with granulated sugar and I like them best that way.

4 medium-size all-purpose potatoes (about 1⅓ pounds)
1 package dry yeast
1 cup warm water
4 cups all-purpose flour
Kosher salt
Corn oil for frying

Place the potatoes in a pot, cover with cold water, and bring to a boil. Cook the potatoes until tender when pierced with a knife, about 15 minutes. Drain, peel, and quarter. Season with salt before mashing until smooth with a potato masher or electric mixer. Transfer to a large bowl.

In a measuring cup, dissolve the yeast in the warm water. Set aside for 5 minutes.

Mix 1 cup of the flour into the mashed potatoes. Stir in the yeast mixture. Mix in 2 cups more of the flour. Turn the dough out onto a floured work surface. Gradually knead in as much of the remaining cup of flour as necessary to form a soft, dry dough. Slice the dough in half to test the center. If it is still sticky, knead in some more flour. Place the dough in a clean bowl. Cover with plastic wrap and then with a clean dish towel. Set aside in a warm place to rise until doubled in size, about 2 hours.

Line a baking sheet with two layers of paper towels and set aside. Fill a medium-size frying pan with corn oil to a depth of 1 inch. Warm the oil over medium-high heat until hot but not smoking.

Gently deflate the risen dough. It will be sticky—lightly dust your fingers with flour. Scoop out a 2-tablespoon-size portion of the dough. Shape it with your fingers to create a doughnut shape.

Place it in the oil. If the oil is hot enough, the dough will rise to the surface and bubble. Fry until golden on both sides, turning once, 3 to 5 minutes on each side. Remove from the oil with a slotted spoon and place on the paper-towel-lined baking sheet to drain before serving. Continue frying the dough in batches of two *zeppole* at a time. Add more oil to the pan as necessary. Allow the oil to return to frying heat before adding more dough. Serve in small batches after allowing to cool slightly.

VARIATION: 1 or 2 chopped anchovies may be mixed with each *zeppole* to create a savory version of this recipe.

PIZZA

MAKES 8 SERVINGS

JOAN: In our neighborhood my mother's pizza was considered the best—quite an accomplishment in a largely Italian community. She began making dough on an almost daily basis at the age of nine or ten and was still doing it at eighty-five. She slowed down a little after suffering a stroke but found making dough to be wonderful physical and psychological therapy. Following my mother's example, I knead the dough by hand, but it may also be prepared in a stand mixer fitted with a dough hook.

For many years my brother Vincent and his wife, Marilyn, lived near my mother. Whenever they were entertaining, she would send over a freshly baked pizza. Marilyn would cut it into small squares to serve with drinks along with other items on an *antipasti* platter. Pizza was also part of my mother's barter system. My cousin Tony has a dental practice and my mother visited his office regularly. He would never accept money for taking care of her, so for a regular checkup she would "pay" him with a homemade pizza. The price of a root canal was two pizzas and some homemade pasta. Tony and my mother both felt they were getting a good deal.

This is our basic recipe for pizza. Of course an infinite number of toppings may be used. Even the marinara sauce is optional, as we found out when, many years ago, an Italian friend and neighbor sent over a pizza that was void of any topping except olive oil, garlic, and strips of sautéed green peppers. It was delicious.

STANLEY: Roll your pizza as thick or thin as you like. My grandmother rolled hers thin enough to be cut with scissors.

1 package dry yeast or 1 cake fresh yeast
2 cups warm water
4 cups all-purpose flour
1 tablespoon kosher salt
4 tablespoons cornmeal
4 tablespoons olive oil
4 cloves garlic (optional), peeled
2 cups Salsa Marinara *(page 125)*
½ teaspoon dried oregano
1 pound mozzarella cheese, grated
½ cup finely grated pecorino Romano cheese

In a measuring cup, combine the yeast with ½ cup of the warm water. Stir until the yeast dissolves.

In a large bowl, combine the flour and salt. Make a well in the center and add the yeast mixture. Mix with a fork while adding enough of the remaining 1½ cups water to form a soft, dry dough.

Turn the dough out onto a lightly floured surface and continue mixing it with your hands. Knead to form a smooth dough, adding more water or flour as necessary to keep the dough from being too sticky. Form into a ball and place in a clean bowl. Cover the bowl loosely with a clean dish towel. Set it aside in a warm place and allow to rise until it has doubled in size, about 2 hours.

Preheat the oven to 400 degrees F.

Divide the risen dough in half. Roll one half of the dough on a lightly floured surface into a rectangle that will fit on a 9 × 13-inch or 12-inch round baking sheet. Sprinkle the baking sheet with 2 tablespoons of the cornmeal. Transfer the rolled dough to the baking sheet. Drizzle with 2 tablespoons of the olive oil. Squeeze 2 of the garlic cloves through a press and sprinkle over the dough. Spread 1 cup of the marinara sauce evenly over the dough to within 1 inch of the edge. Sprinkle ¼ teaspoon of the oregano over the dough. Sprinkle half the mozzarella and half the Romano cheese over the sauce. Bake until the edges and bottom of the dough are lightly browned, about 15 minutes.

While the first pizza is baking, roll out the other half of the dough and top it with the remaining ingredients. Bake the second pizza. Allow each pizza to cool for 5 minutes before slicing so all the cheese doesn't slide to the middle.

VARIATIONS:

- 1 pound Jarlsberg or Fontina, grated, may be substituted for the mozzarella.
- If you have scraps of leftover dough, shape them by hand into thin 4-inch rounds. Warm 2 tablespoons olive oil in a small frying pan set over medium-low heat. When the oil is hot but not smoking, add the dough and fry until golden brown and puffy on one side. Turn and continue browning. Sprinkle with granulated sugar and serve as a snack. Stan's family ate fried dough with fried eggs, as though it was toast.
- Gianni was at our house when we were testing this fried dough recipe for the book. He made a few additional serving suggestions: A delicious sandwich may be prepared by cutting the fried dough in half and filling it with a slice of prosciutto, salami, mortadella, or Asiago cheese. For a savory version, mix 1 finely chopped anchovy into a piece of dough before frying it.

PIZZA RIPIENA

Stuffed Pizza

MAKES 10 SERVINGS

JOAN: My mother made these stuffed pizzas for large family gatherings to be eaten as an appetizer. At Eastertime she would make several to give as gifts to family and friends. The last time I made them with her—when her health was not great—we made six in one day. My mother would buy an eight- to ten-pound ham, boil it for fifteen to twenty minutes, then, trimming away any fat, dice enough meat into cubes to use as filling for three or four *pizze ripiene.* Soppressata or diced ham steaks may be substituted. This pie may be refrigerated for one day. Bring it to room temperature or reheat before serving.

1 package dry yeast or 1 cake fresh yeast
2 cups warm water
4 cups all-purpose flour
1 tablespoon kosher salt
2 tablespoons cornmeal
4 cups ½-inch cubes smoked ham
2 cups ricotta cheese (about 1 pound)
¼ cup finely grated pecorino Romano cheese
2½ cups ½-inch cubes mozzarella cheese (about ¾ pound)
2 large eggs, lightly beaten
Freshly ground black pepper

In a measuring cup, combine the yeast with ½ cup of the warm water. Stir until the yeast dissolves.

In a large bowl, combine the flour and salt. Make a well in the center and add the yeast mixture. Mix with a fork while adding enough of the remaining 1½ cups water to form a soft, dry dough. The dough may be prepared in a stand mixer fitted with a dough hook. Dough prepared this way may require less water.

Turn the dough out onto a lightly floured surface and continue mixing it with your hands. Knead to form a smooth dough, adding more water or flour as necessary to keep the dough from being too sticky. Form into a ball and place in a clean bowl. Cover the bowl loosely with a clean dish towel. Set it aside in a warm place and allow the dough to rise until it has doubled in size, about 2 hours.

Preheat the oven to 350 degrees F. Sprinkle a large (about 9 × 15-inch) baking sheet with the cornmeal and set aside.

In a large bowl, mix together the ham, ricotta, Romano, and mozzarella. Mix in the eggs. Season with pepper and set aside.

Divide the risen dough in half. Roll one half of the dough on a lightly floured surface into a rectangle that is slightly larger than the baking sheet. Transfer the rolled dough to the baking sheet. Spread the filling evenly over the dough to within 1 inch of the edge.

Roll the second half of the dough on a lightly floured surface into a rectangle that will fit on top of the pie. Place it on top of the filled dough on the baking sheet. Gently press the two layers together. Trim away any thick portions of dough to create an even edge. Use the tines of a fork to completely seal the edges.

Bake until the dough is golden brown on the top and bottom, about 1 hour. Allow to cool slightly and set before serving, about 30 minutes.

Gnocchi, Polenta, e Pasta

GNOCCHI, POLENTA, AND PASTA

JOAN: As with most Italians, pasta is a staple of our family's daily life. We eat it all the time, primarily as a first course. The serving portions are modest, with a pound of pasta serving as many as five people. Most of the traditional recipes in this section are simple to prepare, calling for ingredients that I usually keep on hand, such as canned tomatoes, canned Italian tuna, beans, capers, and olives.

GIANNI: My family sometimes ate pasta as a main course, and it was always served with bread. Serving a starch with a starch may seem odd, but I got so accustomed to it that even now I can't eat a bowl of pasta without a slice of bread.

In Italy every small area has differently shaped pastas that are served with a variety of stuffings and sauces. These pastas often have unusual and comical names. One that I think of immediately is called *strozzapreti* or *strangolapreti,* depending on the region you are from. It means "strangle the priests" and is used to describe two very differently shaped pastas. In my region, *strozzapreti* are strands of pasta the width of fettuccine twisted into a coil. In other regions, *strangolapreti* are ricotta dumplings that are so big you almost choke when you eat them. Some pasta shapes, such as *garganelli* or *maccheroni al pettine,* are called the same thing all over Italy but their size varies from region to region. At Le Madri, Stanley watched me prepare *garganelli* the way we do in the Veneto, by twisting a small square of rolled fresh pasta around a thin rod. This simple movement found its way into a kitchen scene in *Big Night. Garganelli* is one of my favorite pasta shapes, along with *bigoli,* a pasta that is found only in my part of Italy. The procedure for making *bigoli,* a thick spaghetti, was always a special event. After kneading and rolling the dough, it was passed through a special tool called a *torchio.* A *torchio* is simply an extruder that creates a thick spaghetti. The *bigoli* was then hung over the back of a chair so it would dry properly before being cooked in duck broth and served with a duck sauce or served with a sauce of oil, garlic, and fresh sardines. Each household had its own special sauce recipe to serve with *bigoli,* which they rarely divulged to non-family members. My father guarded his recipe with such secrecy that now that he has passed away, none of us can remember when he added the special touch of wine that gave his sauce such a unique flavor. These memories of *bigoli,* along with many more, are so strong that I named my culinary consulting company Bigoli, Inc.

STANLEY: Pasta. Pasta. Pasta. It's on everyone's lips these days—literally. Eat it before you run, they say; eat it to lose weight, some say; don't eat it, you'll gain weight, others say; I say, who cares. Eat it, eat it, and eat it. Pasta is one of the simplest yet most complex and varied foodstuffs ever. Each time you make it, you are presented with a clean slate, a blank canvas that is altered by each new and different sauce accompanying it. They say it is like rice, but it is more because pasta can be given so many shapes, sizes, and textures. The pasta recipes that follow are some of the finest I've ever eaten. Try them and let them be an inspiration to someday create your own.

GNOCCHI

Potato Gnocchi

MAKES 6 SERVINGS

GIANNI: On Sundays it is my family's tradition to gather around the big table in our kitchen to prepare and eat gnocchi, a potato-based pasta. My son, nieces, and nephews are very particular about how their gnocchi are served. Some insist on just butter, some want butter and a sprinkling of sugar (I promise, it tastes great), and others prefer a touch of tomato sauce. Naturally, my devoted mother cooks them one batch at a time.

This recipe is for two variations on gnocchi—the regular small ones that are rolled off a fork and larger hand-rolled ones that are stuffed. The stuffed version freezes very well and may be cooked in boiling water directly from the freezer. My nieces and nephews help me prepare this version because they like pressing the cheese into the center of the dough. Both types of gnocchi may be topped with any number of sauces and served as a pasta dish or as a main course.

2 large Idaho potatoes (about 1½ pounds), peeled
Kosher salt
1 large egg plus 1 egg yolk, lightly beaten
2 teaspoons olive oil
¼ teaspoon ground nutmeg
¾ to 1 cup all-purpose flour, as needed
1 cup finely grated Parmesan cheese
Melted butter or heated sauce, for serving

Place the potatoes in a medium-size pot and cover with cold water. Season with salt and bring to a low boil. Cook until the potatoes are very tender when pierced with a fork but not breaking apart, about 35 minutes.

Drain the potatoes and press through a ricer or mash well with the back of a fork. Spread the potatoes out on a work surface and allow to cool. Gather the cooled potatoes into a shallow round, forming a well in the center. Place the beaten egg and yolk, olive oil, salt to taste, and nutmeg in the well. Distribute ¾ cup of the flour and the grated cheese around the outer edge of the round. Use your hands to gradually incorporate all of the ingredients into the potatoes to form a smooth dough. (Making gnocchi is similar to making bread, so the amount of flour you will need will vary. Up to ¼ cup of additional flour may be necessary to make a smooth dough.) Form the dough into a short, thick log.

Bring a large pot of salted water to a boil.

Lightly flour your work surface. Cut the thick log into quarters. Roll each quarter of the dough into a long ½-inch-diameter log. Cut into ½-inch pieces. The gnocchi may be cooked in these cylindrical shapes or individually rolled off a fork to form the traditional gnocchi shape—three or four shallow stripes on one side, a small indentation on the other.

Cook the gnocchi in small batches in the pot of boiling water. They will sink to the bottom of the pot at first. When they rise to the top, they are done. Use a skimmer or slotted spoon to remove them from the water, and set them aside on a warm serving dish until all of the gnocchi are cooked. Toss with butter or sauce and serve immediately.

For stuffed gnocchi, cut the thick log in half. Roll each half into a 2-inch-thick log. Cut a 1-inch-deep slit down the length of the log. Fill this slit with a semisoft cheese (such as Robiola, smoked mozzarella, Brie, Fontina, or Asiago). Firmly pinch the slit closed. Cut the filled log into 3-inch lengths. Firmly pinch the cut ends closed to seal in the cheese. The stuffed gnocchi may be cooked immediately in boiling water following the instructions for traditional gnocchi, or they may be frozen.

To freeze, place the small logs on a baking sheet and place in the freezer. When the logs are firm, they may be transferred to a container and kept frozen for up to 2 months. Cook in boiling water directly from the freezer. Serve as an appetizer topped with butter or your favorite sauce.

VARIATIONS:

- Gnocchi may also be served topped with these warmed sauces: Mushroom Sauce (page 130); Joan's Basic Tomato Sauce (page 124); 2 tablespoons chunky sweet Gorgonzola cheese melted in 1 cup heavy cream until thickened, 6 to 8 minutes.
- For an elegant version of stuffed gnocchi, fill the split log with smoked salmon. Serve topped with sour cream and a dollop of caviar.

GNOCCHI DI SEMOLINA

Roman-Style Semolina Gnocchi

MAKES 4 TO 6 SERVINGS

GIANNI: When we were small children, my mother prepared her own version of *pappetta*, or baby food, for our supper. She would puree assorted cooked vegetables in a small food mill and serve them along with these baked gnocchi. At other times, as a special treat, she would crumble baked gnocchi in a bowl of warm milk and sprinkle it with sugar. To this day, if there is leftover gnocchi or polenta in the house, my mother will prepare it in this way and eat it just before going to bed. She claims it acts as a sedative, guaranteeing her a good night's sleep.

I like this dish because it is very versatile. Roman-style gnocchi are delicious plain, with cheese, or topped with Mushroom Sauce (page 130), shaved white truffles, or a drizzle of truffle oil. They may be served as a main course, preceded by a salad; as an appetizer before a hearty soup; or as a side dish with roasted meat or stews. As a main course I recommend serving three pieces of gnocchi to each person; as an appetizer or side dish, two per person. The gnocchi may be cooked and cooled in the baking pan up to two days in advance of cutting and baking. Cover and store in the refrigerator until ready to proceed with the recipe.

4 cups whole milk
2 tablespoons butter
1/4 teaspoon kosher salt
1/4 teaspoon ground nutmeg
1 1/4 cups semolina flour
3 large egg yolks
6 tablespoons freshly grated Parmesan cheese

Lightly oil a 9 × 13-inch baking pan with olive oil. Set aside.

Warm the milk, 1 tablespoon of the butter, the salt, and the nutmeg in a large saucepan set over medium heat. When the mixture begins to simmer, gradually whisk in the flour. Reduce the heat to medium-low and cook, stirring first with a whisk and then with a wooden spoon, until the mixture becomes thick like polenta, 3 to 5 minutes. Remove from the heat.

Stir in the egg yolks one at a time, mixing well after each addition. Stir in 3 tablespoons of the Parmesan. Pour the mixture into the prepared baking pan. Use a rubber spatula to spread it to an even 1-inch thickness. Set aside to cool completely.

Preheat the oven to 450 degrees F.

Turn the cooled gnocchi out onto a cutting surface. Use a 3-inch circular cookie cutter to cut out twelve pieces of gnocchi, reserving the trimmings. Distribute the trimmings evenly over the bottom of the baking dish. Place the semolina circles, slightly overlapping, on top of the trimmings.

(I don't like to waste any portion of this delicious gnocchi, so I bake and serve some of the trimmings along with each circular portion.) Sprinkle with the remaining 3 tablespoons Parmesan and dot each circle with a portion of the remaining 1 tablespoon butter. Bake until lightly browned, about 10 minutes. Serve immediately.

VARIATIONS:

- 2 tablespoons individual or mixed fresh herbs (such as parsley, basil, marjoram, oregano, or tarragon) may be stirred into the gnocchi just before it is poured into the pan to cool.
- ¼ cup diced ham or black truffles may be stirred into the gnocchi before cooling.
- This gnocchi also makes a great dessert or snack for children. Omit the nutmeg and cheese. Stir ¼ cup sugar, 1 teaspoon pure vanilla extract, and 1 teaspoon grated orange zest into the gnocchi just before it is poured into the pan to cool. Just before serving, cut the gnocchi into circles as instructed. Instead of baking, warm ¼ cup vegetable oil in a sauté pan set over medium heat. Dust the gnocchi generously with flour, dip into an egg that has been beaten with 2 tablespoons milk, and then coat with plain dried bread crumbs. When the oil is hot but not smoking, add the gnocchi and fry until warmed through and crisp, about 4 minutes per side. Serve with sliced fresh fruit or seasonal berries.

POLENTA

MAKES 4 TO 6 SERVINGS

GIANNI: My aunt Angela Santolin was the master of preparing polenta at our house. We had a cast-iron wood-burning stove with rings on top that could be removed to allow a pot to be placed down inside, close to the slow-burning coals. She cooked the polenta in an unlined copper pot. (I don't recommend following her example, mostly because I remember the hours it took to clean the pot with lemon juice, cornmeal, and coarse salt.) She would stir and cook until the polenta *pipava,* or bubbled and sighed. It was then poured onto a *panaro,* a round cutting board, placed in the center of the table. A warm damp cloth was placed on top while the polenta set and cooled a bit. When it was time to eat, my father would use a long thread to cut the polenta into thin slices. It was served to dip or crumble into a stew.

There are many variations on this recipe, but I like to keep it simple. This is meant to be eaten with braised meat or stewed fish or with mushrooms. One of my favorite variations is "messy polenta," which we liked to eat after hiking or skiing: Mix ½ cup cooked white beans or kidney beans and ½ cup Gorgonzola cheese into the cooked polenta and serve immediately.

4 cups water
2½ teaspoons kosher salt
2 tablespoons olive oil
1¼ cups finely ground yellow cornmeal

Bring the water to a boil in a medium-size saucepan. Add the salt and olive oil, reduce the heat to a simmer, and gradually whisk in the cornmeal, a small amount at a time. Reduce the heat to low and cook the polenta, stirring occasionally, until tender, about 30 minutes. Serve immediately, spooned onto serving plates, or pour into a 9 × 13-inch baking pan to cool. The cooled polenta may be sliced for grilling or pan-frying.

VARIATIONS: Add one of the following ingredients to the cooked polenta before serving:

- 2 tablespoons light cream
- 2 tablespoons softened butter
- Freshly ground black pepper
- 1 tablespoon chopped fresh mixed herbs (such as rosemary, sage, thyme, or tarragon)
- ½ cup freshly grated Parmesan, Robiola, Gorgonzola, or Fontina cheese
- ½ pound sautéed sliced mushrooms
- ½ cup roughly chopped walnuts

POLENTA PASTICCIATA AL GORGONZOLA

Lasagna Made with Polenta and Gorgonzola Cheese

MAKES 4 TO 6 SERVINGS

GIANNI: Polenta is the bread of the Veneto region, where I grew up. In fact, people from my area are called *polentoni,* or "polenta people." So it is no surprise that in my home there was always plenty of leftover polenta. It would be refrigerated and sliced to grill or toast and serve with chopped fresh tomatoes or *baccalà* (page 31). It was also used to prepare this simple lasagna, which is delicious as a pasta course before grilled meat or fish.

Look in your local cheese store for dolce latte Gorgonzola, a sweet, mild cheese that doesn't have the hard bite of other Gorgonzolas. Brie, Jarlsberg, Gruyère, or Emmentaler cheese may be substituted.

4 cups water
2½ teaspoons sea or kosher salt
2 tablespoons olive oil
1¼ cups finely ground yellow cornmeal
1½ cups Mushroom Sauce (page 130)
⅓ cup crumbled sweet Gorgonzola cheese
2 tablespoons finely grated Parmesan cheese

Bring the water to a boil in a medium-size saucepan. Add the salt and olive oil, reduce the heat to a simmer, and gradually whisk in the cornmeal, a small amount at a time. Reduce the heat to low and cook the polenta, stirring occasionally, until it is smooth and tender, about 30 minutes. Pour into an 8-inch square baking dish and allow to cool completely.

Preheat the oven to 350 degrees F.

Turn the cooled polenta out onto a cutting surface. Cut the square in half to make two rectangles. Cut each half of the polenta, on the bias, into 8 slices, each about 1½ inches wide. Arrange the slices in a single tightly overlapping row in the baking dish. Spoon 1 tablespoon of the mushroom sauce between each pair of slices, and distribute the remaining sauce over the top of the polenta. Sprinkle with the Gorgonzola. Bake to warm through and melt the cheese, about 20 minutes. Sprinkle with the Parmesan and bake to brown, about 5 minutes. Serve immediately.

VARIATION: Other sauces, such as ragù or marinara, may be substituted for the mushroom sauce.

PENNE CON RUCOLA E POMODORI

Mediterranean Pasta Salad with Arugula and Tomatoes

MAKES 6 TO 8 SERVINGS

GIANNI: I personally love any dish prepared with arugula—hot or cold—and this one is at the top of my list. I eat it topped with Parmesan cheese shavings for a quick lunch. I even enjoy it left over, and have been known to eat it for breakfast on my day off. This entire dish may be prepared a day in advance. Cover and store it in the refrigerator until one hour before tossing and serving.

1 pound penne
6 tablespoons extra virgin olive oil
4 cups packed stemmed arugula, roughly cut or torn
½ cup chopped fresh basil leaves
3 cups peeled ripe tomatoes cut into ½-inch dice (about 4 large tomatoes)
3 teaspoons kosher salt
Freshly ground black pepper
1 tablespoon freshly squeezed lemon juice
Freshly grated Parmesan or ricotta salata cheese

Bring a large pot of salted water to a rapid boil. Add the pasta and cook, until *al dente* following the package instructions. Drain and transfer to a wide serving bowl. Toss with 1 tablespoon of the olive oil. Add the arugula, basil, tomatoes, the remaining 5 tablespoons olive oil, the salt, pepper to taste, and the lemon juice. Toss well. Serve at room temperature, garnished with Parmesan or ricotta salata cheese.

VARIATIONS:

- Fusilli, farfalle, or conchiglie pasta may be substituted for the penne.
- ½ pound diced fresh mozzarella may be added to this recipe. Toss it into the salad along with 1 teaspoon grated lemon zest and 1 tablespoon balsamic vinegar for a zesty, hearty dish.
- Red or yellow cherry tomatoes, or a combination of both, cut in half, may be substituted for the whole tomatoes. You will need about 1½ pints.

INSALATA DI PASTA ALLA NIZZARDA

Pasta Salad Niçoise

MAKES 6 TO 8 SERVINGS

GIANNI: My wife, Laura, and I spent our honeymoon traveling in Spain and France. One day we stopped for lunch in the olive-growing area of Provence. The restaurant was beautiful, the table settings elegant, and the view captivating. Everything was perfect until the waiter brought me the Niçoise salad I had ordered. It seemed as if a cloud had settled around my palate, and the moment was ruined. Not only were the ingredients disappointing but the salad dressing had been prepared with a cheap corn oil.

When we arrived home, I was inspired to create this recipe, which is my own version of a *salade Niçoise.* It is an excellent appetizer and a terrific lunch dish. The entire salad may be prepared one day ahead of time: Toss all of the ingredients together except the dressing made from the remaining olive oil, vinegar, lemon juice, and fresh herbs. Refrigerate overnight and allow the salad to return to room temperature before tossing with the dressing.

¾ pound shell-shaped pasta
4 tablespoons extra virgin olive oil
2 tablespoons balsamic vinegar
1 tablespoon freshly squeezed lemon juice
2 cloves garlic, finely chopped
½ teaspoon kosher salt
½ teaspoon freshly ground black pepper
2 tablespoons drained capers
¼ cup pitted Kalamata or Niçoise olives
½ cup diced roasted red peppers (page 41)
One 7-ounce can solid white tuna packed in olive oil
¼ cup chopped fresh basil leaves
2 tablespoons chopped fresh parsley leaves

Cook the pasta in a pot of rapidly boiling salted water until *al dente,* according to the package instructions. Drain and toss with 2 tablespoons of the olive oil. Spread on baking sheets and set aside to cool.

In a deep serving bowl, whisk together the remaining 2 tablespoons olive oil, the vinegar, lemon juice, garlic, salt, and black pepper. Add the capers, olives, and roasted peppers. Do not drain the tuna, but flake it with a fork. Add the basil and parsley. Add the pasta and toss well. Serve immediately.

VARIATIONS: Many individual ingredients may be added to this basic recipe, such as:

- ½ pound fresh mozzarella, cut into small cubes
- ¼ pound thickly sliced smoked ham, cut into small cubes

continued

- 4 roughly chopped hard-boiled eggs
- Summer vegetables, such as 1 medium-size eggplant, cut into ½-inch-thick strips, grilled, and cut into ½-inch cubes; 1 medium-size zucchini, cut into ½-inch-thick strips, grilled, and cut into ½-inch cubes; 1 cup roughly chopped broccoli florets, blanched in boiling water until just tender, about 1 minute; or ½ cup fresh peas, blanched in boiling water until just tender and bright green, about 2 minutes.

A seaside visit with some of our relatives from Switzerland. My sister Livia is the first child on the left and seated next to her is my sister Catterina. My mother is standing on the right.

INSALATA DI PASTA ESTIVA DELLA SALUTE

Summer Pasta Salad

MAKES 8 TO 10 SERVINGS

GIANNI: My wife, Laura, is a nutritionist and because of her influence I now prepare more vegetable-based dishes than ever before. I came up with this tasty recipe by trying different combinations and flavors. Trust me, there are enough vegetables in this pasta salad to more than meet your daily requirement.

Serve this as a first course before grilled chicken or fish or as a main course for lunch. All of the vegetables, except the tomatoes, may be prepared one day in advance. Store in the refrigerator before tossing with the remaining ingredients.

Do not rinse cooked pasta under cold water. This washes away the pasta's natural starch and flavor and sauces will not adhere as well. Instead, drain the cooked pasta and toss it with a small amount of olive oil. Then spread it on baking sheets and allow it to cool completely.

1 pound short-cut pasta, such as fusilli or penne
4 tablespoons olive oil
½ medium-size eggplant, peeled in intermittent strips and cut into ½-inch cubes (about 3 cups)
2 medium-size carrots, peeled
2 medium-size zucchini, ends trimmed
½ cup fresh or frozen peas
1 red bell pepper, roasted, peeled, seeded, and diced (page 41)
1 yellow bell pepper, roasted, peeled, seeded, and diced (page 41)
2 cups finely diced tender celery hearts
2 cups chopped ripe plum tomatoes (about 4 tomatoes)
3 tablespoons chopped fresh basil leaves
2 tablespoons chopped fresh parsley leaves
1 tablespoon chopped fresh oregano leaves
½ cup extra virgin olive oil
Kosher salt and freshly ground black pepper
6 ounces fresh mozzarella cheese, cut into ¼-inch cubes

Bring a pot of salted water to a boil. Cook the pasta, following the package instructions, until *al dente.* Drain well. Toss the pasta with 1 tablespoon of the olive oil and spread it out in a single layer on baking sheets to cool. Set aside.

Warm the remaining 3 tablespoons olive oil in a large skillet set over high heat. When the oil is hot but not smoking, add the eggplant and cook, tossing frequently, until golden brown and somewhat softened, about 6 minutes. Transfer to a paper-towel-lined plate and set aside.

continued

Fill a 3-quart saucepan with water, salt it, and bring to a boil. Add the carrots and boil to soften slightly, about 5 minutes. Add the zucchini and cook until the vegetables are tender but still firm, about 5 minutes. Add the peas and cook until just tender, about 1 minute. Drain the water from the pan and cover the vegetables with cold water, allowing the water to run for 2 to 3 minutes to cool the vegetables and arrest the cooking.

Cut the cooled carrots and zucchini in half lengthwise and then into ⅛-inch-thick slices. Place in a large serving bowl. Add the drained peas, the eggplant, and the roasted peppers, celery, and tomatoes. Add the basil, parsley, oregano, extra virgin olive oil, and cooked pasta. Toss well to combine. Season with salt and pepper. Gently mix in the mozzarella, and serve.

VARIATION: Blanched asparagus, cut on the bias into 1-inch pieces, makes a nice addition to this salad.

PASTA FRESCA FATTA IN CASA

Homemade Pasta

MAKES ABOUT 1 POUND; ENOUGH FOR 2 RECIPES LASAGNE VERDE

JOAN: Tender homemade pasta is a real treat. My mother prepared it every Sunday when we arrived home from church. She never used a machine to mix the dough or to roll it out. She kneaded the dough by hand and then rolled small pieces until they were very thin. She cut these pieces into strips and spread them out to dry on a clean sheet she had placed across my brother Joe's bed. Later in life she began to use a machine to help with the rolling, but she always mixed the dough by hand.

Stan and I usually make pasta together. I mix it in the food processor and he rolls it through the pasta machine. We arrived at this efficient method during the years when were both working and still wanted to make fresh pasta for dinner. Stan's nephew Pierre suggested I try using a food processor to mix the dough. I found I had to adjust my mother's recipe because the machine blends the dough very differently than when it is kneaded by hand. This is the recipe I arrived at after much trial and error.

1½ cups all-purpose flour
½ teaspoon kosher salt
2 large eggs plus 1 large egg yolk
1 teaspoon olive oil

Place 1 cup of the flour and the salt in a food processor and pulse to combine. Add the eggs, egg yolk, and olive oil, and mix until the dough comes together to form a ball. Turn the dough out onto a lightly floured work surface. Gradually knead the remaining ½ cup flour into the dough by hand. The dough should be smooth, not sticky. Break the dough ball in half to test the center of the dough. If the center is sticky, continue to knead more flour into the dough. Wrap it in plastic and set the dough aside to rest for 5 minutes. (Or wrap it in plastic and refrigerate for several hours. Return to room temperature before proceeding with the recipe.)

Line a large table or work surface (or bed) with a clean sheet or towels. Lightly flour the surface.

Break off one third of the dough. (Rewrap unused sections.) Sprinkle it lightly with flour and pass it through a pasta machine, following the manufacturer's instructions. (Stan's procedure with a hand-crank machine is to begin with the machine set at the widest opening. Pass the dough through and then narrow the opening by one notch, dusting with flour each time so it does not stick to the machine. He continues to narrow the opening one notch at a time until the dough is the desired thickness. For lasagna and cannelloni it is best to stop one short of the narrowest setting on the machine.)

Cut the pasta into 12-inch lengths as wide as you wish. For lasagna the pasta may now be spread out on the table to dry. For long strands of pasta, pass the dough through the cutting portion of the machine and then lay the strands out to dry. (Scraps may be passed through the machine to make shorter strands that may be dried and cooked that day.) Or spread the strands on baking sheets and freeze. Once the strands are stiff, they may be packed in airtight containers and frozen for up to 1 month.

Roll out the remaining two thirds of the dough, one third at a time, following the same procedure.

VARIATION: Cook ½ pound chopped spinach in boiling water until wilted and tender, about 1 minute. Drain thoroughly, squeezing out any excess water. Add to the flour with the eggs. This pasta dough will require up to ½ cup additional flour.

BESCIAMELLA

White Sauce

MAKES 4 SERVINGS; ABOUT 3 CUPS

JOAN: This recipe makes a medium-consistency *besciamella* sauce, which may be used in many recipes in place of cream. It can be prepared a few hours ahead of time and kept at room temperature. Place a piece of plastic wrap or waxed paper directly on the surface of the sauce to prevent a skin from forming.

6 tablespoons (¾ stick) butter
6 tablespoons all-purpose flour
3 cups whole or skim milk, warmed
Kosher salt and freshly ground black pepper
¼ teaspoon ground nutmeg

Melt the butter in a medium-size saucepan set over medium-low heat. When the butter is foaming, whisk in the flour. Gradually whisk in the milk. Cook, whisking frequently, until the sauce thickens, about 20 minutes. Remove from the heat and stir in salt and pepper to taste and the nutmeg.

NOTE: This recipe may easily be cut in half or in thirds when smaller amounts are called for in various recipes throughout this book. Smaller quantities will require less cooking time.

PASSATA DI POMODORO

Uncooked Fresh Tomato Sauce

MAKES 4 SERVINGS

GIANNI: Italians are very proud of their tomatoes, and if you have ever visited Italy in the summer you know why—the tomatoes are sweet and very flavorful. One summer I ate a delicious pasta dish at a restaurant near my hometown. The simple tomato sauce was incredibly fresh and robust. I asked the chef for the recipe but he wouldn't give it to me. I was haunted by the flavor of this dish and had to know the secret of how it was prepared, so a few days later I took the gentleman who had been my waiter out for a drink. I asked him how the sauce was made, and he described a recipe that was so simple, I was certain there must be more to it. I went home and followed his instructions. The sauce was perfect, just as I remembered it from the restaurant. I enjoy it over pasta, but this sauce is also delicious served on bruschetta.

1½ pounds ripe summer tomatoes
½ teaspoon kosher salt
1 pound pasta (spaghetti, linguine, fettuccine)
2 tablespoons extra virgin olive oil

Bring a large pot of salted water to a boil. Use a sharp knife to score the bottoms of the tomatoes with an X. Gently place the tomatoes in the boiling water. When the skin begins to unfurl at the X, remove the tomatoes from the water with a slotted spoon and plunge into a bowl of cold water. Allow the tomatoes to cool slightly; then peel away the skins.

Cut the tomatoes into several small pieces. Remove and discard the seeds. Place the tomatoes in a food mill fitted with a coarse blade. Grind the tomatoes through the mill (or finely chop by hand) into a bowl. Stir the salt into the tomatoes. Transfer to a fine-mesh sieve and place the sieve over a bowl. Allow the tomatoes to drain for several hours at room temperature or overnight in the refrigerator.

Bring a large pot of salted water to a boil. Add the pasta and cook, following the package instructions. Drain well and toss with the olive oil. Distribute evenly among four plates. Discard the water accumulated in the bowl below the tomatoes, and spoon equal portions of the concentrated tomatoes on top of the pasta. Serve immediately.

VARIATION: To warm this sauce, heat 1 tablespoon extra virgin olive oil in a small saucepan until hot but not smoking. Remove from the heat, add the tomatoes, and stir to warm through. Serve immediately.

SALSA DI POMODORO GIANNI

Gianni's Basic Tomato Sauce

MAKES 8 SERVINGS

GIANNI: This recipe makes a slightly chunky tomato sauce. If you like a smoother consistency, cool the sauce and pass it through a food mill, process it with an electric mixer, or pulse it in a blender. I prefer to use fresh peeled and chopped plum tomatoes or ripe summer Jersey tomatoes rather than canned tomatoes. When tomatoes are in season, prepare a double batch and freeze the sauce in several small containers.

1 tablespoon butter
2 tablespoons olive oil
¾ cup diced onions
3 pounds ripe plum tomatoes, coarsely chopped
10 large fresh basil leaves, cut into long thin strips
Kosher salt and freshly ground black pepper

Place the butter and olive oil in a medium-size saucepan set over medium-high heat. When the butter begins to foam, add the onions and cook, stirring frequently, until they have softened but not browned, about 6 minutes. Stir in the tomatoes, crushing them with your hand or the back of a slotted spoon as you add them to the pan. Add half the basil and bring to a boil. Reduce the heat to medium-low and simmer until most of the water has evaporated, about 25 minutes. Season with salt and pepper. Just before serving, stir in the remaining basil. Briskly whisk the sauce to create a chunky puree.

VARIATIONS: Possible additions include 4 cloves garlic, chopped; 1 teaspoon chopped fresh oregano leaves; or a pinch of red pepper flakes or ¼ teaspoon seeded and diced fresh jalapeño pepper—all of which may be added to the sauce after the onions have softened.

Also, 1 medium-size carrot, finely diced, and 1 medium-size celery stalk, finely diced, may be added to the basic recipe along with the onions.

SALSA DI POMODORO JOAN

Joan's Basic Tomato Sauce

MAKES 6 SERVINGS

JOAN: My mother traditionally prepared this sauce using homemade bottled tomatoes. After my father died, we continued to bottle tomatoes for several years, but eventually we stopped. Then my mother began preparing this sauce with store-bought canned tomatoes and found the flavor to be comparable. This sauce is used to flavor and enhance many of the recipes throughout this book.

There are many similarities between this recipe and the one for *Salsa Marinara* on page 125. The most important difference between them is the size pot they are cooked in. The uncovered 12-inch sauté or frying pan I call for in the marinara recipe allows the tomatoes' juices to reduce or cook off, resulting in a thick, densely flavored sauce. In this recipe I call for the sauce to be cooked in an 8-inch covered saucepan so that the tomatoes retain their juices, resulting in a less thick and slightly milder sauce. This basic tomato sauce is most appropriate for use with such dishes as *Ditali con Fagioli* (page 143) and *Ditalini e Piselli* (page 142). Because the sauce freezes well, I recommend making extra to have on hand. This slightly chunky sauce may be cooled and then pureed in the blender for a finer consistency.

¼ cup olive oil
2 cloves garlic, chopped
1 tablespoon chopped onions
1 tablespoon seeded and chopped green bell pepper (optional)
3½ cups canned whole plum tomatoes (about one 28-ounce can)
1 fresh basil leaf
Kosher salt and freshly ground black pepper

Warm the olive oil in a medium-size saucepan (about 8 inches in diameter) set over medium-low heat; then add the garlic, onions, and bell pepper. Cook until softened but not browned, about 2 minutes. Stir in the tomatoes, crushing them with your hands or with the back of a slotted spoon as you add them to the pan. Add the basil and season with salt and pepper. Bring to a boil, cover, and reduce the heat to a gentle simmer. Cook the tomatoes until they sweeten, about 35 minutes. Uncover and continue to simmer for 5 minutes more to thicken the sauce slightly.

SALSA MARINARA

Sailor's-Style Sauce

MAKES 4 SERVINGS

JOAN: The only difference between the Tropianos' marinara sauce and the Tuccis' is the onion. My family put it in and Stan's family left it out. The ingredients for this sauce are essentially the same as in my recipe for Basic Tomato Sauce (page 124). The marinara sauce is cooked in a large uncovered pan so that the tomatoes break down, creating an intensely flavored, thick sauce. The basic tomato sauce is cooked in a small covered saucepan, resulting in a lighter, soupier sauce.

Whenever I shop for canned tomatoes, I look for ones from the San Marzano area of Italy. They are the finest. Marinara sauce may be prepared several days ahead and refrigerated or frozen. Reheat slowly before serving. Serve over pasta or with other dishes as noted throughout the book.

¼ cup olive oil
3 cloves garlic, cut in half
1 tablespoon chopped onions
4 cups canned whole plum tomatoes (about one 35-ounce can)
2 teaspoons chopped fresh oregano leaves or ½ teaspoon dried
3 fresh basil leaves
Kosher salt and freshly ground black pepper

Warm the olive oil in a large sauté or frying pan (about 12 inches in diameter) set over medium-high heat. Add the garlic and onions and cook until the onions are soft but not browned, about 2 minutes. Stir in the tomatoes, crushing them with your hands or the back of a slotted spoon as you add them to the pan. Stir in the oregano and basil, and season with salt and pepper. Simmer until the tomatoes have thickened and sweetened, about 25 minutes (the longer you cook this sauce, the thicker it will become). Remove from the heat and allow to rest so that the sauce thickens slightly and the flavors come together, about 5 minutes.

RAGÙ TUCCI

Meat-Based Tomato Sauce Tucci-Style

MAKES 8 SERVINGS

JOAN: This is the traditional way the Tuccis make ragù. My mother made a lighter version of this same sauce. I call for spareribs and stewing beef, but different cuts of meat may be added depending on what is on hand—pork chops, sausage, pig's feet. It is very delicious with *polpette,* or meatballs, which may be added to the sauce during the last half hour of cooking. The sauce may be prepared two days ahead of serving. Refrigerate it overnight and reheat before tossing with the pasta. It may also be frozen with the meat and meatballs.

STAN: My father's retail monument business operated from March to November. This meant he was at home three to four months of the year. It was a time my mother enjoyed because my father would cook most of the meals. He was an excellent cook and could always find a way to take credit for a good meal or to deflect responsibility for a not-so-perfect one. For example, the ragù turns out excellent because he cooked it even though my mother selected the cuts of meat, or the ragù is excellent even though my mother cooked it because he selected such choice cuts of meat, or the ragù is less than perfect not because of how he cooked it but because my mother selected such inferior cuts of meat, or the ragù is less than perfect because of the way my mother cooked the wonderful meat he had so carefully selected. My father originated the Ragù Catch-22.

¼ cup olive oil
1 pound stewing beef, trimmed of fat, rinsed, patted dry, and cut into pieces
1 pound country-style spareribs, trimmed of fat, cut in half, rinsed, and patted dry
1 cup roughly chopped onions
3 cloves garlic, roughly chopped
½ cup dry red wine
One 6-ounce can tomato paste
1½ cups warm water
8 cups canned whole plum tomatoes (about two 35-ounce cans), passed through a food mill or pureed in the blender
3 fresh basil leaves
1 tablespoon chopped fresh oregano leaves or 1 teaspoon dried

Warm the olive oil in a stew pot set over medium-high heat. Sear the stewing beef until brown on all sides, about 10 minutes. Remove from the pot and set aside in a bowl. Add the spareribs to the pot and sear until they are brown on all sides, about 10 minutes. Remove the ribs and set aside in the bowl with the stewing beef. (If your pot is big enough to hold all of the meat in a single layer, it may be cooked at the same time.)

Stir the onions and garlic into the pot. Reduce the heat to low and cook until the onions begin to soften and lose their shape, about 5 minutes. Stir in the wine, scraping the bottom of the pot clean. Add the tomato paste. Pour ½ cup of the warm water into the can to loosen any residual paste and then pour the water into the pot. Cook to warm the paste through, about 2 minutes. Add the tomatoes along with the remaining 1 cup warm water. Stir in the basil and oregano. Cover with the lid slightly askew and simmer to sweeten the tomatoes, about 30 minutes.

Return the meat to the pot, along with any juices that have accumulated in the bowl. Cover with the lid slightly askew and simmer, stirring frequently, until the meat is very tender and the tomatoes are cooked, about 2 hours. Warm water may be added to the sauce, in ½-cup portions, if the sauce becomes too thick. (If you have made meatballs, they may be added during the last half hour of cooking. The meatballs will soften and absorb some of the sauce.)

NOTE: When preparing ragù for *timpáno,* only the sauce is used and the meat is served as a separate course. The sauce for *timpáno* should be thin, so measure out 7½ cups of prepared sauce and stir in ½ cup water before proceeding with the *timpáno* recipe.

VARIATION: Sweet Italian sausage may be added to this sauce. Sauté it after the spareribs and then proceed with the recipe as written.

RAGÙ TROPIANO

Meat-Based Tomato Sauce Tropiano-Style

MAKES 8 SERVINGS

JOAN: My mother's recipe for ragù was lighter than the ragù Stan's family prepared. She would serve the ragù in the same way Stan's family did—spooning just the tomato sauce over pasta as a first course, followed by the meat as a second course. She also used this sauce when she prepared lasagna. My mother would shred the tender cooked meat into smaller pieces and ladle it between layers of homemade pasta and ricotta cheese for a traditional lasagna casserole. This is her sauce recipe as I recall it.

¼ cup olive oil
½ pound stewing beef, trimmed of fat, rinsed, patted dry, and cut into pieces
½ pound pork chops or spareribs, trimmed of fat, rinsed, and patted dry
2 cloves garlic, finely chopped
1 tablespoon finely chopped onions
½ cup dry red wine
3½ cups canned whole plum tomatoes (about one 28-ounce can), pureed in a blender or food mill
1 fresh basil leaf
Kosher salt and freshly ground black pepper

Warm the olive oil in a medium-size flameproof casserole set over medium-low heat. Add the stewing beef and brown evenly on all sides, about 10 minutes. Remove the beef to a bowl and set aside. Add the pork to the pot and brown evenly on both sides, about 10 minutes. Remove from the pan and add to the bowl with the beef. Stir the garlic and onions into the pot and cook until softened but not browned, about 2 minutes. Add the wine and stir to loosen any bits of meat that may have stuck to the bottom of the pan. Stir in the tomatoes and basil. Return the meat to the pot, along with any juices that have accumulated in the bottom of the bowl. Season with salt and pepper. Bring to a boil, then cover, reduce the heat to medium-low, and simmer until the tomatoes have sweetened and the meat is very tender, about 1½ hours.

MARINARA CON FUNGHI

Tomato Sauce with Mushrooms

MAKES 4 SERVINGS

STAN: Marinara was my father's favorite tomato sauce. He always said he preferred it to ragù. As children none of us agreed with him, but as we got older we appreciated his wisdom—it is lighter and easier to digest.

JOAN: This recipe makes enough sauce for 1 pound of linguine or spaghetti. It may be made one day ahead; refrigerate it and reheat before serving. This sauce is also delicious served with polenta: Cook the polenta and then stir in one third of the sauce. Distribute among four dinner plates and top with remaining sauce.

STANLEY: This is the first sauce I learned to make. It is simple and inexpensive. During the lean years in New York I found it a great comfort nutritionally and economically.

3 tablespoons olive oil
1 clove garlic, sliced
10 ounces white mushrooms, cut into ¼-inch-thick slices
4 cups canned whole plum tomatoes (about one 35-ounce can)
3 fresh basil leaves
1 teaspoon chopped fresh oregano leaves or ½ teaspoon dried (optional)
Kosher salt and freshly ground black pepper
Freshly grated Parmesan or pecorino Romano cheese for garnish (optional)

Warm the olive oil in a large sauté pan set over medium-high heat. Add the garlic and cook until softened and lightly colored, about 2 minutes. Stir in the mushrooms and cook until lightly colored and softened, about 5 minutes. Remove the mushrooms to a plate and set aside.

Add the tomatoes to the sauté pan, crushing them with your hands or the back of a slotted spoon as you stir them into the pan. Add the basil and oregano, and season with salt and pepper. Bring to a boil, then reduce the heat and simmer until the sauce thickens slightly, about 15 minutes. Return the mushrooms to the pan and continue to simmer until the sauce is sweet, about another 15 minutes. Serve over pasta garnished with Parmesan or pecorino Romano cheese if desired.

SALSA AI FUNGHI

Mushroom Sauce

MAKES 6 SERVINGS

GIANNI: I use this sauce in my recipe for Lasagna with Chicken and Mushrooms (page 166). It is also delicious served with Roman-Style Semolina Gnocchi (page 110), Potato Gnocchi (page 108), or over any type of pasta. The sauce may be prepared two days in advance; store it in the refrigerator and reheat before serving.

1 cup dried porcini mushrooms
1½ cups warm water
2 tablespoons olive oil
½ cup thinly sliced onions
3 tablespoons chopped fresh parsley leaves
2 cloves garlic, chopped
Freshly ground black pepper
¼ cup dry white wine
2 cups roughly chopped portobello mushroom caps (about ½ pound)
2 cups roughly chopped cremini mushroom caps (about ½ pound)
3 cups canned whole plum tomatoes (about one 28-ounce can)
Kosher salt

Soak the dried porcini mushrooms in the warm water for 15 minutes.

Warm the olive oil in a medium-size saucepan set over medium-high heat. Add the onions, parsley, and garlic and cook, stirring often, until the onions soften, about 3 minutes. Squeeze the water from the porcini mushrooms. Strain the soaking water through a fine-mesh sieve or coffee filter to remove any grit, and set aside. Roughly chop the mushrooms and add them to the pan. Season with pepper and cook, stirring often, to flavor the mushrooms with the onions, about 2 minutes.

Stir in the wine. When the wine has been absorbed by the mushrooms, stir in the strained mushroom water. Add the chopped fresh mushrooms and bring the sauce to a rapid boil. Stir in the tomatoes, crushing them with your hands or the back of a slotted spoon as you add them to the pan. Reduce the heat to medium-low and simmer the sauce until the tomatoes sweeten, 30 to 35 minutes. Season with salt to taste.

SALSA ALLA MARIA ROSA

Maria Rosa's Sauce

SERVES 6

JOAN: When we were living in Florence, our daughter Gina became friends with a young girl named Mirca. Stan and I in turn became friends with Mirca's parents, Vittorio, who was a policeman, and his wife, Maria Rosa. Almost twenty-five years later we are still friends, phoning throughout the year and visiting whenever we have the opportunity. I think of them whenever I prepare this sauce, which Maria Rosa taught me to make.

Before I learned how to make this simple sauce I had always served pasta with ragù sauce using my mother-in-law's recipe. (Stan used to favor his family's rich ragù. As he has grown older, he has come to prefer my mother's lighter and more easily digested recipe.) I serve *salsa alla Maria Rosa* with penne, farfalle, ziti, or any other long tubular pasta such as rotini or fusilli. I also use it when I prepare *Lasagne Verdi* (page 168), another recipe I learned during our stay in Florence. This sauce freezes very well.

2 tablespoons butter
¼ cup olive oil
1 cup diced carrots (about 2 medium-size carrots)
½ cup diced celery (about 2 small tender stalks)
1 cup diced onions (about ½ large onion)
2 cloves garlic, chopped
2 tablespoons chopped fresh parsley leaves
4 cups canned whole plum tomatoes (about one 35-ounce can)
Kosher salt and freshly ground black pepper

In a large saucepan set over medium heat, melt the butter in the olive oil. When the butter is foaming, add the carrots, celery, onions, and garlic and cook, stirring often, until they have softened, 8 to 10 minutes. Stir in the parsley. Stir in the tomatoes, crushing them with your hands or with the back of a slotted spoon as you add them to the pan. Bring the sauce to a boil. Season with salt and pepper. Reduce the heat to medium-low and simmer, partially covered, until the tomatoes are sweetened and cooked, about 45 minutes.

VARIATIONS:

- To create a less coarse version of this sauce, puree the tomatoes in a blender or food mill before proceeding with the recipe.
- 1 pound ground beef may be added to the sauce before the tomatoes. Cook until the beef is lightly browned and then proceed with the recipe.

PESTO AL BASILICO

Basil Pesto

MAKES 6 SERVINGS

GIANNI: This is a classic summer pasta dish, which may be served before grilled fish or meats. In Liguria, a region of Italy where I have worked, it is usually served over pasta that has been cooked with haricots verts and thinly sliced half-moons of peeled all-purpose potatoes. The beans add a crisp texture to the pasta, while the potatoes add creaminess to the sauce. (Add the vegetables to the pasta during the last five minutes of cooking.) Sometimes broccoli florets are cooked in the same way. If you like to freeze pesto sauce, I recommend preparing this recipe without the cheese. Freshly grated cheese may then be stirred into the thawed sauce before tossing with pasta.

4 cups well-packed fresh basil leaves
1¼ cups well-packed fresh parsley leaves
½ cup pine nuts
6 cloves garlic, peeled
¼ cup very finely grated pecorino Romano cheese
1 cup finely grated Parmesan cheese
2 teaspoons kosher salt
1¼ cups extra virgin olive oil
1 pound pasta (spaghetti, linguine, or fettuccine)

Place the basil, parsley, pine nuts, and garlic in a food processor or blender. Process until the basil and parsley are roughly chopped. Add the Romano, Parmesan, and salt, and process. With the machine running, add the olive oil in a steady stream. Do not over process or the sauce will lose its bright green color. Set aside.

Bring a large pot of salted water to a rapid boil. Add the pasta and cook until *al dente,* following the package instructions. Drain well and toss with a small amount of the pesto. Distribute evenly among plates and top with additional pesto before serving.

VARIATIONS:

- If you like a richer sauce, you may add butter to this basic recipe. Replace ¼ cup of the extra virgin olive oil with softened butter.
- All Parmesan cheese may be used in place of the pecorino Romano.
- If the pesto is slightly brown instead of bright green, add a few leaves of fresh spinach and process. This should help restore the color.
- Use coarsely chopped hazelnuts, toasted in an oven at 350 degrees F for 5 minutes, in place of the pine nuts.

PESTO AL POMODORO PER PASTA O PESCE

Tomato Pesto for Pasta or Fish

MAKES 6 SERVINGS

GIANNI: I prepare this recipe only in the summer, when the tomatoes are ripe and flavorful. It is a delicious lunch dish or pasta course served before grilled fish or meat. This pesto may also be served as a type of salsa with freshly grilled fish: Spoon a portion onto a serving plate and top with the fish and some roughly chopped fresh tomatoes. This pesto may be prepared up to three days in advance; cover and store it in the refrigerator. Return the sauce to room temperature before serving.

¾ cup packed fresh basil leaves
⅓ cup packed fresh parsley leaves
4 cloves garlic, peeled
Kosher salt
½ cup extra virgin olive oil
1 cup peeled, seeded, and finely diced ripe tomatoes (about 3 medium-size tomatoes)
Freshly ground black pepper
1 pound pasta (penne, fusilli, spaghetti, or other pasta of your choice)

Place the basil, parsley, garlic, and salt in a food processor or blender. Turn on the machine and roughly chop the basil and parsley. With the machine running, add the olive oil in a steady stream. Turn off the machine and scrape down the sides. With the machine running again, gradually add the tomatoes. Process just until the tomatoes have been blended into the other ingredients. Season with pepper and set aside.

Bring a large pot of salted water to a boil. Add the pasta and cook until *al dente,* following the package instructions. Drain well and toss with a small amount of the pesto. Distribute evenly among six dinner plates, topping with additional pesto before serving.

VARIATION: ½ pound fresh mozzarella cheese may be thinly sliced and served on top of the sauced pasta.

SPAGHETTI AGLIO E OLIO

Spaghetti with Garlic and Oil

MAKES 4 SERVINGS

STAN: Believe it or not, the Tucci family would cook pasta at picnics! We'd set out early in the morning, loading my father's truck with food, beer, wine, bocce balls, and my uncle's musical instruments. Having secured our favorite spot, we would build a fire. A large cauldron would be filled with water and placed on the fire. Once it came to a boil, we would cook enough pasta for thirty people. My father fashioned utensils made from strong tree branches that would be used by two men to lift and drain the cauldron. Every year these unique utensils were hidden in the park so that they were available for future picnics.

1 pound linguine
½ cup olive oil
3 cloves garlic, cut into ⅛-inch-thick slices
¼ teaspoon paprika
Kosher salt

Bring a large pot of salted water to a boil and cook the pasta, following the package instructions, until *al dente.*

Meanwhile, warm the olive oil in a small sauté pan set over medium-high heat. Add the garlic and cook until it colors slightly but does not brown, about 3 minutes. Remove from the heat and set aside.

Drain the pasta and place in a serving bowl. Add the oil and garlic and toss. Sprinkle with the paprika and serve immediately, adding salt to taste.

SPAGHETTI ALLA CRUDAIOLA

Spaghetti with Fresh Tomatoes

MAKES 4 SERVINGS

JOAN: This is a wonderful pasta to serve in the summer when fresh ripe tomatoes are widely available. The amount of salt you need to add to the tomatoes is determined by how juicy they are.

8 large ripe tomatoes
¾ cup plus 2 tablespoons extra virgin olive oil
1 teaspoon balsamic vinegar
6 fresh basil leaves, torn in half
1 clove garlic, quartered
Kosher salt
1 pound spaghetti or linguine

Cut the tomatoes in half and then into ½-inch-wide wedges. Cut these wedges in half to create chunks. Place them in a large bowl and toss with ¾ cup of the olive oil, the vinegar, basil, and garlic. Set aside for 15 minutes. Then season with salt and let stand until the salt has drawn out the tomatoes' juices, about 10 minutes.

Bring a large pot of salted water to a rapid boil. Cook the pasta until *al dente,* following the package instructions. Drain and toss with the remaining 2 tablespoons olive oil. Distribute among four serving plates. Top with equal portions of the tomato mixture and serve immediately.

VARIATION: ¼ cup Basil Pesto (page 132) may be added to the tomato mixture just before topping the pasta.

PENNE ARRABBIATA

Angry Penne

MAKES 4 SERVINGS

GIANNI: One of my first jobs as a chef in New York City was in a restaurant known for its extensive menu of homemade pastas. Despite the variety we offered, this dish was the most popular—and the most profitable. The ingredients for this classic *arrabbiata,* or angry pasta, are inexpensive but the flavor is rich. I like to prepare this sauce with jalapeño pepper because I like the heat, but it is also good with red pepper flakes. I recommend serving this as a first course followed by a hearty meat dish or stewed fish.

¾ pound penne rigate
5 tablespoons extra virgin olive oil
3 large cloves garlic, minced
¼ teaspoon red pepper flakes or ½ jalapeño pepper, seeded and chopped
1½ cups Gianni's Basic Tomato Sauce (page 123) or use your favorite
2 tablespoons chopped fresh parsley leaves
Kosher salt and freshly ground black pepper
Finely grated Parmesan cheese for garnish (optional)

Bring a large pot of salted water to a rapid boil. Add the pasta and cook, following the package instructions, until *al dente.*

While the pasta is cooking, warm the oil in a medium-size saucepan set over medium-high heat. Add the garlic and red pepper flakes. When the oil is hot but before the garlic has browned, add the tomato sauce and 1 tablespoon of the parsley. Bring to a boil and cook to heat through and evaporate any water, about 2 minutes.

Drain the pasta well and add to the sauce. Add the remaining 1 tablespoon parsley and toss well. Season with salt and pepper. Serve with Parmesan cheese, if desired.

SALSA DISPERATA

Desperate Sauce

MAKES 6 SERVINGS

GIANNI: Some evenings—playing cards at my father's bar or after a soccer game—my friends and I would be having such a good time that we wouldn't want the night to end. So we would extend the evening by going to someone's house to eat. We often prepared this sauce because it was quick—it required only a slice of bread to complete the meal, and there weren't a lot of pots to clean up afterward. A little bit of this spicy sauce goes a long way, and believe me, if you use enough jalapeño, you'll understand why it's called "desperate."

I recommend serving this over a long pasta such as spaghetti, bucatini, fettuccine, or linguine. It is also nice spooned over sautéed veal, chicken breast, or pork chops.

¼ cup olive oil
1 tablespoon finely chopped shallots or onions
2 cloves garlic, chopped
1 tablespoon chopped fresh parsley leaves
1 tablespoon chopped fresh basil leaves
½ jalapeño pepper, seeded and chopped, or ¼ teaspoon red pepper flakes
1 teaspoon finely chopped anchovies (3 to 4 fillets)
2 cups canned whole plum tomatoes, crushed
1 teaspoon chopped fresh oregano leaves or ¼ teaspoon dried
1 teaspoon capers, drained and rinsed
Kosher salt and freshly ground black pepper
1½ pounds spaghetti

Warm the oil with the shallots or onions in a sauté pan set over medium-low heat. When the oil begins to gently bubble, cover the pan and cook to soften the shallots, about 1 minute. Stir in the garlic, parsley, basil, jalapeño or red pepper, and anchovies. When the mixture begins to bubble, add the tomatoes and oregano and cover. Reduce the heat to medium-low and cook to blend the flavors and sweeten the tomatoes, about 15 minutes. Stir in the capers, cover, and cook to flavor the sauce, another 5 minutes. Season with salt and pepper.

While the sauce is simmering, cook the pasta. Bring a large pot of salted water to a boil. Add the pasta and cook, following the package instructions, until *al dente*. Drain and transfer to a deep serving bowl. Add the sauce and toss well to coat the pasta. Serve immediately.

VARIATION: Any of the following ingredients may be added to the sauce along with the capers, or for a hearty sauce, try adding all three: 18 pitted olives, cut in half; 1 roasted bell pepper, roughly chopped; 7 ounces good-quality Italian tuna packed in olive oil (drained).

PIZZOCCHERI DELLA VALTELLINA

Buckwheat Noodles with Swiss Chard, Potatoes, Cabbage, Fontina, and Sage

MAKES 4 MAIN-COURSE SERVINGS; 6 FIRST-COURSE SERVINGS

GIANNI: I recently traveled with my wife, Laura, to Valtellina, an Italian town near the Swiss border. We had a wonderful meal there that included a pasta sauce similar to this one, only it was much heavier and too filling. The combination of ingredients was unusual and the flavor was quite remarkable, so when we returned home I was inspired to create this sauce. My version is lighter and somewhat soupy, but it has the same wonderful flavor, which is perfectly complemented by the buckwheat pasta. The fresh pasta described here will keep for three days in the refrigerator, or it may be dried and stored at room temperature for one week. Health-food stores often carry dried buckwheat or whole wheat fettuccine or pappardelle, which may be substituted for homemade buckwheat pasta.

I prefer to cook with Savoy cabbage, but this recipe may be prepared with tender green cabbage. Savoy cabbage will not take as long to soften, so the cooking time will be slightly shorter.

FOR THE BUCKWHEAT PASTA:

1 cup buckwheat flour
1 cup all-purpose flour
2 large eggs
3 to 6 tablespoons water, as needed

FOR THE SAUCE:

3 tablespoons olive oil
1 cup thinly sliced onions (about 1 medium-size onion)
½ cup ¼-inch-thick slices carrots (about 1 medium-size carrot)
Kosher salt and freshly ground black pepper
¼ cup chopped fresh parsley leaves
4 cups cored, quartered, and thinly sliced Savoy or green cabbage (about 1 pound)
4 cups water
¾ pound all-purpose or new potatoes, peeled, halved, and sliced ½ inch thick (2 cups slices)
2 packed cups roughly chopped Swiss chard leaves
2 tablespoons butter
12 fresh sage leaves
½ pound Fontina cheese, sliced ¼ inch thick and cut into 1-inch squares (2 cups squares)
2 tablespoons extra virgin olive oil

To make the pasta, place the buckwheat flour, all-purpose flour, and eggs in the bowl of a stand mixer fitted with the dough hook. Mix at medium speed, scraping the sides down to incorporate the flour into the eggs. Add 3 tablespoons of the water and continue mixing and incorporating the flour. Add more water as necessary to make a smooth but stiff dough. Compact the pasta dough into a large disk, wrap it in plastic wrap, and refrigerate for at least 30 minutes and up to 1 day.

(The dough may also be made by hand: Stir the flours together in a bowl, then pour onto a work surface. Make a well in the center and place the eggs and 3 tablespoons of the water in the well. Use a fork to slowly work the flour into the liquid ingredients. Knead for 2 to 3 minutes, adding more water if necessary, to make a smooth but stiff dough. Compact the pasta dough into a large disk, wrap in plastic wrap, and refrigerate for at least 30 minutes.)

Cut the chilled pasta dough into quarters. Pass one quarter of the dough through the widest setting of a pasta machine several times, folding it back on itself each time. (It may be necessary to lightly dust the dough with all-purpose flour from time to time so that it does not stick in the machine.) Continue to pass the dough through the machine, narrowing the opening one interval at a time, until you have reached about the fourth interval and have a long, thin sheet of pasta. Cut this long strip into 4-inch-long sections. With a pasta or pizza slicer, cut each section into 1-inch-wide ribbons. Repeat with the other three quarters of the dough. Spread the noodles out on a dish-towel-lined surface to dry until ready to cook (or when dry, wrap individual portions in plastic wrap and refrigerate).

To make the sauce, warm the olive oil in a large-size saucepan set over medium-high heat. Add the onions and carrots, and season with salt and pepper. Cook, stirring frequently, until the onions soften slightly but do not brown, about 8 minutes. Stir in the parsley and cook to flavor the vegetables, about 2 minutes. Add the Savoy cabbage and continue cooking until it has wilted, about 6 minutes. (If you are using green cabbage, add the water at this point and simmer gently to wilt the cabbage, about 10 minutes.) Add the potatoes (and the water if using Savoy cabbage). Bring to a boil. Cover, reduce the heat to medium-low, and simmer until the potatoes are just tender, about 10 minutes. Add the Swiss chard and continue cooking, with the lid off, to wilt the chard and slightly reduce the liquid in the pan, about 5 minutes.

Bring a large pot of salted water to a boil.

In a small sauté pan set over medium-low heat, slowly melt the butter with the sage leaves. Allow the butter to lightly brown and absorb the flavor of the sage, about 4 minutes. Add to the vegetable mixture.

Cook the fresh pasta in the salted boiling water until tender, about 1 minute. Drain well and add to the vegetable sauce, tossing or gently stirring to combine. Season with salt and pepper. Stir in the Fontina cheese, allowing it to melt slightly but to retain its shape. Serve immediately, drizzling each portion with some extra virgin olive oil.

VARIATION: Chopped spinach or collard greens may be used in place of the Swiss chard.

LINGUINE CON CAPPERI ED OLIVE

Linguine with Capers and Olives

MAKES 4 SERVINGS

JOAN: This sauce is similar to puttanesca sauce, which traditionally includes anchovies. Since Stan is not fond of anchovies, I created this recipe, which may be prepared earlier in the day and reheated slowly while the pasta is cooked. It is delicious served as a first course before grilled chicken.

¼ cup olive oil
2 tablespoons chopped onions
1 large clove garlic, quartered
10 kalamata olives, pitted and halved
2 teaspoons capers, drained and rinsed
4 cups canned whole plum tomatoes (about one 35-ounce can)
Kosher salt and freshly ground black pepper
3 fresh basil leaves
1 pound linguine
Freshly grated Parmesan cheese for garnish (optional)

In a large frying pan, warm the oil over medium-low heat. Add the onions and garlic and cook until the onions soften slightly but do not brown, about 5 minutes. Stir in the olives and capers and cook to warm through, about 1 minute. Add the tomatoes, crushing them with your hands or the back of a slotted spoon as you stir them into the pan. Season with salt and pepper, then stir in the basil leaves. Bring the sauce to a low boil, and then simmer slowly until the sauce has thickened and the tomatoes have sweetened, about 30 minutes.

Bring a large pot of salted water to a rapid boil. Add the linguine and cook until *al dente,* following the package instructions. Drain well and toss in a bowl with a ladleful of the sauce. Distribute evenly among four dinner plates. Top with the remaining sauce, and serve immediately. Garnish with grated Parmesan cheese if you like.

ZITI CON BROCCOLI

Ziti with Broccoli

MAKES 4 SERVINGS

JOAN: This recipe is a melding of Tucci and Tropiano cooking. Stan's family prepared this dish with ziti and no garlic. I like garlic, so I added it. Stan found it very strange that my family prepared it with spaghetti broken into 2½-inch lengths, so I bowed to his tradition and prepared it with ziti. He has overcome his initial reluctance, so now I sometimes revert to broken spaghetti.

My mother was able to time the cooking of the broccoli and pasta so precisely that she could boil them together in one pot. I have tried this several times with little success, so I devised this method for guaranteed results.

1 large head broccoli (about 1 pound)
1 pound ziti
¼ cup olive oil
1 clove garlic (optional), chopped
Freshly ground black pepper
Extra virgin olive oil to drizzle on each portion

Trim off 2 to 3 inches of the tough broccoli stems and discard. Cut the broccoli florets away from the remaining tender stems. Cut the florets into large bite-size pieces. Cut the tender stems into short sections and then into thin bite-size lengths. Set all of the prepared broccoli aside.

Bring a large pot of salted water to a boil. Add the stems and then the broccoli florets. Cook until tender but firm, about 4 minutes. Remove with a slotted spoon to a bowl and set aside.

Add the pasta to the same water and cook, following the package instructions, until *al dente.* Reserve 1 cup of the cooking water before draining the pasta.

Return the drained pasta to the pot and toss with the olive oil. Add the garlic, broccoli, and ½ cup reserved cooking water. Toss, adding more olive oil and water if the mixture is too dry. Serve immediately, garnished with freshly ground pepper and drizzled with extra virgin olive oil.

VARIATION: The garlic may be lightly sautéed in 1 tablespoon olive oil and tossed with the drained pasta and broccoli.

DITALINI E PISELLI

Ditalini Pasta with Peas

MAKES 4 SERVINGS

STAN: The first time I ever ate this dish was as a young boy, when I was visiting with my uncle Gasper and aunt Candidia. My mother had prepared it at home, but I had never tasted it. Because my mother tolerated my suspicions about this dish, I assumed my uncle and aunt would too, so I boldly announced, "I don't eat that." My uncle Gasper was not amused and made it clear that *ditalini e piselli* was the only dish being offered for dinner that evening. He persuaded me to taste it, and since then it's been one of my favorites.

JOAN: Two of my children, Gina and Stanley, enjoy this dish, but when my younger daughter, Christine, was little, she couldn't decide how she felt about it. One week she would eat all the peas and leave the pasta, another week she would eat all the pasta and leave the peas. Sorting the peas from the ditalini, which is a short tubular pasta, was a time-consuming task, but somehow Christine managed.

½ pound ditalini pasta
1½ cups Basic Tomato Sauce (page 123 or 124)
2 cups frozen or drained canned peas
Kosher salt and freshly ground black pepper
Freshly grated Parmesan cheese for garnish (optional)

Bring a large pot of salted water to a boil. Cook the pasta until *al dente,* following the package instructions. Reserve ½ cup of the cooking water before draining the pasta.

Meanwhile, in a large saucepan set over medium-high heat, bring the tomato sauce to a simmer. Add the peas and simmer until tender, about 5 minutes. Add the drained pasta to the sauce. Stir in enough of the reserved pasta water to create a slightly soupy sauce. Season with salt and pepper, and serve immediately. Garnish with Parmesan if desired.

DITALE CON FAGIOLI

Ditale with Beans

MAKES 4 TO 6 SERVINGS

STAN: One of the first dinners I had with Joan, at her parents' house, was pasta with beans. When I got home I told my parents that the Tropianos made this dish quite differently than we did, but that it was very tasty. My father asked how it was prepared. When I told him it was served in a light tomato liquid, he responded immediately, saying, "That's just how my mother prepared it in Italy."

JOAN: This is a quick *pasta fagioli* recipe, especially since the sauce may be prepared up to one day in advance. Add the beans and celery and warm the sauce while the pasta is cooking. I like to use ditale, but any tubular pasta may be substituted. This dish has a souplike consistency and should be served immediately so the pasta doesn't soak up all the sauce.

¼ cup olive oil
1 clove garlic, chopped
4 cups canned whole plum tomatoes (about one 35-ounce can)
Kosher salt
1 fresh basil leaf
1 pound ditale pasta
1 tender 5-inch-long celery stalk with leaves, cut into 1-inch pieces
One 19-ounce can cannellini beans, drained and rinsed
Freshly ground black pepper
Freshly grated Parmesan cheese for garnish (optional)

Warm the olive oil in a large-size saucepan set over medium-high heat. Add the garlic and cook until lightly colored but not browned, about 2 minutes. Stir in the tomatoes, crushing them with your hands or the back of a slotted spoon as you add them to the pan. Season with salt, stir in the basil leaf, and bring to a boil. Reduce the heat to a simmer, cover, and cook until the tomatoes sweeten, about 30 minutes.

Bring a large pot of salted water to a boil. Cook the pasta until *al dente,* following the package instructions. Reserve 1 cup of the cooking water before draining the cooked pasta.

Meanwhile, stir the celery and beans into the sauce. Return to a simmer, cover, and cook until the beans are heated through and have blended with the tomato sauce, about 10 minutes.

Add the drained pasta to the bean sauce, and stir in enough of the reserved cooking water as necessary to make a soupy consistency. Simmer until the ingredients are combined, about 2 minutes. Serve immediately, garnished with pepper and, if you like, Parmesan cheese.

continued

VARIATION: I often use dried beans to make this dish and I like to prepare the beans using the following quick-soak method. Place the dried beans in a saucepan and fill the pan with cold water to a level 2 inches above the beans. (If you like, a few tender celery leaves may be added to the beans.) Cover the pot and bring the water to a boil. Allow the beans to boil for 2 minutes. Remove from the heat and let the beans stand, covered, for one hour. Reserve 1 cup of the cooking liquid before draining the beans and proceeding with the recipe.

Circa 1957, the christening of the Vincenzo Tropiano *barge on the occasion of Pop's retirement from the New York Trap Rock Corporation.* On the left: *Sister Angie with sister-in-law Natalie observing Mom and Pop at the christening.*

SPAGHETTI E LENTICCHIE

Spaghetti with Lentils

MAKES 4 SERVINGS

JOAN: Being basically a vegetarian, my mother prepared this dish all the time. She used tomatoes she had grown and bottled, along with items that she kept on hand in the pantry. The lentils may be prepared one day in advance and then combined with the sauce.

1 cup dried brown lentils, rinsed and picked over
½ pound spaghetti, broken into 1- to 1½-inch pieces
1½ cups Basic Tomato Sauce or Salsa Marinara (page 123, 124, or 125) or your own favorite tomato sauce
Freshly ground black pepper

Place the lentils in a medium-size saucepan. Fill the pan with cold water to a level 1 inch above the lentils. Slowly bring to a simmer, and cook until the lentils are just tender, about 20 minutes. Remove from the heat and set aside.

Bring a large pot of salted water to a boil. Cook the spaghetti until *al dente,* following the package instructions. Reserve ½ cup of the cooking water before draining the pasta.

Meanwhile, drain the lentils and combine them with the tomato sauce in a saucepan large enough to hold the pasta. Bring to a simmer, cover, and cook until the lentils have blended with the sauce, about 10 minutes. Add the drained pasta, along with the reserved pasta water to make a liquid consistency. Season with pepper. Simmer the pasta and sauce together to allow the flavors to combine, about 3 minutes. Serve immediately.

NOTE: Lentils should not have much water left after cooking; draining may not be necessary.

FARFALLE AL FORNO

Pasta Casserole

MAKES 6 SERVINGS

JOAN: This is one of my grandchildren's favorite dishes. I created this recipe because I wanted a dish that would serve a group and still allow me time to visit with company. It may be prepared one day in advance—just cover and refrigerate overnight. Allow the casserole to return to room temperature before baking.

4 tablespoons (½ stick) butter
¼ cup all-purpose flour
2 cups whole or skim milk
Kosher salt and freshly ground black pepper
⅛ teaspoon ground nutmeg
1 pound Swiss chard, tough stems removed and discarded and leaves coarsely chopped
1 pound farfalle pasta
2 cups Salsa Maria Rosa *(page 131)*
½ cup grated Fontina cheese
½ cup grated Jarlsberg cheese
½ cup grated mozzarella cheese
¼ cup finely grated Parmesan cheese

Preheat the oven to 350 degrees F.

Melt the butter in a medium-size saucepan set over medium-low heat. Whisk in the flour, then slowly whisk in the milk. Cook the sauce, whisking frequently, until it thickens, about 10 minutes. Season with salt and pepper, and stir in the nutmeg. Cover with plastic wrap and set this *besciamella* sauce aside.

Bring a large pot of salted water to a boil. Add the Swiss chard and cook until tender but firm, 8 to 10 minutes. Remove with a slotted spoon to a fine-mesh sieve. Drain, pressing out any excess water. Set the Swiss chard aside.

Return the water to a boil. Add the pasta and cook until *al dente,* following the package instructions. Drain well and place the pasta in a large bowl. Toss the pasta together with the Swiss chard, 1 cup of the *salsa Maria Rosa,* the *besciamella* sauce, and the grated Fontina, Jarlsberg, and mozzarella cheeses.

Spread the remaining 1 cup salsa over the bottom of a large casserole or baking dish. Spread the pasta mixture on top of the salsa, and sprinkle with the Parmesan. Bake until the sauce is bubbly and the casserole is warmed through, about 30 minutes.

VARIATION: Penne, mezzani, or penne rigate pasta may be substituted for the farfalle.

Venetian Seafood Salad (page 55) and Bread Sticks (page 89)

Delicious Vegetable Tart (page 38) and Stuffed Pizza (page 104)

Poached Eggs on Country Bread with Pecorino Toscano (page 64) and Eggs with Tomato (page 66)

Timpáno alla Big Night (page 172) and a slice of Vegetarian Timpáno (page 175)

Green Lasagna (page 168)

Lasagna with Chicken and Mushrooms (page 166)

Fettuccine with Asparagus and Shrimp (page 154)

Veal Stew (page 209)

Chicken with Sausage and Peppers (page 231)

Stuffed Roasted Rabbit (page 220) and Risotto with Vegetables and Fine Herbs (page 187)

Broiled Bluefish (page 244)

Celery Salad (page 285), Carrot Salad (page 288), and Beet Salad (page 287)

Concetta's Stuffed Artichokes (page 264)

Clockwise from the top: Walnut Bread (page 96), Maria Pia's Easter Bread (page 98), Rosemary Focaccia (page 91), and focaccia topped with ripe plum tomatoes (page 91)

Plum and Polenta Cake (page 307)

Peaches and Wine (page 319) and Fried Cookies (page 298)

FARFALLE AI CARCIOFI, PATATE, E PROSCIUTTO

Farfalle with Artichokes, Potatoes, and Prosciutto

MAKES 4 MAIN-COURSE SERVINGS; 6 FIRST-COURSE SERVINGS

GIANNI: My mother doesn't garden, but she has many older women friends who do. These women continue to plant vegetable gardens large enough to feed a growing family even though their children have moved away or tend their own gardens. My mother's friends know that she is a good, inventive cook and so they bring her their extra vegetables. This is one of the dishes she prepares in the late fall, at the beginning of the artichoke season, from these friendly donations.

Potatoes are a traditional ingredient in northern Italian cooking, just as the tomato is crucial to the unique flavors of southern Italian cooking. In this recipe the potatoes create a creamy sauce that does not compete with the subtle flavor of the artichokes.

4 large artichokes (or one 9-ounce package thawed frozen artichoke hearts, or one 15-ounce can artichoke bottoms, drained and quartered)
1 tablespoon freshly squeezed lemon juice (for fresh artichokes)
¼ cup extra virgin olive oil
1 cup thinly sliced onions (about 1 medium-size onion)
1 cup julienned prosciutto, pancetta, or bacon (about 3 ounces)
2 tablespoons chopped fresh parsley leaves
2 medium-size all-purpose potatoes, peeled, halved, and sliced ¼ inch thick (about 2 cups)
Kosher salt and freshly ground black pepper
2 cups chicken broth or water
1 pound farfalle
¼ cup freshly grated Parmesan cheese
1 tablespoon extra virgin olive oil

If using fresh artichokes, peel off and discard the hard outer leaves. Cut off the top of each artichoke at the point where the leaves become almost white. Discard the top. Cut the remaining artichoke into ⅛-inch-thick wedges. Remove any fine hairs (choke) from each wedge. Place the trimmed artichoke pieces in a bowl of cold water along with the lemon juice. Set aside.

Warm the olive oil in a large skillet or large-size saucepan set over medium heat. Add the onions, cover, and cook until limp, 5 to 8 minutes. Stir in the prosciutto and cook to soften, about 1 minute. Stir in the parsley and potatoes. Drain the fresh artichokes, pat dry, and stir them into the pan. Season with salt and pepper. Cover and cook to allow the flavors to combine, about 2 minutes. Add the broth or water and simmer slowly, with the lid on, until the potatoes and artichokes are tender, 5 to 10 minutes. Remove the lid and continue cooking until the liquid has been reduced by three fourths, about 10 minutes. (If you are using frozen or canned artichokes, add them at this point, allowing them to warm through while the sauce reduces.)

Meanwhile, bring a large pot of salted water to a boil. Add the pasta and cook, following the package instructions, until *al dente.* Drain, and stir the pasta into the vegetable mixture. Gently stir the pasta and sauce over low heat to coat and thicken slightly. Add the Parmesan and adjust the seasoning with salt and pepper. Distribute among plates or pasta bowls, drizzle with the extra virgin olive oil, and serve.

VARIATIONS:

- Other pastas that hold sauce well, such as rigatoni, fresh fettuccine, or fusilli, may be substituted for farfalle.
- 1 tablespoon chopped fresh mint, thyme, or marjoram leaves may be sprinkled on top of the pasta along with the Parmesan cheese.
- The prosciutto may be eliminated to make a flavorful vegetarian pasta.
- Broccoli or cauliflower may be added to the sauce: Add 1 head trimmed cauliflower florets to the salted boiling water along with the pasta and cook until the pasta is *al dente.* Trimmed broccoli florets will require less cooking time than cauliflower and may be added to the pasta during the last 5 minutes of cooking.

FUSILLI CON RICOTTA, PROSCIUTTO, E SPINACI

Fusilli with Ricotta, Prosciutto, and Spinach

MAKES 6 SERVINGS

GIANNI: My mother sold an assortment of meats in the *bottega di alimentari,* or little grocery store, that she ran. Customers only wanted to purchase the best cuts of pancetta, salami, mortadella, or prosciutto and were not interested in the small end pieces. However, I learned from my mother that these are good cuts for cooking. She would bring them home to use in soups, stuffings, and sauces such as this one.

This creamy sauce is also a delicious filling for cannelloni (page 161) and for *Bucaneve di Recoaro* (Pasta Roll, page 159). It may be prepared up to two days in advance. Refrigerate it and let it return to room temperature before tossing with pasta or filling cannelloni. This sauce reheats well even after it has been tossed with the pasta: Place the leftover pasta in a saucepan set over medium heat, add ½ cup hot water, and cook to warm through, stirring frequently.

2 tablespoons olive oil
2 cups finely chopped onions
1 pound spinach, washed well and tough stems removed
1 cup ricotta cheese
1 cup finely chopped prosciutto (about 6 ounces)
1 cup finely grated Parmesan cheese
Freshly ground black pepper
½ cup plain dried bread crumbs
2 teaspoons extra virgin olive oil
1 pound fusilli

Warm the olive oil in a saucepan set over medium-high heat. Add the onions and cook, stirring occasionally, until softened but not browned, about 5 minutes. Add the spinach and cook until wilted, about 5 minutes. Remove from the heat and cool completely.

Squeeze out any liquid retained by the spinach by pressing it between your hands or by placing it in a fine-mesh sieve and pressing on the spinach with the back of a spoon. Place the spinach in a food processor. Add the ricotta and prosciutto and process until smooth. Stir in the Parmesan and season with pepper. Set aside.

Preheat the oven to 350 degrees F. In a bowl, toss together the bread crumbs and extra virgin olive oil. Spread on a baking sheet. Toast the bread crumbs in the oven, stirring once or twice, until lightly browned, about 8 minutes. Set aside.

Bring a large pot of salted water to a boil. Cook the fusilli until *al dente,* following the package instructions. Reserve ½ cup of the cooking water before draining well. Return the drained pasta to the pot. Stir in the sauce and the reserved cooking water. Heat together over low heat, stirring constantly, until the sauce is creamy and evenly coats the pasta, about 3 minutes. Serve immediately, topped with the toasted bread crumbs.

VARIATIONS:

- 1 pound chopped broccoli florets, broccoli di rape, or asparagus may be used in place of the spinach.
- 1 pound cauliflower florets that have been boiled until tender, about 10 minutes, may be used in place of the spinach. Puree 4 anchovy fillets in the processor along with the cauliflower and the other ingredients in the original recipe.

LINGUINE CON TOPOLINI

Linguine with Veal Rolls

MAKES 6 SERVINGS

JOAN: Stan's mother originated the recipe for these savory veal rolls. After your guests have eaten this delightful meal, you can inform them that *topolini* is the Italian word for "mice"! The rolls are most delicious when prepared several hours in advance and then slowly warmed through while the pasta is cooking. The veal and sauce may be cooled and refrigerated overnight or frozen for up to one month.

Spoon the sauce onto the pasta and serve it as a first course, and then serve the veal rolls as a second course with a vegetable side dish. Or if you prefer, the pasta and veal rolls may be served together as one course.

1½ pounds veal scaloppine
3 cloves garlic, finely chopped
6 tablespoons finely chopped provolone cheese
6 tablespoons grated pecorino Romano cheese
6 tablespoons chopped fresh parsley leaves
Kosher salt and freshly ground black pepper
½ cup olive oil
½ cup roughly chopped tender celery leaves
1 cup dry white wine
2 cups chicken broth
1½ pounds linguine
Freshly grated pecorino Romano cheese for garnish

Cut the scaloppine into squares measuring about 3 inches across. Pound each piece, flattening it to form a slightly larger square, about 4 inches.

Sprinkle each veal square with equal portions of the garlic. Then sprinkle with about I teaspoon each of provolone, Romano, and parsley. Season with salt and pepper. Roll each square snugly by folding up a ¼-inch-wide flap of veal on opposite sides of the square, then rolling the veal into a small sausage shape. Tie snugly with butcher's string.

Warm the olive oil in a large frying pan set over medium-high heat. When the oil is hot but not smoking, add half the veal rolls and cook until well browned on all sides, about 8 minutes. Remove the veal to a plate and set aside. Cook the remaining veal rolls in the same manner, remove to the plate, and set aside.

Add the celery leaves to the pan and cook, stirring constantly, to soften slightly, about 2 minutes. Add the wine and stir, loosening any pieces of meat that may have stuck to the bottom of the pan. Add the chicken broth, and return the veal rolls to the pan along with any juice that has accumulated on the plate. Bring to a boil and then simmer gently until the meat is cooked through, about 20 minutes. Turn the veal rolls two or three times while they cook to keep them evenly moist.

Bring a large pot of salted water to a boil. Add the linguine and cook until *al dente,* following the package instructions. Drain the pasta and return it to the pot. Spoon a small amount of the veal sauce onto the pasta and toss.

Distribute the pasta equally among six plates. Top with more sauce and serve, garnishing with freshly grated pecorino Romano cheese.

Serve the veal as a second course, removing the strings and spooning any remaining sauce over the meat.

VARIATION: This dish may also be prepared using boneless chicken breasts. Slice each breast in thirds horizontally, creating three thin slices. Cut and pound the chicken as necessary to achieve the recommended dimensions given for the veal scaloppine. Proceed with the recipe as written.

SPAGHETTI CON POMODORO E TONNO

Spaghetti with Tomato and Tuna

MAKES 4 SERVINGS

JOAN: The basic tomato sauce for this recipe—excluding the tuna—may be made in advance and kept in the refrigerator for one week or frozen for future use. The tuna should sit in the sauce for ten to fifteen minutes before being ladled over the pasta so that the flavor develops. If it sits longer than that, however, the tuna absorbs too much of the tomato and the sauce gets too thick.

¼ cup plus 2 tablespoons olive oil
1 tablespoon roughly chopped onions
4 cups canned whole plum tomatoes (about one 35-ounce can)
Kosher salt and freshly ground black pepper
2 fresh basil leaves
One 6-ounce can Italian tuna packed in olive oil
1 pound spaghetti or linguine

Warm ¼ cup of the olive oil in a small saucepan set over medium-high heat. Add the onions and cook, stirring, until softened, about 3 minutes. Add the tomatoes, crushing them well with the back of a slotted spoon or by squeezing them through your fingers while adding them to the pan. Season with salt and pepper, and stir in the basil. Cover and bring to a boil. Reduce the heat to medium-low and simmer until the sauce thickens, about 20 minutes. Remove the cover and simmer to sweeten the tomatoes, an additional 5 minutes. Drain half of the olive oil from the canned tuna. Flake the tuna into the tomato sauce. Cover and simmer to heat through, 8 to 10 minutes. Remove from the heat and set aside while the pasta cooks.

Bring a large pot of salted water to a boil. Add the pasta and cook until *al dente,* following the package instructions. Drain, then toss the pasta with the remaining 2 tablespoons olive oil. Add about 3 ladlesful of sauce and continue tossing. Distribute evenly among four dinner plates. Ladle the remaining sauce on top, and serve immediately.

VARIATION: Fresh tuna may be used: Warm 1 tablespoon olive oil in a nonstick sauté pan set over medium-high heat. Add a 6-ounce tuna steak and cook until medium to medium rare, about 2 minutes per side. Flake the cooked tuna into the sauce during the last 15 minutes of cooking time. Proceed with the basic recipe.

FETTUCCINE CON ASPARAGI E GAMBERETTI

Fettuccine with Asparagus and Shrimp

MAKES 4 SERVINGS

GIANNI: This elegant but simple spring pasta is the type of dish I prepare for myself at home. The sauce cooks in the time it takes to boil the pasta. The shrimp may be replaced by bay scallops, crabmeat, lobster, or squid. Or substitute thinly sliced white mushrooms for the seafood to create a purely vegetarian meal.

A simple way to peel the fresh tomatoes called for in this recipe is to plunge them into the boiling water the pasta will be cooked in. It will not affect the flavor of the pasta and eliminates boiling up as a second pot of water.

1 pound fettuccine
12 medium-size asparagus (about 1 pound)
5 tablespoons extra virgin olive oil, plus extra to drizzle on top of the pasta
2 tablespoons finely diced shallots
2 small cloves garlic, thinly sliced
⅛ teaspoon red pepper flakes
1 tablespoon chopped fresh parsley leaves
1 tablespoon chopped fresh basil leaves
¾ pound medium-size shrimp, shelled, deveined, and sliced in half lengthwise
Kosher salt and freshly ground black pepper
½ cup dry white wine
1 cup peeled and roughly chopped ripe tomatoes (1 large or 2 plum tomatoes)

Bring a large pot of salted water to a boil and add the fettuccine. Cook until *al dente,* following the package instructions.

Meanwhile, cut 1 inch off the bottoms of the asparagus. Use a vegetable peeler to trim away the tough outer layer of the asparagus, beginning about 1 inch below the tender tip. Cut the asparagus on an acute angle to create 2-inch-long slices. Set aside.

Warm 3 tablespoons of the olive oil in a large sauté pan set over medium-high heat. Add the shallots, garlic, red pepper flakes, parsley, and basil and cook, stirring frequently, to flavor the oil with the aromatics, about 1 minute. Stir in the asparagus and shrimp, and season with salt and pepper. Cook, stirring and tossing frequently, until the shrimp are pink, 2 to 3 minutes. Add the wine and cook until it evaporates, about 1 minute. Add the tomatoes and return the sauce to a gentle boil. Drain the pasta and add it to the sauce. Stir in the remaining 2 tablespoons olive oil. Gently toss to coat the pasta with the sauce. Serve immediately, placing the shrimp decoratively on top of the pasta and drizzling with additional extra virgin olive oil.

VARIATIONS:

- Canned whole plum tomatoes may be substituted for fresh ripe tomatoes.
- ½ pound shelled fresh or frozen peas, or young summer zucchini that has been finely julienned or diced into ¼-inch pieces, may be substituted for the asparagus.
- 2 thin, round slices seeded fresh jalapeño pepper may be substituted for the red pepper flakes. Remove the pepper slices from the pan just before tossing the pasta with the sauce.

My mother and me at the shore near Venice, which is about an hour from our home in Mason Vicentino.

FETTUCCINE CON GAMBERETTI E POMODORO

Fettuccine with Shrimp and Tomato

MAKES 4 SERVINGS

JOAN: A simple, quick, but outstandingly delicious meal. If you don't have marinara sauce in the freezer, it will take about thirty minutes to prepare before proceeding with the rest of the recipe. If you have the marinara sauce already made, just warm it on the stove before adding the shrimp.

My daughter Gina has a simple and very tasty variation on this dish that does not call for marinara sauce. She follows the basic recipe, adding ½ cup chopped fresh parsley and ¼ cup chopped fresh basil to the shrimp. Toss the pasta with the sauce, along with an additional ¼ cup olive oil. Cover and set aside for 5 minutes to allow the pasta to absorb the flavor of the sauce.

1 pound fettuccine
¼ cup plus 1 tablespoon olive oil
2 cloves garlic, cut in half
1 pound large shrimp, shelled and deveined
½ cup dry white wine
4 cups warm Salsa Marinara *(page 125), or your favorite tomato sauce*
2 fresh basil leaves
Kosher salt and freshly ground black pepper

Bring a large pot of salted water to a boil. Cook the pasta until *al dente,* following the package instructions.

Meanwhile, warm ¼ cup of the olive oil in a large sauté pan set over medium-high heat. Add the garlic and cook to flavor the oil but do not brown, about 2 minutes. Add the shrimp and cook, stirring constantly, until they turn pink, about 1 minute. Add the wine and simmer, allowing the shrimp to absorb the wine, about 1 minute. Stir in the marinara and basil, and season with salt and pepper. Reduce the heat to medium-low and gently simmer the sauce until the shrimp are cooked through but not chewy, about 5 minutes.

Drain the pasta and place in a serving bowl. Toss with the remaining 1 tablespoon olive oil. Distribute the pasta equally among four dinner plates. Top with equal portions of the sauce, and serve immediately.

LINGUINE ALL'ARAGOSTA ARRABBIATA

Linguine with "Angry Lobster"

MAKES 4 SERVINGS

GIANNI: I've always heard that if you make a lobster angry it will lose weight and you will end up with no meat. Therefore I always treat my lobsters gently before cooking them. What makes these lobsters angry comes after they're cooked: the spicy red pepper flakes, garlic, and herbs.

I serve this pasta in the main part of the lobsters' shells. After cooking the lobsters and removing the meat, I cut them each in half lengthwise with a heavy, sharp knife. I place each lobster half, with the cavity facing up, on a serving plate and then fill the cavity with the cooked pasta.

The lobster may be cooked and the meat removed from the shells one day in advance. Cover and refrigerate the meat and shells overnight, bringing them to room temperature before finishing the dish.

2 fresh lobsters (about 1½ pounds each)
1 pound linguine
⅔ cup extra virgin olive oil
⅓ cup minced shallots
¼ cup minced garlic
½ cup chopped fresh parsley leaves
⅓ cup chopped fresh basil leaves
1 teaspoon red pepper flakes
Kosher salt and freshly ground black pepper
½ cup dry white wine
1 cup chopped canned tomatoes (with some of the juice)

Bring a large pot of water to a boil. Add the lobsters, cover, and cook until the shells are bright red, about 15 minutes. Drain and set aside to cool.

Separate the claws from the body and extract the claw meat. Set aside. Cut the lobsters in half lengthwise. Remove the tail meat and roe. Chop the tail and claw meat into bite-size pieces and set aside. Finely chop the roe and set aside. Discard the green tomalley, and rinse the shells thoroughly under cold running water. Reserve the shells until ready to serve.

Bring a large pot of salted water to a boil. Add the linguine and cook until *al dente,* following the package instructions. Reserve ½ cup of the pasta cooking water before draining.

Warm ⅓ cup of the olive oil in a large saucepan set over medium-high heat. Add the shallots and cook to flavor the oil, stirring frequently, about 30 seconds. Stir in the garlic, ¼ cup of the parsley, half the basil, and the red pepper flakes. Cook to soften the garlic slightly, about 2 minutes. Add three quarters of the lobster meat and all of the roe. Cook, stirring frequently, to flavor the lobster with the aromatics, about 2 minutes. Season with salt and pepper. Add the wine and bring to a boil. Add the tomatoes and bring to a simmer, stirring frequently. Stir in the remaining lobster meat. Add the drained pasta, the remaining ¼ cup parsley, the remaining basil, and the remaining ⅓ cup olive oil. Toss to coat the pasta with the sauce. If the pasta seems dry, add the reserved pasta water. Spoon onto plates and serve immediately.

LINGUINE CON VONGOLE

Linguine with Clam Sauce

MAKES 4 SERVINGS

STAN: This was one of my father's favorite sauces to make. He preferred to open the clams himself, collecting the juice and chopping the clam meat. In the summer when we had large outdoor parties, we often served a bushel of raw clams on ice. Any remaining clams were prepared following my father's methods and frozen. They defrost quickly, providing a meal in the time it takes to cook the pasta.

JOAN: If your fish market will open the clams and reserve the juice, it will save a lot of preparation time. If not, wash the clamshells thoroughly. Open the clams over a large bowl to catch the juices. Cut the clams into ½-inch pieces, removing and discarding the dark sac, and set aside. Strain the juice through a fine-mesh sieve to remove sand and shells. Add the clams to the strained juice. Begin to prepare the sauce when the pasta is halfway cooked.

1 pound linguine
½ cup plus 1 tablespoon olive oil
6 cloves garlic, finely chopped
¼ cup dry white wine
18 littleneck or chowder clams
Kosher salt and freshly ground black pepper
1 tablespoon chopped fresh parsley leaves

Bring a large pot of salted water to a boil and cook the pasta, following the package instructions, until *al dente.*

Meanwhile, warm ½ cup of the olive oil in a high-sided saucepan set over medium-high heat. Add the garlic and cook until softened, about 2 minutes. Add the wine and allow it to cook away slightly, about 1 minute. Add the clams and their juice, and season with salt and pepper. Cook until the broth froths to a level of 1 to 2 inches. Remove from the heat. Stir in the parsley.

Drain the pasta and toss in a serving bowl with the remaining 1 tablespoon olive oil. Distribute evenly among six dinner plates. Top with equal portions of the sauce, and serve immediately.

VARIATION: This same dish may be prepared without removing the clams from their shells, making for a less formal, hands-on meal. Warm the olive oil in a pot large enough to hold the clams in a single layer. Add the garlic and cook until softened but not browned, about 2 minutes. Add the wine and allow to simmer and sweeten, about 2 minutes. Add the clams and parsley, and cover the pot. Cook until the clams open, about 5 minutes. Season with salt and pepper. Remove from the heat and spoon over cooked pasta. Be sure to discard any unopened clams.

BUCANEVE DI RECOARO

Pasta Roll

MAKES 6 TO 8 SERVINGS

GIANNI: I was taught this recipe by Guiotto Sergio, a fellow chef who was at the Recoaro Terme Culinary Institute with me. In the early spring we could see women gathering fresh dandelion greens out in the open fields and hillsides near the school. These bitter greens are one of the first fresh vegetables to appear at the farmer's markets and are used in salads, cooked as side dishes, or used for pasta sauces. This is my favorite method for preparing these greens. Because dandelion greens are not as widely available in America, I have used spinach in this recipe. Broccoli rabe would also make a good substitute.

The recipe begins with homemade pasta, and the finished roll may be prepared several days in advance of serving. Allow the cooked roll to cool before wrapping it in plastic wrap and storing it in the refrigerator. Remove the plastic wrap and rewrap the roll in a clean dish towel before reheating it in boiling water for about 10 minutes. I recommend serving two slices as an appetizer or three as a pasta course.

1 pound fresh spinach, dandelion greens, or broccoli rabe
1 recipe Homemade Pasta (page 119)
¼ cup ricotta cheese
1½ cups grated Asiago cheese
1 cup diced pancetta, prosciutto, or Canadian bacon
1 large egg
¼ teaspoon ground nutmeg
Kosher salt and freshly ground black pepper
12 large fresh sage leaves
4 tablespoons (½ stick) butter
Grated Asiago or Parmesan cheese for garnish

Rinse the spinach, dandelion greens, or broccoli rabe well to remove any dirt or sand. Trim off and discard the stems. Place a small amount of water in the bottom of a large saucepan. Add the greens and cook over medium heat until wilted, about 4 minutes. Strain the greens in a fine-mesh sieve, pressing and squeezing to remove all the liquid. Thinly slice the greens and set aside (there should be 1 well-packed cup of greens).

Use a pasta machine to roll out two thin sheets of pasta measuring about 4 inches wide by 15 inches long. Lay a clean dish towel or tightly woven piece of cheesecloth horizontally on your work surface. Place one sheet of pasta on top of the cloth, approximately 1 inch from the bottom edge. Place the second sheet of pasta above the first, overlapping the long edges of the two pieces by about ¼ inch. Use a small amount of water to moisten this seam, pressing gently with your fingers to seal it securely. Set aside.

continued

In a medium-size bowl, mix together the ricotta, Asiago, greens, and pancetta. Stir in the egg. Add the nutmeg, season with salt and pepper, and mix well. Spread this mixture over the entire surface of the pasta, to within ¼ inch of each edge. Begin rolling up the pasta from the bottom of the long edge, lifting the cloth gently to help form a long, snug 1½- to 2-inch-diameter roll. Position the roll seam side down, and wrap the cloth around it. Secure the ends of the cloth close to the ends of the roll with butcher's string or plastic bag ties. Set aside.

Bring a fish poacher or other long pot filled with salted water to a rapid boil. Reduce the heat to a simmer and submerge the pasta roll in the water. Cover and gently simmer until the roll is heated through, about 35 minutes.

Meanwhile, place the sage leaves and butter in a small saucepan set over low heat. Melt the butter slowly, allowing it to absorb the flavor of the sage.

When the roll is cooked through, remove it from the water and carefully unwrap. Cut the roll on a slight angle into ½-inch-thick slices. Place two or three on a plate, and spoon a small amount of the sage butter on top. Garnish with additional grated Asiago or Parmesan cheese, and serve.

VARIATION: This roll may be served with a fresh tomato sauce in place of the sage butter.

CANNELLONI IN DUE MANIERE

Cannelloni with Two Stuffings

MAKES 8 TO 10 SERVINGS

GIANNI: Tasty homemade cannelloni are versatile, and because they may be prepared one day in advance, great to make when you are entertaining. Cannelloni are a terrific dish for a buffet. This recipe will prepare twenty cheese-filled and twenty meat-filled cannelloni. Serve one of each kind as an appetizer, or two of each kind as a pasta course. If you are planning to freeze the cannelloni, prepare a slightly thinner *besciamella* sauce, as it will thicken while it cools.

Another variation is to serve cannelloni as a passed appetizer with cocktails. After rolling the cannelloni as described below, cut each long roll into 1-inch sections. Place them filling side down on a baking sheet. Sprinkle with Parmesan cheese and bake in a preheated oven at 350 degree F, until heated through and lightly browned, about ten minutes.

1 recipe Homemade Pasta (page 119)
Double recipe Besciamella *(page 121)*
1 cup finely grated Parmesan cheese
1 recipe Spinach Ricotta Filling (recipe follows)
½ cup Basic Tomato Sauce (page 123 or 124)
1 recipe Meat Filling (recipe follows)

Bring a large pot of salted water to a boil. Preheat the oven to 400 degrees F.

Roll out the homemade pasta as instructed. Cut each long strip of pasta into pieces that are 4 inches by the width created by your pasta machine. There will be about 40 pieces. Cook the pasta in batches just until tender, about 3 minutes. Cool the cooked pasta under cold running water. Drain and lay out on a dish towel to dry.

Butter two large baking dishes. Evenly spread a thin layer of *besciamella* sauce on the bottom of each dish and set aside.

Place a piece of cooked pasta on a dry cloth with the short end toward you. Dust the top end of the pasta with a small amount of Parmesan. Place 2 tablespoons of the ricotta filling ½ inch above the short end of the pasta and spread it to within ¼ inch of either edge. Roll the pasta up toward the Parmesan-dusted edge to form a neat roll. Place each completed roll, seam side down, in one of the prepared baking dishes. When all of the cheese-filled cannelloni are rolled and in the baking dish, top with half of the remaining *besciamella* sauce. Dot ½ teaspoon of the tomato sauce in the center of each cannelloni. (The cannelloni may be covered and frozen at this point. When reheating frozen cannelloni, bake at 350 degrees F for 15 minutes, then broil to brown as described below.)

continued

Fill the remaining pasta with the meat filling, following the same procedure. Arrange in the other prepared baking dish and cover with the remaining *besciamella* sauce.

Sprinkle the remaining Parmesan on top of both dishes of cannelloni before baking. Cook until the sauce begins to bubble, about 10 minutes. Turn on the oven broiler and cook until lightly browned, about 3 minutes. Serve immediately.

VARIATION: The shape of homemade pasta that has been cut and boiled in the method used for cannelloni is called *fazzoletti,* which means "handkerchief." *Fazzoletti* may also be used to prepare individual portions of an informal lasagna: Place a sheet of cooked pasta on a serving plate. Top with sauce, such as *Calamari Affogati in Brodetto* (page 53) or ragù (page 126 or 128), and lay another piece of pasta on top. Top with more sauce, and serve immediately.

Fazzoletti lasagna may be frozen: Place individual portions of this informal lasagna a few inches apart on a baking sheet and place in the freezer to set, about 30 minutes. Transfer to an airtight container and store for up to 1 month. Place the frozen *fazzoletti* in a preheated oven at 300 degrees F and bake to soften, about 10 minutes. Increase the temperature to 350 degrees F and cook until browned, 8 to 10 minutes. Serve immediately.

• • •

SPINACH RICOTTA FILLING

2 tablespoons olive oil
½ cup finely chopped onions
1 pound fresh spinach, washed well and tough stems removed
2 cups ricotta cheese
¾ cup finely grated Parmesan cheese
¼ cup finely ground plain dried bread crumbs
Kosher salt and freshly ground black pepper

Warm the olive oil in a skillet set over high heat. Add the onions and cook, stirring constantly, to wilt them, about 2 minutes. Add the spinach and cook, stirring frequently, to wilt the spinach, about 4 minutes. Remove from the heat and cool completely.

Squeeze out any liquid retained by the spinach by pressing it between your hands or by placing it in a fine-mesh sieve and pressing on it with the back of a spoon. Place the spinach in a food processor and chop. Add the ricotta and process to combine. Stir in the Parmesan and bread crumbs, season with salt and pepper, and set aside.

VARIATIONS: Use 1 cup ricotta and 1 cup grated smoked mozzarella, grated Fontina, or grated Asiago cheese in place of the 2 cups ricotta.

MEAT FILLING

GIANNI: I was taught this recipe by my mother. If she had any leftover filling, she would make tiny *polpette,* or fried meat cakes. She would stir about ¼ cup bread crumbs into the meat to form a dough and then scoop out rounded tablespoons and shape them into small patties. The patties were then dipped in a lightly beaten egg and rolled in more bread crumbs. My mother fried them in olive oil and we would eat them for a snack. Delicious.

2 tablespoons olive oil
1½ cups roughly chopped celery
1½ cups roughly chopped carrots
1½ cups roughly chopped onions
½ cup roughly chopped fresh parsley leaves
3 cloves garlic, crushed
¼ cup roughly chopped fresh sage leaves
¼ cup roughly chopped fresh rosemary leaves
1 pound stewing beef, veal, lamb, pork, or venison, trimmed of fat and cut into cubes
Kosher salt and freshly ground black pepper
½ cup dry red wine
1 cup water
½ cup dried porcini mushrooms
1 large egg, lightly beaten
½ cup freshly grated Parmesan cheese

Warm the olive oil in a medium-size saucepan set over medium-high heat. Stir in the celery, carrots, onions, and parsley. Cook, stirring occasionally, to soften the onions, about 5 minutes. Add the garlic, sage, and rosemary and continue cooking until the onions begin to brown, about 10 minutes. Stir in the meat. Cook, stirring occasionally, to brown the meat, 6 to 8 minutes. Season with salt and pepper, then add the wine, water, and mushrooms. Cover, and reduce the heat to a simmer. Cook until most of the water has evaporated and the meat is beginning to fall apart, about 1 hour.

Remove the cover and increase the heat to medium. Stir the meat and cook to make sure all the water has evaporated, about 10 minutes. Remove from the heat and allow to cool. Place in a food processor and process until very smooth. Blend in the egg and cheese. Taste, and season with more salt and pepper if necessary. Set aside.

VARIATIONS:

- When preparing this filling with lamb, 1½ cups roughly chopped cabbage may be added to the celery, carrots, and onions at the beginning of the recipe.
- When preparing this filling with venison, ½ cup currants or raisins that have been soaked for 5 minutes in boiling water and drained may be stirred into the completed puree.

MANICOTTI

Stuffed Crêpes

MAKES 24 CRÊPES

JOAN: During our stay in Italy in 1974, we visited my cousin Catherine in Calabria. I worked with her in the kitchen and watched as she made these light, delicious stuffed crêpes. Before that I had used this stuffing to make cannelloni or stuffed shells. This is a terrific first course or buffet dish. It may be prepared earlier in the day or may be frozen for several weeks before bringing to room temperature and baking.

FOR THE CRÊPES:

3 large eggs

1¾ cups water

1½ cups all-purpose flour

Kosher salt

Olive oil for the pan

FOR THE FILLING:

2 pounds whole-milk or part-skim ricotta cheese

1 cup grated mozzarella cheese (about 4 ounces)

1 large egg

2 teaspoons chopped fresh parsley leaves

½ cup Besciamella *(page 121)*

½ cup chopped cooked spinach (about ½ pound), all liquid squeezed out

4 tablespoons finely grated pecorino Romano or Parmesan cheese

Kosher salt

1½ cups Basic Tomato Sauce (page 123 or 124), pureed in a blender

Grated pecorino Romano or Parmesan cheese for serving (optional)

To prepare the crêpes, in a large bowl, beat the eggs until frothy. Beat in a small portion of the water, followed by a small portion of the flour. Continue adding water and flour, beating after each addition, to make a smooth batter. Season with salt.

Line a baking sheet with waxed paper or plastic wrap. Set aside.

Brush an 8-inch crêpe or nonstick pan with olive oil. Warm the pan over medium-high heat. Pour ¼ cup of the batter into the pan. Swirl the batter around the pan to evenly coat the bottom, and pour any excess batter back into the bowl. The batter should cover the bottom of the pan in a thin layer. Cook the crêpe until bubbles appear, about 1 minute. Flip the crêpe over and cook the other side for an additional minute. Remove to the prepared baking sheet and continue cooking crêpes, placing waxed paper or plastic wrap over each one on the baking sheet. (If the crêpes begin to stick to the pan, brush it with more oil.) With this batter you will be able to make 24 crêpes.

To prepare the filling, in a large bowl, stir together the ricotta, mozzarella, egg, parsley, *besciamella,* and spinach. Stir in 1 tablespoon of the Romano cheese and season with salt.

Preheat the oven to 350 degrees F. Divide ½ cup of the tomato sauce between two large baking dishes, and spread to cover the bottom with a thin layer.

Spread a rounded tablespoon of the filling across the bottom third of each crêpe. Roll the crêpe closed and place, seam side down, in one of the prepared baking dishes. Continue filling crêpes and arranging them in the baking dishes, making sure that their sides do not touch. Spread a generous teaspoon of tomato sauce across the top of each crêpe. Sprinkle with the remaining 3 tablespoons Romano cheese. Cover the baking dishes with aluminum foil and bake until the crêpes puff, about 20 minutes. Remove the foil and bake until lightly browned, about 5 minutes. Serve immediately, with remaining warm tomato sauce and grated Romano or Parmesan cheese if desired.

LASAGNE DI POLLO E FUNGHI MISTI

Lasagna with Chicken and Mushrooms

MAKES 8 SERVINGS

GIANNI: In Italy lasagna is traditionally served for holidays and special occasions. If you prepare homemade sauce and pasta, it can be a very labor-intensive dish. I wanted to create a recipe that was less work, and because I don't like to have the same dish for every holiday, I wanted a dish with a different flavor. This recipe eliminates the need to prepare a ragù sauce, and the chicken and mushrooms complement each other very well. It may be served as a pasta course before roasted pork or grilled fish. When served with bread and a tossed green salad, this lasagna makes a meal all by itself. It may be baked up to one day in advance. Cover it and refrigerate overnight, then allow to return to room temperature before reheating. It also freezes well, so try doubling the recipe and freezing one pan.

TO PREPARE THE CHICKEN:

1 whole boneless, skinless chicken breast, split
Kosher salt and freshly ground black pepper
2 teaspoons butter
2 teaspoons olive oil
3 fresh sage leaves

FOR THE BESCIAMELLA:

4 tablespoons (½ stick) butter
½ cup all-purpose flour
4 cups whole milk, at room temperature
Pinch of ground nutmeg

TO ASSEMBLE THE LASAGNA:

12 strips lasagna pasta, dried or fresh, cooked al dente *and rinsed in cold water*
1 recipe Mushroom Sauce (page 130)
⅓ cup freshly grated Parmesan cheese
¼ cup chopped fresh parsley leaves

The chicken breast should be about ½ inch thick. If necessary, place it between two sheets of plastic wrap and pound to achieve the desired thickness. Season the chicken on both sides with salt and pepper. Heat the butter and oil together in a medium-size sauté pan set over medium heat. When the butter is foaming, add the sage leaves and then place the chicken in the pan. Cook over medium heat so that the chicken slowly browns on one side, about 5 minutes. Turn and continue cooking until browned and cooked through, about 5 more minutes. Remove from the pan and allow to cool. Dice into ½-inch cubes (there should be about 1½ cups).

To prepare the *besciamella,* melt the butter in a 2-quart saucepan set over medium-high heat. When the butter is foaming, whisk in the flour. Gradually whisk in the milk and nutmeg. Reduce the heat to medium and continue whisking until the sauce thickens, about 8 minutes. (If you plan to bake the lasagna a day before serving, or if you plan to freeze it, the sauce may be of a slightly thinner consistency because it will thicken as it cools. To make a thinner sauce, cook for less time.) Remove from the heat and set aside.

Preheat the oven to 350 degrees F. Butter a 9 × 13-inch baking pan.

Evenly spread ½ cup of the *besciamella* over the bottom of the prepared pan. Place three lasagna noodles side by side on top of the sauce. Spread a layer of *besciamella* on top of the noodles. Spread one quarter of the mushroom sauce on top of the *besciamella.* Sprinkle half the chicken on top of the mushroom sauce. Sprinkle with some of the Parmesan and parsley. Top with three lasagna noodles and spread a layer of *besciamella* on top of the noodles. Spread one quarter of the mushroom sauce on top of the *besciamella.* Sprinkle the remaining half of the chicken on top of the mushroom sauce. Sprinkle with Parmesan and parsley. Top this layer with three lasagna noodles. Spread a layer of *besciamella* on top of the noodles. Spread one quarter of the mushroom sauce on top of the *besciamella.* Sprinkle with Parmesan and parsley. Place the final layer of noodles on top. Spread with the remaining *besciamella,* then the remaining mushroom sauce, and sprinkle with the remaining Parmesan and parsley.

Bake until bubbly and lightly browned on top, about 30 minutes. Allow to cool for 10 minutes before slicing and serving.

LASAGNE VERDI

Green Lasagna

MAKES 8 SERVINGS

JOAN: I learned how to make this dish the year we were living in Florence. The first time I made it at home, Stan and the kids loved it. I watched the results of my day's work disappear in five minutes! This dish tops the request list when I prepare family birthday dinners.

I make Homemade Pasta (page 119), but this recipe is also very tasty made with commercial fresh pasta or with dried pasta. Either way I recommend using a combination of both egg, or standard yellow, noodles and spinach, or green, noodles for a colorful and flavorful dish. I prefer to leave my homemade noodles the width they are when they come out of the pasta machine. I trim them to fit the length of the pan. This way I need only two of these wider noodles to complete each layer of lasagna. The directions in this recipe are based on using commercial pasta that is narrower, so each layer will require three noodles. The lasagna may be prepared, cooled completely, and refrigerated for two days before baking and serving. It may also be frozen and should be defrosted before baking.

STANLEY: During our stay in Italy we found ourselves in Bologna—the only city, it seemed, where there was an orthodontist who could replace my sister's retainer. During this day trip we ate lunch at a restaurant that specialized in *lasagne verdi.* I can only say that to this day, it remains one of the finest meals I have ever eaten.

1 recipe Salsa alla Maria Rosa *(page 131)*
1 recipe Besciamella *(page 121)*
1 cup finely grated Parmesan cheese
7 standard lasagna noodles, cooked al dente, *chilled in cold water, and drained on dish towels*
8 green lasagna noodles, cooked al dente, *chilled in cold water, and drained on dish towels*

Preheat the oven to 350 degrees F. Butter a 9 × 13-inch baking pan.

Ladle ½ cup of the *salsa alla Maria Rosa* over the bottom of the prepared pan. Place three standard lasagna noodles side by side on top of the sauce. Spread a layer of one quarter of the remaining *salsa alla Maria Rosa* on top of the noodles. Spread one quarter of the *besciamella* on top of the salsa. Sprinkle with ¼ cup of the Parmesan. Top with three green lasagna noodles, and spread a layer of *salsa alla Maria Rosa,* a layer of *besciamella,* and another ¼ cup of the cheese on top of these noodles. Top this layer with three standard lasagna noodles, and spread a layer of salsa, a layer of *besciamella,* and ¼ cup cheese on top of these noodles. For the final layer, place one standard lasagna noodle in the center and a green lasagna noodle on either side of it. Top with the remaining *salsa alla Maria Rosa,* remaining *besciamella,* and the remaining ¼ cup Parmesan.

Bake until bubbly and lightly browned on top, about 30 minutes. Allow to cool slightly before cutting.

TIMPÁNO

JOAN: One of the most impressive characters in Stanley's movie *Big Night* has no lines. It is the extravagant *timpáno* that is created as the centerpiece of an excessive meal. *Timpáno* (as it is said in Calabrian dialect)—or *timballo*—has been prepared for feasts and festivals in Italy for centuries. It is generally believed to have entered the lexicon of traditional Italian cooking from Morocco through Sicily.

The Tucci family recipe was brought to the United States by Apollonia Pisani, Stan's maternal grandmother. She grew up in Serra San Bruno, a small hill town in Calabria. If you saw *Big Night*, you have an idea of the wonderful visual impression *timpáno* can make. It is also intensely flavorful and well worth the process of preparing the components to fill the drum of pasta dough.

The process begins with a search for the perfect pot. We have baked timpános in various sizes and in all types of pots and pans. The Tuccis traditionally used a white enamel tub, the kind that every hardware and houseware store used to carry. The enamel finish conducted the heat very well, so the *timpáno* cooked evenly, didn't stick, and browned nicely. This type of pot is now very hard to come by. Stan and I have searched all over—New York City's Chinatown, an Italian-run department store in Toronto, a gourmet cooking shop in Seattle, and, of course, whenever we have traveled to Italy. When we find one we think will work, we bring it home to test. If the *timpáno* comes out well, we guard that pot carefully, wrapping and storing it away for future use. In fact, Stan's sister Dora uses permanent marker to put her name on the bottom of her prized *timpáno* pot so she can be sure to get it back after a family dinner.

We anticipated that finding the right pan would be a challenge for readers who wanted to create their own timpános, so we located a company that manufactures enameled bowls in a variety of sizes. The *timpáno* we baked in a six-quart container from CGS International came out perfectly, so we have written the following recipe to fill that bowl (see page 172). However, we have baked *timpános* in other materials—Corningware, Le Crueset pots, and even in terra-cotta baking dishes—and they worked with varying success. The only material that isn't right for *timpáno* is stainless steel, because the dough will not brown.

This recipe will feed twelve to sixteen people. The proportions may be adapted to fit a smaller or larger container. The ragù sauce and the meatballs freeze well, so they may be prepared ahead or leftovers may be saved for future use. Preparing these ingredients ahead of time will also make the process of assembling the *timpáno* less time-consuming on the day you plan to serve it to your guests. We have frozen a whole *timpáno* in the pot it will be baked in, with great success. A frozen *timpáno* will take three days to fully defrost in the refrigerator before it can be covered with aluminum foil and baked as directed in the recipe.

There is a fair amount of drama associated with creating a *timpáno*. Lots of questioning—"Is there enough sauce?" "Is this the right amount of salami [or cheese or egg]?" "Is it done?" "Should we have used the other pan?" "Will it crack when we flip it over?" "Is it cool enough to slice?" "Is it as good as the last one we made?" "Next time . . ." I can imagine generations of Tuccis past, present, and future asking those same questions, and that adds to my enjoyment of *timpáno*.

STAN: When I was growing up, my family would organize large picnics. My mother would bake a *timpáno* as the centerpiece of the meal, which also included chicken sautéed at home in lemon, olive oil, rosemary, and garlic and kept warm by the campfire. My mother baked the *timpáno* at home also, and then wrapped it in layers of newspaper and a heavy tablecloth so it would stay warm but not become soggy. Of course there always was salad, bread, and cheese to round out the meal.

We set up our picnic spot early in the day. One day, a few hours after we had established our spot, we saw another large Italian family setting up their picnic nearby. After a while we noticed they were eating something that looked very familiar. Some of the adult members of our family were dispatched to verify, and sure enough, they were eating *timpáno*. More important, they were from my family's hometown of Serra San Bruno. This was the only time anyone in the family ever met someone outside of our extended family who prepared *timpáno*. The Tucci family is now quite large, and as a result *timpános* are made today by family members from New York to Scottsdale to Seattle.

When Joan and I bake a *timpáno*, we each take responsibility for different components. Joan cooks the ragù sauce, makes and fries the meatballs, and boils the eggs and pasta. I slice the cheese and salami and prepare the dough, rolling it out on our round kitchen table. I also take responsibility for greasing the *timpáno* pot. I always worry that the *timpáno* will stick, and I generally apply enough olive oil so that the *timpáno* spins in the pot when it is done baking. Slicing the baked *timpáno* is also my job. I like to cut a small circle in the center, about 3 inches in diameter, and then cut pie-shaped pieces to this center. It makes it easier to remove each piece, and the whole *timpáno* seems to hold together better. There is one final, important secret to baking a *timpáno:* You must open the oven and check on its progress regularly—even when it is covered with foil and you can't tell anything. We all do it, and I'm convinced it affects the *timpáno*'s baking.

GIANNI: I had the opportunity to watch the Tuccis create their *timpáno* when we were testing recipes for this book. For me it epitomized the way I cook because everything about creating a *timpáno* is summed up in the expression I use so often: "It depends." It depends on the type of pot on how thick the sauce is, on how thickly the salami is sliced, on the kind of oven it is baked in, and so on. The process of assembling the *timpáno* and then discussing it while we ate it added to the festive mood and left our stomachs and our hearts feeling full.

I have included in this section a recipe for a vegetable *timpáno*. Instead of dough, the shell is made from grilled eggplant. The filling is essentially a pasta primavera composed of lots of pasta, fresh vegetables, and herbs in a light *besciamella* sauce. This *timpáno* is a variation on one I learned when I was working at a wonderful hotel in Venice. Every summer this hotel hosted an incredible Feast of the Pirates on the Lido. Guests, dressed as pirates, were brought by boat from Venice to the beach. The chefs would already be there, cooking rabbit and lamb over open pit fires. In anticipation of the feast, we would bake twenty timpános very similar to this a day or two in advance and bring them with us to the Lido. We warmed them by the fire and served slices as a first course before the grilled meats. Following in Stan's family tradition, I recommend my *timpáno* recipe for picnics. It travels well in its springform pan and is delicious served warm or at room temperature.

STANLEY: I can't remember when the idea to use *timpáno* as the centerpiece of the meal in *Big Night* came to us. I can only say that I'm glad it did. Structurally and creatively, it gave us a strong focus for the meal and had repercussions that we never anticipated. During the first screenings we were amazed at the audience's reactions to this dish. They were exactly those of the characters in the film—audible gasps of awe and wonder. After the release of *Big Night,* people literally begged my mother and me for the recipe. We always refused to give it because we hoped we could someday do so in a cookbook.

Though many *Big Night timpáno* recipes have been printed in various magazines and newspapers since the film's release, they are impostors. This is the *true* recipe for our *timpáno.* Good luck and *buon appetito!*

TIMPÁNO ALLA BIG NIGHT

Drum of Ziti and Great Stuff

MAKES 16 SERVINGS

JOAN: Our traditional *timpáno* is baked in a round enamelware pan that is wider on top than it is on the bottom. This type of pan is our first choice to bake *timpáno* and we knew from experience that finding such a pan might be difficult. We tested several 6-quart containers, the size pan this recipe is written for, and found three that we recommend here. CGS International makes a 6-quart enamelware bowl that is appropriate. If you cannot find their products in a local housewares store, contact them directly by calling (800) 777-0747. The Chantal Cookware Corporation manufactures an enamelware 8-quart lidded casserole. The principal drawbacks to this casserole are its depth and its straight sides, which make it difficult to remove the baked *timpáno* without its breaking. Chantal's products are widely available or can be ordered by calling (800) 365-4354. While shopping at Zabar's, New York City's renowned food and housewares store, we came across an enamelware 4-quart chili pot that was sold with four small bowls. We used the small bowls to bake mini-timpános, each of which served four people. The General Housewares Corporation manufactures this set, which may be ordered by calling (800) 457-2665. All three of these products baked excellent, well-browned timpános.

The dough for *timpáno* is rolled out into a thin round, the diameter of which is determined by the pan you are baking it in. Add together the diameter of the bottom of the pan, the diameter of the top of the pan, and twice the height of the pan. The total will equal the approximate diameter needed. The dough may be kneaded in advance and set aside or refrigerated overnight. Return it to room temperature before rolling it out. Place the rolled dough in the *timpáno* baking pan while the pasta is cooking.

The meat used in preparing the ragù sauce is generally served for dinner the night before the *timpáno* is baked because no one has room for anything other than salad after eating *timpáno.*

FOR THE DOUGH:

4 cups all-purpose flour

4 large eggs

1 teaspoon kosher salt

3 tablespoons olive oil

½ cup water

TO PREPARE THE PAN:

Butter

Olive oil

FOR THE FILLING:

2 cups ¼ × ½-inch Genoa salami pieces

2 cups ¼ × ½-inch sharp provolone cheese cubes

12 hard-boiled eggs, shelled, quartered lengthwise, and each quarter cut in half to create chunks

2 cups little meatballs (page 201)

8 cups Ragù Tucci (page 000 or 126), prepared following Note on page 127

3 pounds ziti, cooked very al dente *(about half the time recommended on the package) and drained (18 cups cooked)*

2 tablespoons olive oil

⅔ cup finely grated pecorino Romano cheese

4 large eggs, beaten

To make the dough, place the flour, eggs, salt, and olive oil in a stand mixer fitted with the dough hook. (A large-capacity food processor may also be used.) Add 3 tablespoons of the water and process. Add more water, I tablespoon at a time, until the mixture comes together and forms a ball. Turn the dough out onto a lightly floured work surface and knead to make sure it is well mixed. Set aside to rest for 5 minutes.

(To knead the dough by hand, mix the flour and salt together on a clean, dry work surface or pastry board. Form these dry ingredients into a mound and then make a well in the center. Break the eggs into the center of the well and lightly beat them with a fork. Stir in 3 tablespoons of the water. Use the fork to gradually incorporate some of the dry ingredients into the egg mixture. Continue mixing the dry ingredients into the eggs, adding the remaining water I tablespoon at a time. Knead the dough with your hands to make a well-mixed, smooth, dry dough. If the dough becomes too sticky, add more flour. Set aside to rest for 5 minutes.)

Flatten the dough out on a lightly floured work surface. Dust the top of the dough with flour and roll it out, dusting with flour and flipping the dough over from time to time, until it is about 1⁄16 inch thick and is the desired diameter.

Generously grease the *timpáno* baking pan with butter and olive oil. Fold the dough in half and then in half again, to form a triangle, and place it in the pan. Open the dough and arrange it in the pan, gently pressing it against the bottom and the sides, draping the extra dough over the sides. Set aside.

Preheat the oven to 350 degrees F.

To prepare the filling, have the salami, provolone, hard-boiled eggs, meatballs, and ragù at room temperature. Toss the drained pasta with the olive oil and 2 cups of the ragù. Distribute 6 generous cups of the pasta on the bottom of the *timpáno*. Top with I cup of the salami, I cup of the provolone, 6 of the hard-boiled eggs, I cup of the meatballs, and ⅓ cup of the Romano cheese. Pour 2 cups of the ragù over these ingredients. Top with 6 cups of the remaining pasta. Top that with the remaining 1 cup salami, 1 cup provolone, 6 hard-boiled eggs, 1 cup meatballs, and ⅓ cup Romano cheese. Pour 2 cups of the ragù over these ingredients. Top with the remaining 6 cups pasta. (The ingredients should now be about 1 inch below the rim of the pot.) Spoon the remaining 2 cups ragù over the pasta. Pour the beaten eggs over the filling. Fold the pasta dough over the filling to seal completely. Trim away and discard any double layers of dough.

Bake until lightly browned, about 1 hour. Then cover with aluminum foil and continue baking until the *timpáno* is cooked through and the dough is golden brown (and reaches an internal temperature of 120 degrees F), about 30 minutes. Remove from the oven and allow to rest for 30 or more minutes. The baked *timpáno* should not adhere to the pan. If any part is still attached, carefully detach with a knife. Grasp the baking pan firmly and invert the *timpáno* onto a serving platter. Remove the pan and allow the *timpáno* to cool for 20 minutes. Using a long, sharp knife, cut a circle about 3 inches in diameter in the center of the *timpáno,* making sure to cut all the way through to the bottom. Then slice the *timpáno* as you would a pie into individual portions, leaving the center circle as a support for the remaining pieces.

TIMPÁNO DI VEGETALI

Vegetarian Timpáno

MAKES 12 SERVINGS

GIANNI: Despite its spectacular presentation, this dish is much simpler to prepare than you might think. All of the components may be prepared in advance. The eggplant may be broiled or baked one day ahead. The sauce may be prepared one day in advance. Refrigerate the eggplant and sauce overnight and bring to room temperature before filling the *timpáno*. In fact, the *timpáno* maintains its shape best if it is baked earlier in the day and then reheated before serving.

4 medium-size eggplants (about 1½ pounds each), cut lengthwise into ½-inch-wide strips with the peel removed from every other piece
Kosher salt
3 tablespoons butter
½ cup plain dried bread crumbs
2 tablespoons all-purpose flour
1 cup cold milk
½ cup plus 2 tablespoons olive oil
1 cup diced onions
1 cup seeded and diced red bell pepper
1 cup seeded and diced green bell pepper
1 cup seeded and diced yellow bell pepper
Freshly ground black pepper
1 cup quartered and thinly sliced carrots
¾ cup thinly sliced tender celery
3 cups halved and thinly sliced zucchini
2 tablespoons chopped fresh basil leaves
2 tablespoons chopped fresh parsley leaves
2 cups canned whole plum tomatoes
1 cup fresh or frozen peas
¾ pound penne, ziti, or fusilli pasta
2 cups diced mozzarella cheese
½ cup freshly grated Parmesan cheese

Generously sprinkle the eggplant slices with kosher salt, place them in a colander, and set aside to drain for 2 hours.

Generously grease a 10-inch springform pan with 2 tablespoons of the butter. Sprinkle the bread crumbs on the bottom and sides of the pan. Do not knock out the excess crumbs. Set aside.

Melt the remaining 1 tablespoon butter in a small saucepan set over medium heat. Whisk in the flour; then gradually whisk in the milk. Bring to a simmer and cook this *besciamella* sauce, whisking regularly, until it thickens, about 8 minutes. Remove from the heat and set aside.

Bring a large pot of salted water to a boil. Reduce the heat and hold at a low simmer until you are ready to cook the pasta.

Warm 2 tablespoons of the olive oil in a sauté pan set over medium-high heat. Add the onions and bell peppers and cook, stirring, until slightly softened but not browned, about 5 minutes. Season with salt and pepper. Add the carrots and celery and continue cooking, stirring frequently, until they have softened slightly, about another 10 minutes. Stir in the zucchini, basil, and parsley and cook to soften slightly, 2 to 3 minutes. Stir in the tomatoes, crushing them with your hand or the back of a slotted spoon as you add them to the pan. Bring to a boil, then reduce the heat to a simmer. Cook until the tomatoes have sweetened slightly, about 10 minutes. Stir in the peas and *besciamella* sauce, and cook until the peas are tender, 5 minutes. Continue to gently cook the vegetables over low heat, stirring occasionally, while the pasta boils.

Return the water to a boil. Add the pasta and cook for 2 minutes longer than recommended on the package. Drain well and stir into the vegetable sauce. Remove from the heat and transfer to a wide bowl. Allow the sauce to cool to room temperature.

Preheat the oven broiler, or a gas or charcoal grill. Pat the eggplant slices dry with paper towels. Lightly brush the eggplant slices with the remaining ½ cup olive oil. Brown under the broiler or on the grill, about 5 minutes per side.

Preheat the oven to 350 degrees F.

Line the prepared springform pan with overlapping slices of eggplant, alternating the peeled and unpeeled slices, allowing each slice to overhang the edge of the pan by about 3 inches. Line the center of the pan with eggplant, alternating the peeled and unpeeled slices, overlapping the ends of the side pieces. There should be a few pieces of eggplant remaining to fill the top of the *timpáno.*

Stir the mozzarella and Parmesan cheeses into the cooled vegetable sauce. Fill the eggplant shell with the pasta/vegetable mixture, pressing down with the back of a wooden spoon to compact it in the pan. Fold the eggplant slices that are hanging over the edge of the pan back over the filling. Patch the center of the *timpáno* with a few remaining slices of eggplant. Cover with aluminum foil and bake for 15 minutes. Remove the foil, increase the oven temperature to 400 degrees F, and continue baking until warmed through, another 15 minutes. Remove from the oven and allow to rest for 10 minutes before removing the outer ring of the springform pan and placing on a serving platter. Serve immediately. (If you are baking it ahead of time, leave the *timpáno* in the pan, cover, and store at room temperature. Reheat before serving.)

VARIATIONS:

- This vegetable sauce may be tossed with fusilli, ziti, or penne and served as a pasta course.
- The vegetable sauce, without the fusilli, ziti, or penne, also makes a nice filling for lasagna. Spoon ½ cup of the sauce onto the bottom of a baking dish. Top with 3 precooked lasagna noodles. Top with sauce and continue layering, using a total of 12 precooked lasagna noodles. Bake at 350 degrees F until the sauce bubbles, about 35 minutes.
- 1 cup diced vegetables, such as string beans, artichokes, mushrooms, or asparagus, can be added.
- For a spicier version, add ½ teaspoon chopped jalapeño pepper or ¼ teaspoon red pepper flakes when cooking the onions and bell peppers.

Riso e Risotto

RICE AND RISOTTO

JOAN: There are three types of rice recipes in this section—those prepared with long-grain or basmati rice and risottos prepared with arborio rice. My mother never made risotto, so I learned how from Stan's family. In fact, I believe the first time my mother tasted risotto was when Stan's mother made it for her. My mother loved it but was never interested in learning how make it on her own. Once I felt confident preparing *risotto alla Milanese,* I began to experiment with other recipes, such as the *risotto con gamberetti* (Risotto with Shrimp). I like to serve risotto in place of pasta as a first course before meat, chicken, or fish.

GIANNI: A lot of rice is grown in the Veneto region of Italy, where I grew up. The rice is inexpensive and of very high quality, so people cook with it two or three nights a week. They make winter soups using rich broth and cooked rice, spring risottos with fresh peas and parsley, and in the summer they make rice salads. There are rice dishes to choose from in every season.

I consider making risotto an art rather than a science. It begins with shopping for the rice. In the United States I look for brands marked Carnaroli; if that is not available, I purchase a Vialone Nano rice or superfino arborio rice, both of which may be found in most supermarkets. The rice you buy is important because different varieties absorb liquid at different rates. That is why when people ask me how much liquid they should add to the rice, I find it difficult to say because I cook risotto by eye. If it is still tough after you've added all the liquid called for in the recipe, you'll need to add more, so I recommend having excess hot liquid available. The following recipes call for more liquid than you will most likely use.

There are two other important steps to remember when cooking risotto. First, make sure to "toast" the rice with the oil and onions before adding any liquid. "Toasting" seals the rice grains and helps to keep them from overcooking. Second, test the rice for the desired texture after it has cooked for twelve to fifteen minutes. Risotto may be served *al dente,* with a slight crispness to the bite, or with a softer consistency—the choice is yours. In Italy we call a risotto of perfect consistency *all'onda,* which means "on the wave" and describes the movement the rice should make as you spoon it onto a plate. Just don't overcook risotto or it will turn into paste.

STANLEY: In one of the first scenes in *Big Night,* risotto is used as a metaphor for prejudice and a preconception of what "Italian" food really is. Though risotto is now quite popular in this country, this was not true in the 1950s, the period in which *Big Night* is set. Because it is Northern Italian in origin and most of the Italians who emigrated to America were from the poorer South, most Americans were unfamiliar with risotto until even the last decade. Preparing risotto requires your focused attention for about twenty minutes, so I like to open a bottle of wine and gather my family and friends around the stove to keep me company while I stir.

INSALATA DI RISO

Rice Salad

MAKES 4 SERVINGS

JOAN: The year we lived in Florence, I shopped at the local *tavola calda* (specialty food store), which carried a number of prepared salads. This was one of young Stanley's favorites. I asked the owner for his recipe and then went home and made it myself. It has long been one of our standard lunch dishes.

1 cup long-grain rice
2½ cups cold water
3 tablespoons freshly squeezed lemon juice (from about 1 lemon)
2 tablespoons red wine vinegar
Kosher salt and freshly ground black pepper
¼ cup olive oil
1 cup frozen peas
2 tablespoons chopped fresh parsley leaves

Place the rice and water in a small saucepan over medium-high heat. Cover and bring to a boil. Reduce the heat to low, and simmer until the rice is tender and most, if not all, of the water has been absorbed, about 20 minutes. If water remains, drain the rice before placing it in a serving bowl.

In a small bowl whisk together the lemon juice and vinegar, and season with salt and pepper. Gradually whisk in the olive oil. Pour a small portion of this dressing onto the rice and toss. Set the rice aside to cool.

Place the peas in a colander. Pour 3 to 4 cups of hot water over them to defrost and cook slightly. Drain, then stir the peas and parsley into the cooled rice. Whisk the remaining dressing before pouring it over the rice and tossing to coat evenly. Serve at room temperature.

RISO CON POMODORO

Rice with Tomato Sauce

MAKES 6 SERVINGS

STAN: I grew up in a duplex house with my sisters, Dora and Rosalinda, and my brother, Frank. My mother's parents lived next door with my two unmarried uncles and my unmarried aunt. Since the local schools I attended were all within easy walking distance, my siblings and I always went home for lunch. This dish was among many my mother would prepare for us; others included frittata, *Mozzarella in Carrozza* (page 35), and *Pastina con Uova* (page 69).

JOAN: My mother served this dish as a quick no-meat supper on Friday evenings. As kids we loved its creamy texture and found it quite filling. It was not enough of a meal for my father, so he would follow it with some of mother's freshly baked bread, olives, slices of provolone, and a salad.

1 cup long-grain rice
2½ cups cold water
1½ cups Basic Tomato Sauce (page 123 or 124) prepared with green bell peppers
Freshly grated Parmesan or pecorino Romano cheese for garnish (optional)

Place the rice and water in a small saucepan over medium-high heat. Cover and bring to a boil. Reduce the heat to low, and simmer the rice until it is tender and all of the water has been absorbed, about 20 minutes. Stir the tomato sauce into the cooked rice. Cook the rice mixture over low heat to blend the flavors, about 5 minutes. Serve hot, topped with cheese.

RISO CON ZUCCHINI

Rice with Zucchini

MAKES 4 SERVINGS

JOAN: I know it's not Italian, but I love the flavor of basmati rice. I experimented with different ways of cooking it and came up with this recipe. The zucchini adds nice flavor to this simple dish, which I serve with grilled chicken or fish. The rice may be cooked and mixed with the onion and zucchini several hours in advance. Add the cheese just before baking.

1 cup brown basmati rice
2½ cups cold water
2 tablespoons olive oil
½ cup roughly chopped onions
2 cups roughly chopped zucchini
Kosher salt and freshly ground black pepper
½ cup grated Jarlsberg cheese
¼ cup finely grated Parmesan cheese

Place the rice and water in a small saucepan over medium-high heat. Cover and bring to a boil. Reduce the heat to low and simmer the rice until it is tender, about 20 minutes. If there is water left in the pan, do not drain it off.

Preheat the oven to 350 degrees F.

Warm the olive oil in a medium-size sauté pan set over medium heat. Add the onions and cook, stirring, until softened, about 5 minutes. Add the zucchini and season with salt and pepper. Cook until the white portion of the zucchini has softened but the green rind remains firm, about 5 minutes.

In a small casserole, mix together the cooked rice, zucchini, and grated cheeses. Cover and bake until the cheeses have melted, 15 to 20 minutes. Serve immediately.

VARIATIONS: Asiago, Gruyère, or Monterey Jack cheese may be substituted for the Jarlsberg.

RISO ALLA SALVIA

Rice with Sage

MAKES 6 SERVINGS

GIANNI: Most Americans use arborio rice only when preparing risotto. However, it is also very delicious if you cook it as you would conventional rice and blend it with herbs and butter. It makes a delicious side dish in place of potatoes or beans.

As a young chef, on my day off I wanted to eat well but didn't have the energy to cook an elaborate meal. So I would cook some rice according to this recipe and add a drained 3.5-ounce can of Italian tuna, 2 teaspoons rinsed capers, and 6 pitted, chopped olives. With a little extra virgin olive oil drizzled on top, I had created a simple and delicious dinner.

2 cups arborio rice
2 tablespoons butter or olive oil
12 fresh sage leaves
½ cup freshly grated Parmesan cheese

Bring a medium-size saucepan of salted water to a boil. Add the rice and cook, uncovered, until tender, about 15 minutes.

Melt the butter in a small sauté pan set over low heat. Remove from the heat and add the sage leaves. Set aside.

Reserve ¼ cup of the cooking water before draining the rice. Return the drained rice to the saucepan. Stir in the reserved water, melted butter with sage leaves, and cheese. Blend together well, and serve.

VARIATIONS:

- Other soft-leaved herbs such as basil, parsley, or marjoram may be substituted for the sage.
- Boiled arborio rice may be used in place of pasta in any of the pasta salad recipes found in this book. Cook the rice, run it under cold water, and toss with the recipe of your choice.

RISO E LATTE DI "BERTILLA"

Rice with Milk

MAKES 4 TO 6 SERVINGS

GIANNI: I named this dish for my mother, Maria-Bertilla, who would make it for me as an after-school snack. I savored each bite, slowly spooning around the cooled edges of the bowl toward the center until each morsel was eaten. I now serve it to my own son, Christian. I have warned him, as my mother warned me, to blow on each spoonful to avoid burning his tongue.

4 cups milk
1½ cups water
2 cups arborio rice
Kosher salt
1 tablespoon butter or olive oil

Bring the milk and water to a boil in a large saucepan set over medium-high heat. Stir in the rice and salt to taste. Simmer until the rice has absorbed most of the liquid, about 20 minutes. Remove from the heat and allow to cool for 2 minutes. The rice should be creamy and, when poured into bowls, should be *all'onda,* which means "wavy." Top each portion with a little butter or olive oil. Serve immediately.

RISOTTO ALLA MILANESE

Traditional Risotto from Milan

MAKES 6 SERVINGS

JOAN: In Italy they sell small paper packages of powdered saffron. When Stan and I shop on Arthur Avenue in the Bronx, I am often able to purchase this type of Italian saffron. However, in the United States it is more typical to find saffron threads sold in small vials, and these also may be used to prepare this dish. It is traditional to serve *risotto alla Milanese* with osso buco. It may also be served as a first course before chicken or other veal dishes.

STANLEY: My wife, Kate, and I serve risotto cakes for lunch on top of a green salad or for brunch with fried eggs. To the leftover risotto I add an egg and enough bread crumbs to form a soft dough. Shape the risotto into patties about 3 inches in diameter and ½ inch thick. Heat 3 tablespoons olive oil in a sauté pan set over medium-high heat. When the oil is hot but not smoking, add the risotto cakes. Cook until warmed through and golden brown on both sides, about 8 minutes altogether. Serve immediately.

8 cups hot chicken broth
½ teaspoon powdered saffron or 20 saffron threads
2 tablespoons butter
2 tablespoons olive oil
½ cup roughly chopped onions
2 cups arborio rice
½ cup dry white wine
¼ cup finely grated Parmesan cheese

Measure out ½ cup of the hot broth, stir in the saffron, and set aside. Keep the remaining broth warm in a medium-size saucepan set over medium-low heat.

Melt the butter in the olive oil in a large saucepan set over medium heat. Add the onions and cook, stirring, until they have softened but not browned, about 5 minutes. Add the rice and stir to coat with the butter, oil, and onions. Add the wine and cook, stirring continuously, until the wine evaporates, about 1 minute. Stir in the saffron broth and cook, allowing the rice to absorb it, about 2 minutes. Add the remaining broth, ½ cup at a time, stirring after each addition and allowing the rice to absorb the broth before adding more. Cook until the rice is tender but *al dente,* about 20 minutes. Stir in the Parmesan and serve immediately.

VARIATION: Dried porcini mushrooms make a nice addition to this risotto. Soak 1 cup chopped dried porcini in 1 cup warm water. After the saffron broth has been added to the rice, strain the mushrooms through a fine-mesh sieve, reserving the liquid. Stir the mushrooms and the strained liquid into the risotto, allowing the rice to absorb the liquid before proceeding with the recipe.

RISOTTO CON ASPARAGI

Asparagus Risotto

MAKES 4 SERVINGS

GIANNI: Recoaro Terme is a small resort town in the foothills of the Dolomite Mountains. It is known for its mineral water, which flows, warmed from the earth, into a fountain in the center of town. It is also home to the Recoaro Terme Culinary Institute, where I went to study at the age of fourteen. Four nights of the week, the Culinary Institute provided dinner. The other three nights my roommates and I cooked for ourselves. I would prepare this "lazy" risotto with the basic ingredients we always had on hand—rice, onion, canned vegetables, Parmesan cheese, olive oil, and sometimes parsley. If we didn't have any chicken broth in the pantry, I would use water—and never found the flavor lacking. Canned asparagus may sound gross but they provide lots of flavor and make the rice very creamy. I also prepare this dish using canned peas or crushed plum tomatoes. Of course this risotto may be prepared using fresh ingredients, but remember, it was meant to be a "lazy" meal.

2 tablespoons olive oil
1 small onion, minced
2 tablespoons chopped fresh parsley leaves
2 cups arborio rice
One 15-ounce can asparagus (do not drain)
4 cups hot chicken broth
Tips from 8 fresh asparagus stalks (optional)
Kosher salt and freshly ground black pepper
1 tablespoon butter (optional)
1 tablespoon extra virgin olive oil
⅓ cup finely grated Parmesan cheese

Warm the olive oil in a medium-size saucepan set over medium heat. When the oil is hot but not smoking, stir in the onion and cook, stirring frequently, until soft but not browned, about 5 minutes. Stir in 1 tablespoon of the parsley and all of the rice. Stir to toast lightly and coat the rice with oil. Stir in the canned asparagus with its liquid, plus 2 cups of the chicken broth. Bring to a boil, then reduce the heat to simmer. Add more chicken broth, ½ cup at a time, stirring frequently and allowing the rice to absorb the liquid after each addition, until the rice is *al dente,* about 15 minutes. (If you use fresh asparagus tips, add them with the last ladleful of broth.) The rice should have a slight resistance to the bite. If it seems too hard, add a little bit more liquid and continue cooking for another minute or two.

Remove from the heat and season with salt and pepper. Add the remaining 1 tablespoon parsley, the butter, extra virgin olive oil, and cheese. Whip with a wooden spoon to bring out the creaminess of the rice and to incorporate all the ingredients. Adjust the seasoning with salt and pepper if necessary. Serve immediately.

continued

VARIATIONS:

- White canned asparagus may be used in place of green asparagus.
- 2 teaspoons chopped fresh tarragon leaves stirred in at the end of the recipe make a nice addition to this risotto.
- Fresh asparagus may be used. Chop the tips off 1 pound asparagus and set aside. Roughly chop the remaining portion of the asparagus, discarding any woody stems. Stir the chopped asparagus into the risotto along with the first 2 cups of broth, and proceed with the recipe as written. Add the asparagus tips along with the parsley, butter, olive oil, and cheese.
- Some evenings after finishing classes at the Culinary Institute, my roommates and I would make an even simpler version of this recipe. We would cook the onion and parsley in olive oil, add the rice, and gradually stir in 6 cups of chicken stock. After seasoning with salt and pepper, we would stir in ½ cup grated or crumbled cheese. We used whatever cheese we had on hand—Fontina, Gorgonzola, Gruyère. These creamy cheeses added texture and flavor to this one-dish meal.

RISOTTO DI VEGETALI ALLE ERBETTE FINI

Risotto with Vegetables and Fine Herbs

MAKES 4 SERVINGS

GIANNI: I learned how to make this dish at the Excelsior Hotel on the Lido in Venice when I was eighteen years old. It is visually stunning, and in every bite you will find a little something different. Although the types and quantities of vegetables used in this recipe may vary, I would not use strong-flavored vegetables such as fennel, broccoli, cauliflower, cabbage, garlic, or even mushrooms, which would overpower the other flavors.

2 teaspoons chopped fresh basil leaves
2 teaspoons chopped fresh parsley leaves
½ teaspoon chopped fresh thyme leaves
½ teaspoon chopped fresh sage leaves
1 tablespoon plus 2 teaspoons butter
2 tablespoons olive oil
½ cup diced shallots or onions
12 small artichoke hearts, cut in half (frozen hearts or canned artichoke bottoms may be used)
4 string beans, ends trimmed and cut into 2-inch pieces
2 tablespoons finely diced tender celery
1¼ cups halved and thinly sliced zucchini (about 1 small zucchini)
1¼ cups halved and thinly sliced carrots (about 2 medium-size carrots)
¼ cup fresh or frozen peas
½ cup 1-inch lengths asparagus (about 3 stalks)
½ cup chopped fresh or canned plum tomatoes (about 2 tomatoes)
2 cups arborio rice
5 cups hot chicken broth
Kosher salt and freshly ground black pepper
1 tablespoon extra virgin olive oil
⅓ cup freshly grated Parmesan cheese

In a small bowl, mix together the chopped herbs and set aside.

In a large saucepan set over medium-high heat, melt 2 teaspoons of the butter in the olive oil. Add the shallots, cover, and cook until they are soft but not browned, about 5 minutes. Add all of the vegetables and half of the herb mixture, stirring to combine. Add the rice, stirring to toast lightly and coat with the oil. Add 2 cups of the chicken broth. Bring to a rapid boil, then reduce the heat to a gentle boil. Add the remaining broth, ½ cup at a time, stirring frequently and allowing the rice to absorb the liquid after each addition, until the rice is *al dente,* about 15 minutes. The rice should have a slight resistance to the bite. If it seems too hard, add a little more liquid and continue cooking for another minute or 2.

Remove from the heat and season with salt and pepper. Stir in the remaining herbs, the remaining 1 tablespoon butter, the extra virgin olive oil, and the Parmesan. Whip with a wooden spoon to bring out the creaminess of the rice and to incorporate all the ingredients. Cover and allow to rest for a few minutes before serving.

My father's grandmother, Cunegonda, weaving little baskets. People filled these small baskets with the short pieces of vine used to tie up the grape plants in the vineyards.

RISOTTO DI ZUCCA CON ARAGOSTA E SALVIA

Risotto with Butternut Squash, Lobster, and Sage

MAKES 4 TO 6 SERVINGS

GIANNI: Naturally sweet butternut squash and seafood create the unique flavor of this beautiful, creamy risotto. Adding pumpkin puree to enrich the chicken broth saves the time of preparing a vegetable broth, and the small amount of seafood called for makes this dish a relatively inexpensive way to serve lobster to a group. Serve this risotto with a green salad, a loaf of bread, and a dry white wine.

STANLEY: If memory serves me correctly, this was the first dish Gianni ever cooked for me while I was doing research at Le Madri. I knew then I was in the hands of a master.

8 cups chicken broth
¼ cup canned pumpkin puree
3 tablespoons olive oil
½ cup diced onions
1 pound butternut squash, peeled, seeded, and diced into ¼-inch cubes (about 3 cups)
2 cups arborio rice
1 teaspoon chopped fresh sage leaves
½ pound cooked lobster meat, cut into small bite-size pieces (about 1 cup)
Kosher salt and freshly ground black pepper
2 tablespoons brandy or cognac
1 tablespoon chopped fresh parsley leaves
2 tablespoons unsalted butter

In a large saucepan, whisk together the chicken broth and pumpkin puree. Bring to a boil, then reduce the heat to medium-low and leave the broth at a gentle simmer.

In a large high-sided sauté pan, warm 1 tablespoon of the olive oil over medium heat. Stir in the onions and cook until softened but not browned, about 5 minutes. Stir in the squash and cook to flavor with the onions, about 2 minutes. Stir in the rice, sage, and 2 cups of the simmering broth. Bring to a boil, stirring frequently, then reduce the heat to a simmer.

When the rice has absorbed the liquid, add half the lobster meat and ½ cup of the simmering broth. Stir the rice until the liquid is absorbed. Continue adding the remaining broth, ½ cup at a time, stirring after each addition and allowing the rice to absorb the liquid before adding more. After 15 minutes, taste a grain of rice. It should have a slight resistance to the bite. If it seems too hard, add a little more broth and continue cooking for another minute or 2. When the rice has absorbed the last of the broth, add the remaining lobster. Remove from the heat.

continued

Season with salt and pepper. Stir in the brandy, parsley, butter, and remaining 2 tablespoons olive oil. Whip with a wooden spoon to bring out the creaminess of the rice and to incorporate all the ingredients. Cover and allow to rest for 5 minutes before serving.

VARIATIONS:

- Culls (lobsters without claws) or single lobster tails may be used for this recipe. You will need about 1½ pounds lobster in the shell.
- An additional ¼ pound chopped butternut squash may be substituted for the pumpkin puree.
- Crabmeat or shrimp may be substituted for the lobster.
- Parmesan cheese may be served as a garnish.

RISOTTO CON GAMBERETTI

Risotto with Shrimp

MAKES 4 SERVINGS

STAN: Zia Maria, one of my great-aunts, brought her recipe for *risotto alla Milanese* from Lombardy when the family emigrated to Vermont. She used local wild mushrooms to prepare her risotto, and her recipe is a family staple that has now been passed down through three generations of Tuccis. Joan created this variation using delicate shrimp, which beautifully accent the pearly white arborio rice.

1 pound medium-size shrimp, peeled and deveined, shells reserved
1 medium-size onion, quartered
1 celery stalk, cut into thirds
1 carrot (optional), cut into thirds
4 sprigs fresh parsley
Kosher salt
5 cups water
4 tablespoons olive oil
1 clove garlic, chopped
2 tablespoons unsalted butter
¼ cup chopped onions
1 cup arborio rice
½ cup dry white wine
1 fresh or canned plum tomato, peeled, seeded, and diced
¼ cup finely grated Parmesan cheese (optional)

In a large saucepan, combine the shrimp shells, quartered onion, celery, carrot, parsley, salt to taste, and water. Bring to a boil, then simmer gently, with the lid slightly askew, for 25 minutes. Strain through a fine-mesh sieve. Discard the shells and vegetables. When you are ready to prepare the risotto, warm the broth to a gentle simmer.

Warm 2 tablespoons of the olive oil in a large high-sided sauté pan set over medium heat. Add the garlic and cook until lightly colored, about 1 minute. Add the shrimp and cook until they turn light pink, about 4 minutes. Remove the shrimp from the pan to a plate and set aside.

Add the remaining 2 tablespoons olive oil, 1 tablespoon of the butter, and the chopped onions to the sauté pan. Cook over medium-high heat until the onions have softened but not browned, about 5 minutes. Add the rice, stirring to coat it with the olive oil. Stir in 1 cup of the simmering broth. When the rice has absorbed the broth, add the wine and tomato and stir until the wine has been absorbed by the rice. Add the remaining broth, ½ cup at a time, stirring frequently and allowing the rice to absorb the liquid after each addition, until the rice is *al dente,* 15 to 20 minutes. Add the reserved shrimp along with the last ladleful of broth and any juices that may have accumulated on the plate. The rice should have a slight resistance to the bite. If it seems too hard, add a little more liquid and continue cooking for another minute or two. Remove the rice from the heat and briskly stir in the remaining 1 tablespoon butter and the cheese. Serve immediately.

VARIATIONS:

- The shrimp may be peeled and the broth prepared several hours ahead of time.
- Chicken stock may be substituted for the shrimp broth, although this will alter the delicate flavor slightly.

NOTE: Leftover shrimp broth may be frozen in an airtight container for up to 3 months.

My father, Stanislao (left), *with Zio Emilio Politi in snow shoes.*

Carne

MEAT

JOAN: My father made his own sausage at the end of the summer, when the pigs we had fattened up were butchered. My mother cooked veal cutlets and occasionally made a steak or pork chops, though they were not served "American style"—with a vegetable and potato on the side. Instead, we always began with a pasta dish. This was followed by the meat course accompanied by a simply cooked vegetable. We finished with a green salad followed by nuts and fresh fruit. I maintain this tradition and find that pacing the meal in this way leaves me feeling less full.

GIANNI: Most of the meat my family ate was given to us by friends who raised cows and pigs or hunted deer and pheasant. My father rented out our trattoria for parties, cooking the meals for these events himself. If there was any meat left over, my mother would grind it together with some of the leftover vegetables. She would add some bread crumbs and eggs and fry these *polpettine,* or burgers, for supper.

STANLEY: The Italian Futurists believed in the abolition of pasta because they said it "slowed down" the Italian people. They believed in a diet consisting mostly of meat. Some of their bizarre recipes called for a variety of meats cooked and served together. They felt this high-protein diet would propel them to be more aggressive and therefore successful in every way. I am inclined to believe it would only constipate and become boring after a while. Though the Futurists' art had great impact culturally, luckily their dietary suggestions did not.

What Italians do so well is serve all courses in perfect proportion. When meat is served, it is generally not an enormous slab slathered in a fatty gravy, but a portion large enough to satisfy, complementing what came before and what will come after. This is one of the reasons Italians live long and healthy lives. That and the daily consumption of red wine.

FILETTO DI BUE AL PROSCIUTTO

Beef Tenderloin with Prosciutto

MAKES 6 TO 8 SERVINGS

GIANNI: This dish is very good when served with Mashed Potatoes and Artichokes (page 274). Domestically cured prosciutto may be purchased for this recipe; because it will be roasted along with the meat, there is no need to purchase an imported brand. You may even use pancetta or American bacon instead.

2 tablespoons canola or vegetable oil
1 large carrot, halved lengthwise and cut into 2-inch pieces
1 medium-size onion, quartered
2 celery stalks, halved lengthwise and cut into 2-inch pieces
One 2½- to 3-pound beef tenderloin or Chateaubriand
2 tablespoons Dijon mustard
1 tablespoon roughly chopped fresh rosemary leaves
1 tablespoon roughly chopped fresh sage leaves
Kosher salt and freshly ground black pepper
12 very thin slices prosciutto
1 tablespoon all-purpose flour
½ cup dry red wine
1 cup chicken broth

Preheat the oven to 500 degrees F. Grease a small roasting or baking pan—one that will hold the beef snugly—with the oil.

Arrange the carrot, onion, and celery on the bottom of the prepared pan. Place a wire rack in the pan and set aside.

Rub the beef all over with the mustard. Sprinkle the rosemary, sage, and salt and pepper to taste all over the beef. Place 6 to 8 slices of the prosciutto, slightly overlapping, on a clean work surface. Place the beef on top of the prosciutto. Wrap the prosciutto up and over, and use the remaining slices of prosciutto to completely enclose the beef. Secure the prosciutto around the beef by gently tying the roast with butcher's string.

Place the roast on the rack and cook in the oven until browned on top, about 15 minutes. Turn the roast and continue cooking until browned and medium-rare, about 15 minutes more. (An internal thermometer should register about 130 degrees F for medium-rare beef.) Transfer the meat to a platter and set aside to rest for 10 minutes before removing and discarding the string. Carve into 1-inch-thick slices.

Meanwhile, set the roasting pan over high heat (or transfer the contents to a wide saucepan). Stir in the flour, wine, and broth, bring to a boil and cook, stirring constantly, to slightly thicken the juices in the pan, about 5 minutes. Strain through a fine-mesh sieve and spoon over the sliced roast.

BISTECCA ORIGANATA

Steak Oreganato

MAKES 6 SERVINGS

JOAN: Stan's mother cooked steak this simple, quick, flavorful way.

1 top round beef steak (2½ to 3 pounds)	*Kosher salt and freshly ground black pepper*
2 tablespoons butter	*½ cup dry red wine*
2 tablespoons olive oil	*½ teaspoon dried oregano*

The steak should be ½ inch thick. If necessary, pound it between two sheets of waxed paper to achieve this thickness.

Warm the butter and olive oil together in a large sauté or cast-iron pan set over medium-high heat. When the butter is foaming rapidly, add the steak and fry to brown on one side, about 3 minutes. (If the steak is larger than your sauté pan, cut it in half.) Turn, and season with salt and pepper. Brown the other side, about 3 minutes. Remove from the pan to a warm platter and set aside.

Add the wine and oregano to the pan, scraping up any meat that may have stuck to the bottom. Simmer to sweeten the wine, about 1 minute. Meanwhile, cut the meat into six equal portions. When the wine sauce is ready, pour it over the meat and serve immediately.

BRACIOLE

Stuffed Beef Rolls

MAKES 6 SERVINGS

JOAN: There are many variations on this basic recipe, and it seems that every southern Italian family has their own version. I prefer to stuff several pieces of beef round pounded to ⅛-inch thickness, brown them, and then add them to a simple tomato sauce. Stan's mother would stuff a whole flank steak with chopped hard-boiled eggs, parsley, cheese, and garlic. She browned it before adding it to the other meats she used in her ragù recipe.

Either way, the tomato sauce is served over pasta as a first course, and the meat is sliced and served as a second course, followed by salad. This entire recipe may be prepared in advance. Cover and refrigerate for up to three days or freeze for up to one month.

6 pieces beef round for braciola (about 1½ pounds total)
Kosher salt and freshly ground black pepper
6 cloves garlic, minced
½ cup freshly grated pecorino Romano cheese
½ cup finely chopped fresh parsley leaves
¼ cup olive oil
½ cup finely chopped onions
½ cup dry red wine
4 cups canned whole plum tomatoes (about one 35-ounce can), pureed in a blender

Place each piece of meat between two sheets of waxed paper and pound until it is about ⅛-inch thick. Season with salt and pepper. Sprinkle the pieces evenly with equal portions of the garlic, cheese, and parsley. Gently roll up the meat, pressing the filling into it, to make a tight roll. Tuck in the ends and secure the rolls with butcher's string. Set aside.

Warm the olive oil in a wide, deep saucepan set over medium heat. When the oil is hot but not smoking, add the onions. Cook until softened but not browned, about 4 minutes. Remove the onions from the pan with a slotted spoon and set aside. Add the beef rolls to the pan and cook until browned on all sides, about 8 minutes. Return the onions to the pan. Add the wine and cook, scraping to loosen any meat that has stuck to the bottom of the pan. When the wine has reduced slightly, about 1 minute, remove the meat rolls from the pan to a plate and set aside.

Add the tomatoes to the saucepan. Season with salt and pepper and simmer to warm through, about 10 minutes. Return the meat rolls to the pan, along with any juices that have accumulated on the plate. The meat should be completely submerged in the sauce. Simmer gently, with the cover of the pan slightly askew, until the meat is tender and the sauce has thickened, about 1½ hours.

VARIATION: ½ cup whole pine nuts may be added to the stuffing.

BRASATO AL BAROLO

Braised Italian-Style Pot Roast

MAKES 4 SERVINGS

GIANNI: In Italy it is possible to find inexpensive Barolo wines that are perfect to cook with. Unfortunately, that is not the case in America. Because you don't want to pour a fifteen-dollar bottle of wine over a four-dollar piece of meat, I recommend cooking with a flavorful inexpensive red wine and reserving the Barolo to serve with dinner. For tender, flavorful meat, it is best to prepare this dish several hours or, even better, a full day ahead of time. Reheat it in the oven before serving with mashed potatoes or polenta.

I begin this recipe by preparing a *sacchetto di spezie,* a little bag of herbs and spices.

FOR THE *SACCHETTO DI SPEZIE:*

One 5-inch sprig fresh thyme
5 fresh parsley stems
2 dried bay leaves or 1 fresh bay leaf
One 5-inch sprig fresh rosemary
2 juniper berries, crushed

FOR THE POT ROAST:

One 2-pound piece shoulder of beef, bottom round, or pot roast
Kosher salt and freshly ground black pepper
All-purpose flour for dusting
5 tablespoons butter
1 cup roughly chopped celery (about 2 stalks)
1¼ cups roughly chopped Spanish onion (1 medium-size onion)
½ cup roughly chopped carrot (1 medium-size carrot)
1 bottle (750 ml) dry red wine
½ cup dried porcini mushrooms, roughly chopped and soaked in 1 cup warm water
1 tablespoon tomato paste
2 cups canned whole or crushed plum tomatoes
Chicken broth or water if needed
2 tablespoons arrowroot or cornstarch
¼ cup dry red or white wine

To make the *sacchetto di spezie,* combine all the ingredients in the center of a piece of cheesecloth that is large enough to hold the herb sprigs, and tie in a bundle with butcher's string. Set aside.

Preheat the oven to 350 degrees F.

Season the beef with salt and pepper, then lightly dust with flour. Melt the butter in a large (6-quart) flameproof casserole set over medium-high heat. When it is foaming, add the beef and brown it on all sides, 5 minutes. Add the celery, onions, carrot, and *sacchetto di spezie.* Cook, stirring occasionally, until the vegetables soften slightly, about 2 minutes. Raise the heat to high and add the bottle of wine. Cook until the wine begins to boil, about 2 more minutes, skimming off any fat that rises to the surface.

Strain the porcini mushrooms through a fine-mesh sieve, reserving the liquid. Rinse the mushrooms under cold running water to remove any grit, and add them to the casserole along with the strained mushroom liquid, tomato paste, and tomatoes. The liquid should just cover the meat. If it does not, add chicken broth or water. Cover the casserole and bake in the oven until the meat is cooked through and tender, about 2 hours. Remove the meat from the casserole to a cutting board, cover with aluminum foil, and set aside.

Strain the broth through a fine-mesh sieve and discard the vegetables and *sacchetto*. Pour the broth back into the casserole and set it over high heat. Bring to a boil and add the arrowroot or cornstarch and the 1/4 cup wine. Cook to reduce and thicken the liquid, about 5 minutes. Carve the meat into 1/4-inch-thick slices. Serve immediately, spooning some of the broth over each portion.

VARIATION: If you have any leftover meat, shred it and stir it into any remaining sauce. Heat through and serve as a delicious pasta sauce over cooked penne.

CASSERUOLA LOMBARDA

Milanese Casserole

MAKES 6 SERVINGS

GIANNI: I ate this meal with my family and friends on cold autumn evenings, lingering over glasses of wine and helping ourselves to generous portions of the stew. Those evenings frequently ended with singing, and the one tune we all knew was the local army song. For generations each Italian army regiment has had its own song, and because all Italian boys are required to serve, everyone learns the words. Our local Alpini troop is stationed near the Dolomite Mountains, so our song is about being cold and sad during the war.

I generally consider most variations of this type of stew to be too heavy. So I have created a recipe that is rich in flavor and won't leave you feeling overly full. Be sure to tightly pack all of the ingredients into a heavy-bottomed casserole so that the broth is absorbed by the meat and vegetables and does not just boil away. Serve this one-dish meal with polenta or a crusty bread to dip into the sauce. It may be prepared a day in advance and reheated before serving.

2 tablespoons olive oil
1 cup roughly chopped onions
¾ cup roughly chopped shallots
⅓ pound slab bacon, cut into ½-inch chunks
½ cup roughly chopped fresh parsley leaves
2 teaspoons sweet paprika
2 bay leaves
1 pound cabbage, trimmed, cored, and roughly chopped
3 medium-size carrots, cut into ½-inch-thick slices
Kosher salt and freshly ground black pepper
6 lean beef short ribs
6 links sweet sausage
3 cups chicken broth
2 cups water or 1 cup water and 1 cup dry white wine
2 Idaho potatoes, peeled, balved, and each half cut into 6 pieces

Warm the olive oil in a flameproof casserole set over medium-high heat. Add the onions and shallots and cook, stirring, until softened, about 8 minutes. Stir in the bacon and continue cooking until it has softened and begun to brown, about 3 minutes. Stir in the parsley, paprika, bay leaves, cabbage, and carrots, and season with salt and pepper.

Season the short ribs with salt and pepper, then add them to the casserole. Add the sausage, pressing down on the meat to tightly compact all the ingredients in the pan. Pour in the broth and water. Cover and bring to a boil. Reduce the heat to a low boil and cook, skimming off any fat that accumulates on top of the stew, until the meat begins to become tender, 1 to 1½ hours. Then add the potatoes and continue cooking until they are soft and the meat is cooked through, about another hour.

VARIATIONS:

- Country-style pork spareribs may be used in place of beef ribs. They will take about half as long to cook through.
- Parsnips or turnips may be cut in the same manner as the potatoes. Add them to the stew with the potatoes or in place of them.

POLPETTE

Meatballs

MAKES 4 SERVINGS

STAN: On occasion my mother would not feel like cooking a large meal, and then we would have one of our favorite dishes: freshly fried *polpette.* These were served with salad and lots of crusty Italian bread with butter. This was the only time that butter ever appeared on the table.

JOAN: These meatballs may be eaten as Stan suggests, or they may be lightly sautéed and added to the recipe for ragù meat sauce (page 126). They are also an important ingredient in *timpáno* (page 172). Dried bread is an essential ingredient in this recipe. I purchase long, thin loaves of unseeded Italian white bread. Set aside leftover bread 2 or 3 days out of wrapper before you plan to prepare these meatballs.

Ten 1-inch-thick slices Italian bread
1 pound ground beef chuck
2 tablespoons chopped fresh parsley leaves
2 cloves garlic, finely chopped
1 large egg
5 tablespoons finely grated pecorino Romano cheese
Kosher salt and freshly ground black pepper
2 tablespoons olive oil

Arrange the bread on a cookie sheet and allow it to dry out, uncovered, about 3 days. Place the dried bread in a bowl and cover with warm water. Set aside until the bread softens, about 5 minutes.

In another bowl, combine the meat, parsley, garlic, egg, cheese, and salt and pepper to taste, using your hands to mix the ingredients. Remove and discard the crust from each slice of bread. Squeeze the water out of the bread, and breaking it into small pieces, add it to the meat. Work the bread into the meat until they are equally combined and the mixture holds together like a soft dough.

Warm the olive oil in a large frying pan set over medium-high heat. Scoop out a heaping tablespoon of the meat mixture. Roll it between the palms of your hands to form a ball about 1½ inches in diameter. (Meatballs that are being prepared for *timpáno* should be very small. Use a ½ teaspoon to scoop out the dough and form it into ½-inch balls.) Cook one meatball until well browned on all sides, about 8 minutes. (A meatball that sticks to the pan is not ready to be turned.) Taste the meatball, and if needed, adjust the seasoning of the remaining mixture by adding more cheese or salt and pepper. Proceed to cook the meatballs in small batches. As each batch is completed, remove it to a warmed serving plate. Serve when all the meatballs are cooked.

continued

VARIATION: Meatballs that will be added to ragù sauce should be slightly undercooked (about 6 minutes), as they will finish cooking in the sauce. Add the meatballs to the ragù during the last half hour of cooking.

Some of the pan juices from cooking the meatballs may be used to flavor the ragù sauce: Discard half of the oil and cooking juices left in the pan. Pour the remaining half of the pan juices into the ragù sauce. Add 2 tablespoons water to the pan and stir with a wooden spoon to remove any meat that may have stuck to the bottom of the pan. Pour this into the ragù sauce as well.

Mercato Centrale in Firenze, 1973. This was our source for excellent produce and meat the year we lived there.

PEPERONI RIPIENI

Stuffed Peppers

MAKES 6 SERVINGS

STAN: In the summer my family would visit my aunt Maria and uncle Emilio at their camp in Roxbury, Vermont. Those long car trips, on pre-interstate roadways, were made more enjoyable by having a picnic with stuffed pepper sandwiches. Less than an hour into the trip, we would be begging my mother for these sandwiches. These stuffed peppers also make a hearty main course, preceded by pasta and followed by a salad.

JOAN: It is important to dry the bread used in this recipe for several days. We have bread with almost every meal. If there is any left over, I place it in a basket and let it dry until it is hard. I then either use it in recipes such as this one or grind it in the food processor to make bread crumbs.

1 long loaf Italian bread (not seeded), cut into 1-inch-thick slices
2 tablespoons olive oil
1 pound ground beef chuck
2 cloves garlic, diced
1 extra-large egg
¼ cup finely grated pecorino Romano cheese
Kosher salt and freshly ground black pepper
2 tablespoons chopped fresh parsley leaves
2 cups Basic Tomato Sauce (page 123 or 124) or your own favorite tomato sauce
3 large green bell peppers, cut in half lengthwise and stems and seeds discarded
¼ cup water

Arrange the bread on a cookie sheet and allow it to dry out, uncovered, for about 3 days.

Preheat the oven to 400 degrees F.

Place the dry bread in a large bowl and cover with warm water. Set aside to soak until the bread softens, about 5 minutes.

Use the olive oil to grease a baking dish that is large enough to hold the pepper halves in one layer.

In a large bowl, combine the meat, garlic, egg, cheese, salt and pepper to taste, and parsley, using your hands to mix the ingredients. Remove and discard the crust from each slice of bread. Squeeze the water out of the bread, and breaking it into small pieces, add it to the meat. Use your hands to work the bread into the meat until they are equally combined and the mixture holds together like a soft, moist dough.

Add ½ cup of the tomato sauce to the meat mixture. Mix well. The original meat mixture will now have doubled in size. Divide the filling equally among the pepper halves, mounding it high, and place each filled pepper in the prepared baking dish. Top each pepper with 1 tablespoon of the tomato sauce. Pour the water and ¼ cup of the tomato sauce around the peppers. Cover with aluminum foil and bake until the peppers soften slightly, about 15 minutes.

Remove the foil and baste the peppers with additional tomato sauce. Continue to bake, uncovered, adding sauce and basting occasionally, until the peppers are soft and the meat has browned, 1½ to 2 hours.

VARIATIONS:

- The peppers may be placed in a baking dish and cooked in a microwave oven for 5 minutes to soften slightly before stuffing. This will shorten the baking time by 20 to 30 minutes.

- Red bell peppers may be used instead of green. However, they will bake more quickly. After the initial 15-minute baking period, uncover and cook until softened, about 1 hour.

- To make a lower-fat version of this dish, substitute ground turkey breast for the ground chuck and 2 egg whites for the whole egg.

- Sometimes I will make additional stuffing and use it to prepare a *polpettone,* or meat loaf. To this basic mixture add enough marinara or ragù sauce to make a very moist mixture. Place in a covered casserole and bake in a preheated oven at 375 degree F for 1 hour. It makes a fine meat dish for dinner, but we like it best cooled and sliced for sandwiches.

ROLLATINI DI CAVOLO RUSTICO

Italian Cabbage Rolls

MAKES 4 SERVINGS

GIANNI: My mother, Maria-Bertilla, had a fundamental household law: No leftover meat of any kind was ever thrown away. She did this to save money but also because she could create a whole new meal out of those leftovers. In place of the ground meat called for in this recipe she would grind together small portions of cooked pork, chicken, and beef to add to the other filling ingredients. My mother served cabbage rolls as a side dish with fish or chicken, or as an appetizer. I even enjoyed them cold for lunch—making for a double leftover meal.

Only the easy-to-roll soft outer leaves of Savoy cabbage are used when preparing this dish. Reserve the remaining cabbage for soup or salad. If Savoy cabbages are not available, other cabbages may be substituted, but they will take longer to blanch and the thick spine of the leaf may need to be trimmed to ease rolling. The cabbage rolls may be cooked up to one day in advance. Refrigerate overnight and reheat before serving.

1 head Savoy cabbage
Four ½-inch-thick slices country bread, crusts removed and discarded, dried overnight or for up to 3 days (½ pound dried bread)
1½ cups milk
½ pound ground beef, veal, or pork (or a mixture of these meats)
1 large egg
2 tablespoons chopped fresh parsley leaves
Kosher salt and freshly ground black pepper
¼ teaspoon dried oregano
2 tablespoons olive oil
¼ cup diced pancetta (about 2 ounces)
2 cups chopped canned plum tomatoes
2 tablespoons extra virgin olive oil

Bring a large pot of salted water to a boil. Select 12 of the largest outside cabbage leaves. Add 6 of the leaves to the boiling water. Allow the water to return to a boil and blanch the leaves until just tender, about 10 minutes. (Green cabbage will take about 15 minutes to blanch.) Drain, pat dry, and set aside. Repeat with the remaining 6 leaves.

Soak the bread in the milk for 10 minutes.

Place the meat in a medium-size mixing bowl. Squeeze the milk out of the bread and knead the bread it into the meat. Add the egg, parsley, salt and pepper to taste, and the oregano. Knead these into the meat to form a moist dough.

Divide the mixture evenly among the blanched cabbage leaves. Fold the long sides of each cabbage leaf toward the center. Roll the soft top portion of the leaf toward the center. Bring the spiny bottom portion of the leaf over the top, and then roll the leaf over so it is seam side down on the work surface.

Warm the olive oil in a large sauté pan set over medium heat. Stir in the pancetta and cook until it begins to color, about 2 minutes. Add the cabbage rolls, seam side down, and season with salt and pepper. Cook until they begin to sizzle, about 3 minutes. Add the tomatoes and bring to a simmer. Reduce the heat to low, cover, and cook slowly until the cabbage has softened and the filling is cooked through, about 45 minutes. Use a slotted spoon to transfer the cabbage rolls to a serving platter. Stir the extra virgin olive oil into the tomatoes and spoon over the rolls. Serve immediately.

VARIATION: Thin slices of Asiago or cheddar cheese may be placed over the rolls during the last few minutes of cooking. Allow to melt slightly. Spoon the tomato sauce onto individual serving plates, and top with one or two cabbage rolls.

COSTOLETTE FARCITE AL PROSCIUTTO E FONTINA

Veal Chops Stuffed with Fontina and Prosciutto

MAKES 4 SERVINGS

GIANNI: My father prepared this dish at his trattoria when people came to celebrate special occasions, such as their children's baptism or first Holy Communion. He liked this recipe for many reasons. The chops could be stuffed, breaded, and refrigerated several hours in advance, leaving him free to attend to his patrons, pouring wine and serving appetizers. The veal cooked quickly on the trattoria's large stove, which meant he didn't have to spend a long time in the kitchen. And, knowing that most people were not likely to prepare this generous, rich dish for themselves at home, he was sure they would leave happy and full.

Thickly sliced pork chops or boneless chicken breast may also be stuffed and cooked this way. Any of these variations may be topped with Joan's recipe for Sautéed Mushrooms (page 270). I recommend serving asparagus, steamed artichokes, spinach, or an arugula salad with sliced tomato as a side dish.

4 veal chops cut from the rack, bone in (about ½ pound each)
4 fresh sage leaves
3½ ounces Fontina cheese, cut into 4 equal pieces
8 very thin slices prosciutto
2 teaspoons extra virgin olive oil
½ cup all-purpose flour
3 large eggs, beaten
About 1½ cups plain dried bread crumbs
3 tablespoons butter
3 tablespoons canola oil
Kosher salt and freshly ground black pepper
1 lemon, quartered

Have the butcher cut each chop in half horizontally, leaving it still joined together by the bone, to form a pocket. Place each chop between two layers of plastic wrap and pound to a ¼-inch thickness. Open the pocket and place a single sage leaf on the bottom portion of each chop. Layer 1 slice of Fontina between 2 slices of prosciutto inside each chop. Drizzle the top slice of prosciutto with ½ teaspoon of the olive oil. Close the pocket by gently pulling the top section of meat slightly over the bottom section.

Dredge the chops in the flour, shaking off any excess. Dip the chops into the beaten eggs and then into the bread crumbs, coating well. Arrange the chops on a baking sheet and press the pocket of each chop firmly closed with the side of a wide knife. Allow the chops to sit for at least 5 minutes before cooking. (Refrigerate if it will be more than 30 minutes before cooking. Bring to room temperature before proceeding with the recipe.)

In a large sauté pan set over medium-high heat, warm the butter and the canola oil together. When the butter is hot and foaming, add the chops. Cook until well browned, about 5 minutes, and then turn. Season with salt and pepper, and reduce the heat to medium. Continue cooking until the other side is well browned, about 7 minutes. Remove the chops from the pan and drain on paper towels before serving each chop with one of the lemon quarters.

VARIATION: Truffle oil may be substituted for the olive oil drizzled inside the chops.

SPEZZATINO DI VITELLO

Veal Stew

MAKES 6 SERVINGS

JOAN: I created this stew to appeal to the different eating habits of my three children: a vegetarian, a meat lover, and one who will eat everything. Like most stews, it is best when cooked a day in advance, then warmed up slowly before serving. Polenta, plain fettuccine, or egg noodles make a good bed for the stew. Double the recipe when you need to feed a large group or if you want to have some on reserve in the freezer.

2½ pounds lean veal stew meat
¼ cup all-purpose flour
⅓ cup olive oil
½ cup sliced onions
1 clove garlic, cut in half
2 cups dry white wine
2 cups Salsa Marinara (page 125) or your own favorite tomato sauce
3 small yellow onions, peeled and left whole, or 3 medium-size yellow onions, quartered
1 teaspoon chopped fresh thyme leaves
2 tablespoons chopped fresh rosemary leaves
3 large fresh sage leaves, torn in half
1 fresh or dried bay leaf
Kosher salt and freshly ground black pepper
4 medium-size all-purpose potatoes, peeled and cut into eighths
4 large carrots, cut into ¾-inch-thick slices
1 cup fresh or frozen peas

Place the veal and flour in a large bowl or sealable plastic bag. Toss to coat the veal lightly with the flour. Toss the meat in a strainer to remove any excess flour. In a deep flameproof casserole, warm the olive oil over medium heat. Cook the veal in the oil, a few pieces at a time, browning on all sides, about 5 minutes per batch. Remove the cooked pieces to a plate and reserve.

When all the veal has been browned and removed from the casserole, reduce the heat to medium-low, and add the sliced onions and the garlic. Cook, stirring frequently, until softened but not browned, about 1 minute. Add 1 cup of the wine and stir, scraping the bottom of the pan clean.

Return the veal to the pan, along with any juices that have accumulated on the plate. Add the remaining 1 cup wine, the marinara sauce, onions, thyme, rosemary, sage, and bay leaf. Season with salt and pepper. The veal should be immersed in liquid; add more wine if necessary. Cover the pan and simmer the stew over low heat, stirring frequently, until the meat is tender, 30 to 45 minutes.

Add the potatoes and carrots, cover, and continue simmering until the vegetables are tender but not mushy, about 50 minutes. Stir the stew frequently, making sure that none of the meat is sticking to the bottom of the pan. Remove the cover and stir in the peas. Simmer until they are tender, 5 to 7 minutes. (The stew may be set aside before adding the peas. Refrigerate overnight. Reheat slowly, stirring frequently, before adding the peas.)

VARIATION: I pound mushrooms, quartered and sautéed in olive oil until browned but still firm, may be added to the stew along with the peas.

Summer 1967, Mom and Pop Tropiano (center) *visiting his sisters and their children in Cittanova, Italy.*

OSSOBUCO CON VERDURINE E FUNGHI

Stewed Veal Shanks with Mushrooms

MAKES 6 SERVINGS

GIANNI: This dish is at the top of my list of favorites. Excellent stews and braised meats require patience—that is why I cook them in the oven, where it is easier to maintain uniform heat. The oven heat allows the meat to simmer very gently, so it holds to the bone and does not fall apart. For a truly rich flavor, I recommend that you prepare this ossobuco a day ahead, refrigerate it overnight, and reheat in the oven the next day.

When shopping for veal shanks, request ones cut from the center. These have more meat and less bone. Ask the butcher to securely tie the meat so it does not fall off the bone. Serve accompanied by *Risotto alla Milanese* (page 184), Risotto with Vegetables and Fine Herbs (page 187), gnocchi (potato or semolina), or mashed potatoes.

6 pieces center-cut veal shank (8 to 10 ounces each, 1 to 1½ inches thick)
3 tablespoons all-purpose flour, plus additional for dredging
Kosher salt and freshly ground black pepper
4 tablespoons canola oil
1 tablespoon butter
½ cup finely diced celery
½ cup finely diced carrots
1 cup finely diced onions
1 cup dry white wine
1 cup dried porcini mushrooms, soaked for at least 15 minutes in 1 cup warm water
1 teaspoon plus 1 tablespoon finely chopped fresh sage leaves
1 teaspoon plus 1 tablespoon finely chopped fresh rosemary leaves
2 cups drained and chopped canned whole plum tomatoes
3 cups chicken broth or water
1 tablespoon finely chopped lemon zest

Preheat the oven to 350 degrees F.

Dust the veal with flour, shaking off any excess. Season with salt and pepper. Warm 2 tablespoons of the oil in a large flameproof casserole or sauté pan set over medium-high heat. Cook the veal, browning it evenly on both sides, about 5 minutes per side. Transfer the meat to a platter and set aside.

Drain off any juices remaining in the pan. Place the pan over medium-high heat and melt the butter in the remaining 2 tablespoons oil. When the butter begins to foam, add the celery, carrots, and onions. Cook, stirring occasionally, until the vegetables have softened but not browned, about 5 minutes.

continued

Return the veal to the pan, along with any juices that have accumulated on the plate. Stir in the 3 tablespoons flour, then add the wine. Remove the porcini mushrooms from the water, reserving the water. Squeeze the mushrooms gently to remove excess moisture, roughly chop them, and add them to the pan. Bring to a boil and cook to sweeten the wine, about 1 minute.

Reduce the heat to a simmer and add 1 teaspoon of the sage, 1 teaspoon of the rosemary, the chopped tomatoes, and the chicken broth. Strain the mushroom water through a fine-mesh sieve or coffee filter and add to the pan. Season with salt and pepper. Slowly return the liquid to a boil, shaking the pan to combine all the ingredients. Transfer to the oven and cook until the meat feels soft when gently probed, about 1½ hours.

Just before serving, combine the remaining tablespoon each sage and rosemary and the lemon zest. Sprinkle this mixture over the individual portions of the ossobuco.

POLPETTONE ALLA ROMANA

Roman-Style Meat Loaf

MAKES 6 TO 8 SERVINGS

GIANNI: The first time I tasted this dish was when a Roman friend prepared it for me. He enjoyed it thickly sliced for dinner or thinly sliced in a sandwich the following day. This meat is also delicious cooked as individual hamburger patties. I like to form the mixture into two small loaves so that the meat holds together well when sliced. One large loaf may require 20 minutes additional baking time. I also prepare this meat loaf using ground pork, adding 1 tablespoon of fennel seeds to the mixture along with the fresh herbs.

¼ pound day-old crustless white bread
1 cup water
1½ pounds ground veal
1 cup ricotta cheese
3 tablespoons finely grated Parmesan cheese
3 large eggs
¼ teaspoon ground nutmeg
2 tablespoons chopped fresh parsley leaves
2 tablespoons chopped fresh sage leaves
2 tablespoons chopped fresh rosemary leaves
Kosher salt and freshly ground black pepper
2 tablespoons butter, melted
2 tablespoons canola oil
1 cup dry white wine
Three 5-inch sprigs fresh rosemary

Preheat the oven to 350 degrees F.

Cut the bread into 1-inch cubes. Place in a bowl and cover with the water. Allow the bread to absorb the water and become very soft, about 5 minutes. Gently squeeze all the water out of the bread. Place the bread in a large bowl (discard the water).

Add the veal to the bread and work them together to form an even mixture. Stir in the ricotta and Parmesan and mix well. Add the eggs and mix well. Add the nutmeg, parsley, sage, rosemary, salt to taste, and generous grindings of pepper. Mix well.

Divide the mixture in half, and shape each half into a loaf measuring approximately 10 inches long by 3 inches wide. Pour the melted butter, canola oil, and wine into a large baking dish. Place the meat loaves in the baking dish, leaving at least an inch between them. Distribute the rosemary sprigs in the dish. Bake until browned and cooked through, about 40 minutes.

Remove the loaves to a warm platter, cover with aluminum foil, and set aside. Strain the liquid left in the baking dish through a fine-mesh sieve into a saucepan. Bring to a boil over medium-high heat and cook to reduce by half, 6 to 8 minutes.

Cut the meat loaf into 1-inch-thick slices and arrange on a platter or dinner plates. Spoon some of the sauce over each portion, and serve immediately.

AGNELLO CON CARCIOFINI

Stewed Lamb with Artichokes

MAKES 4 SERVINGS

GIANNI: In my travels I often have the opportunity to observe other chefs at work. On one occasion I watched an experienced chef from Rome prepare this dish, and I thought it was very strange—especially the process of mixing lemon juice and egg yolks into the stew at the end. However, when I tasted it, I found it was quite delicious and unique. The use of lean meat from the leg of lamb gives this stew a light and subtle flavor. It may be prepared two days in advance up to the point where the lemon juice and eggs are added. Simply reheat and then complete the recipe. Spoon this stew over a wide pasta noodle such as pappardelle. It may also be served preceded by Asparagus Risotto (page 185) and accompanied with sautéed escarole.

10 medium-size to small artichokes, or 9 ounces thawed frozen artichoke hearts, or one 15-ounce can artichoke bottoms, quartered
1 tablespoon plus 1 teaspoon freshly squeezed lemon juice
3 tablespoons olive oil
3 cloves garlic, crushed
2 pounds boneless leg of lamb, trimmed of fat and cut into 1½-inch cubes
½ cup chopped fresh parsley leaves
Leaves from two 5-inch sprigs fresh thyme
¾ cup dry white wine
1½ cups warm chicken broth
2½ teaspoons kosher salt
Freshly ground black pepper
2 large egg yolks

Remove the tough outer leaves of the artichokes. Trim ¼ inch off the tops of the artichokes and discard. Cut the artichokes in half. Remove any of the fine choke from the center and discard. Slice each half lengthwise into ¼-inch-thick slices. Place in a bowl of cold water mixed with 1 tablespoon of the lemon juice. Set aside. (Skip this step if using frozen or canned artichokes.)

Warm the olive oil in a large flameproof casserole set over medium-high heat. Add the garlic and cook until lightly browned, about 2 minutes. Remove and discard the garlic. Adjust the heat to high and add the lamb. Cook until browned on all sides, about 5 minutes. Stir in ¼ cup of the parsley and all of the thyme. Add the wine and allow it to evaporate, about 2 minutes. Remove the artichokes from the water, pat dry, and stir into the stew. Cover and cook to soften slightly, about 3 minutes. Pour in the warm broth and cover. Reduce the heat to medium-low and simmer until the lamb is tender, about 1 hour. Season with the salt and pepper to taste.

In a small bowl, whisk together the egg yolks and remaining 1 teaspoon lemon juice. Remove ¼ cup of the broth from the stew and gradually whisk it into the egg mixture. Gradually add the egg mixture to the stew, stirring constantly. Stir in the remaining ¼ cup parsley, and serve immediately.

VARIATIONS:

- 5 shallots, quartered, may be browned with the meat.
- 1 cup quartered cremini mushroom caps may be browned with the meat.

I'm cooking as a guest chef at the James Beard Foundation.

STUFATINO DI AGNELLO IN BRODETTO CON PATATE E VERDURE

Lamb in Broth with Potatoes and Vegetables

MAKES 4 SERVINGS

GIANNI: Lamb is not a common ingredient in Italian cooking, and so for many families the only time of year they eat lamb is during the Easter holiday. The meat is usually cut into large cubes, seasoned with salt and pepper, slid onto skewers, and cooked on a rotisserie. I prefer to stew lamb, flavoring it with wine and vegetables. I serve each portion with a thick slice of country bread to soak up the broth and complete the meal.

1¼ pounds boneless leg of lamb, trimmed of fat and cut into 1-inch cubes
Kosher salt and freshly ground black pepper
¼ teaspoon ground cumin
2 tablespoons butter
½ cup dry white wine
½ cup chicken broth
1 tablespoon prosciutto, cut into 1- by ¼-inch julienne (about ½ ounce)
1 large all-purpose potato, peeled, halved, and cut into 1- by ¼-inch julienne (about 1 cup)
1 small onion, halved and cut into 1- by ¼-inch julienne (about ½ cup)
1 small celery stalk, cut into 1- by ¼-inch julienne (about ½ cup)
1 small carrot, cut into 1- by ¼-inch julienne (about ½ cup)
1 tablespoon chopped fresh parsley leaves
4 teaspoons freshly squeezed lemon juice
3 tablespoons freshly squeezed orange juice

In a large bowl, toss the lamb with salt and pepper to taste and the cumin. Warm 1 tablespoon of the butter in a flameproof casserole set over medium-high heat. Sear the lamb, a few pieces at a time, removing pieces to a plate as they are evenly browned, about 5 minutes per batch. When all of the lamb has been seared and set aside, pour off any fat that has accumulated in the casserole. Reduce the heat to medium and add the wine to the casserole, stirring while it evaporates to loosen any meat that may have stuck to the bottom of the pan. Pour in the chicken broth. When the broth begins to boil, return the lamb to the pan along with any juices that may have accumulated on the plate. Reduce the heat to medium-low, cover, and simmer to cook the lamb through, about 25 minutes.

Warm the remaining 1 tablespoon butter in a large sauté pan set over medium heat. Add the prosciutto and cook to warm through, about 2 minutes. Add the potato, onion, celery, and carrot strips, and continue cooking until slightly softened, about 5 minutes.

Remove the lamb from the broth and set aside. Strain the broth and return it to the casserole. Return the lamb to the casserole along with any juices that have accumulated on the plate. Stir the vegetables into the lamb. Stir in the parsley, lemon juice, and orange juice, bring to a boil, then remove from the heat. Cover, and allow to rest for 10 minutes before serving.

VARIATIONS:

- Shallots cut in half and *cipolline* (flat Italian onions) left whole may be added to the sauce.
- Peeled turnips, Jerusalem artichokes, or parsnips may also be added to the sauce. Cut all the vegetables into 1-inch-long, ¼-inch-wide strips, using about ½ cup of each vegetable.

ARISTA DI MAIALE ALLA FIORENTINA

Pork Tenderloin with Fennel and Rosemary

MAKES 6 SERVINGS

GIANNI: Fennel is a widely used vegetable in Italy and it is becoming quite popular in the United States. People who are not familiar with fennel often ask me how to cook with it. At the end of this recipe you will find a few other ideas for cooking with fennel. In this recipe it is finely diced and cooked with the pork. The pork absorbs the fennel's sweet, pungent flavor while mellowing its natural licorice zest. Either pork tenderloin or boneless loin of pork may be used when preparing this recipe. Serve it with roasted potatoes and a simply prepared winter green, such as escarole or broccoli di rape.

1 tablespoon chopped fresh rosemary leaves
2 cloves garlic, finely chopped
1 bulb fresh fennel, finely diced
3 tablespoons canola or vegetable oil
2 pork tenderloins (1½ pounds each)
1 sprig fresh rosemary
Kosher salt and freshly ground black pepper
½ cup finely diced carrots
½ cup finely diced celery
½ cup roughly chopped onions
1½ cups chicken broth or water

Preheat the oven to 375 degrees F.

Toss the rosemary in a bowl with the garlic, fennel, and 1 tablespoon of the oil, stirring to make a paste. Spread half the mixture on top of one of the pork tenderloins. Place the second tenderloin on top. Firmly tie the two tenderloins together with butcher's string. With a sharp knife, make several large holes or angled incisions in the tenderloins and stuff the remaining fennel mixture into these incisions. Cut the rosemary sprig into thirds and tuck under the string. Season the tenderloin with salt and pepper on all sides.

Warm the remaining 2 tablespoons oil in a large flameproof casserole set over medium-high heat. Sear the tenderloin until browned on all sides, 6 to 8 minutes. Distribute the carrots, celery, and onions around the meat. Place the casserole in the oven and bake until the meat reaches an internal temperature of 155 degrees F on a meat thermometer, about 30 minutes.

Remove the tenderloin from the casserole to a warm plate, wrap in aluminum foil, and set aside.

Set the casserole over medium-high heat. Stir the chicken broth into the vegetables and bring to a boil. Boil, stirring frequently, to loosen any meat that has stuck to the bottom of the casserole. Allow the sauce to reduce slightly, about 5 minutes. Strain the sauce through a fine-mesh sieve into a bowl. Press firmly on the vegetables with the back of a spoon to extract all of their flavor. Discard the vegetables and reserve the sauce. Remove the butcher's string and thinly slice the pork.

Arrange the pork on a platter or individual plates. Spoon the sauce over the slices of pork, and serve immediately.

NOTE: Here are a few other simple ideas for cooking with fennel:

- The leafy part of the fennel bulb may be used as an herb in place of dill; it is a flavorful addition to marinades for fish or meat.
- To make a simple salad, thinly slice a fennel bulb and toss it with orange sections, thinly sliced red onion, arugula, and a mild vinaigrette.
- Pureed fennel is an excellent accompaniment to fish. Warm 2 tablespoons olive oil in a small sauté pan set over medium-high heat. Add 1 fennel bulb, cut into wedges, 1 shallot, diced, and 1 teaspoon fresh thyme leaves. Cover and cook until tender, about 15 minutes. Puree these ingredients in a blender or processor. Stir in the grated zest of 1 orange and 2 tablespoons extra virgin olive oil. Place a dollop in the center of each diner's plate, and top with a portion of grilled fish. Use a vegetable peeler to shave a few slices of raw fennel over the fish, and garnish with a few fennel leaves.

VARIATION: When using a pork loin, ask the butcher to butterfly the meat. Lay the pork out flat and spread half the fennel mixture on top. Roll the loin and tie securely with butcher's string. Proceed with the recipe as given, and cook until the meat reaches an internal temperature of 155 degrees F, about 1 hour.

ARROSTO DI CONIGLIO RIPIENO

Stuffed Roasted Rabbit

MAKES 6 SERVINGS

GIANNI: Rabbit is eaten in Italy almost as often as chicken. Like many of our neighbors, my family raised rabbits and pigeons with the understanding that they would one day make a fine meal. My brother, Mario, was very fond of the rabbits and treated them like pets. Eventually my father would have to debate with him to determine which of the rabbits would be sacrificed for dinner. This recipe is one way my father would prepare rabbit. By the time we sat down at the table Mario had usually adopted a new rabbit, and he enjoyed the meal as much as the rest of us.

Most American butchers can order rabbit with a few days' notice. Ask the butcher to remove the bones, or using a sharp knife, cut the meat away by following the shape of the bones. (Reserve the bones to make a sauce.) The meat is then pounded into a neat rectangle, stuffed, and roasted. Because rabbit stays very tender, it may be cooked one day ahead of time and reheated before serving. Serve this dish with roasted potatoes or vegetables, or with sautéed vegetables such as broccoli di rape or escarole. Butterflied loin of pork pounded to a thickness of about ¼ inch is also delicious prepared this way. Cook the pork until it reaches an internal temperature of 155 degrees F on a meat thermometer, about 1½ hours.

1 boned rabbit, bones reserved and skin removed
1 tablespoon chopped fresh sage leaves
2 tablespoons chopped fresh parsley leaves
1 tablespoon chopped fresh rosemary leaves
Kosher salt and freshly ground black pepper
1 boneless, skinless chicken breast half, cut lengthwise into 1-inch-wide strips
½ cup pitted prunes
2 tablespoons olive oil
1 carrot, roughly chopped
1 celery stalk, roughly chopped
1 tablespoon all-purpose flour
½ cup dry white wine
1 cup chicken broth

Preheat the oven to 325 degrees F. Generously grease a long sheet of aluminum foil with butter. Set aside.

Place the rabbit between two sheets of waxed paper or plastic wrap. Pound the meat into a large thin rectangle. Transfer the meat to the center of the aluminum foil, with the long end facing you. In a small bowl, mix together the sage, parsley, and rosemary. Sprinkle half the herb mixture on the rabbit. Season with salt and pepper.

Arrange the strips of chicken breast in a single long line down the center of the rabbit. Arrange the prunes on top of the chicken. Sprinkle with the remaining herb mixture. Roll the rabbit into a neat, tight log. Fold the foil tightly around the rabbit, and twist the foil closed at both ends. Place in a roasting pan.

In a large bowl, toss the rabbit bones with the olive oil, carrot, and celery. Distribute this around the rabbit in the roasting pan. Bake until the rabbit is cooked through and reaches an internal temperature of 160 degrees F on a meat thermometer, about 1½ hours. Remove from the oven, transfer the rabbit in foil to a cutting board, and set aside.

Set the roasting pan over high heat (or transfer the contents to a wide saucepan). Stir in the flour, wine, and broth. Bring to a boil and cook, stirring constantly, to slightly thicken the juices in the pan, about 5 minutes. Strain through a fine-mesh sieve and set aside.

Slice the rabbit into 1½-inch-wide portions. Spoon the sauce over the sliced meat, and serve.

VARIATIONS:

- 6 to 8 thin slices prosciutto may be placed on the aluminum foil and wrapped around the rabbit as you roll the stuffed meat.
- Cubes of apples or pears may be substituted for the prunes in the stuffing.

COSCIOTTO DI AGNELLO

Grilled Butterflied Leg of Lamb

MAKES 6 TO 8 SERVINGS

JOAN: In my family there was no squeamishness about butchering chickens or other animals we had raised. We took this in stride and we all helped out. But the year we were planning to get married, Stan offered to help slaughter a lamb. The whole process proved to be more than Stan could handle. He turned white, crawled to the cellar steps, and put his head between his knees to avoid passing out. My mother looked at me and asked, "You're going to marry *him*?" We all laughed at Stan's expense. Needless to say, we don't butcher our own meat today. However, this memory serves to remind me of how much hard work both my parents put into feeding our family.

1 boneless butterflied leg of lamb (about 4 pounds off the bone)
¼ cup olive oil
2 cloves garlic, crushed
2 fresh sage leaves
Two 5-inch sprigs fresh rosemary, cut in half
Two 5-inch sprigs fresh oregano, torn into pieces, or ¼ teaspoon dried oregano
½ cup dry red wine
1 medium-size onion, cut into 1-inch-thick slices
1 tablespoon balsamic vinegar
½ lemon, quartered

Place the lamb in a large glass baking dish or sealable plastic bag. In a medium-size bowl, mix together the olive oil, garlic, sage, rosemary, oregano, wine, onion, and vinegar. Add the lemon sections, squeezing them gently to release some of the juice. Pour this over the lamb, cover, and refrigerate for at least 2 hours, basting the meat occasionally. Allow the meat to return to room temperature before grilling.

Prepare a grill that has a cover. Cook the meat on the grill, covered, basting once or twice with the marinade, until well browned on one side, about 12 minutes. Turn the meat over and baste once. Cover the grill and cook the meat for 12 minutes more for medium to medium-rare, and 15 minutes for medium-well to well-done meat. (Rare lamb registers 160 degrees F on a meat thermometer; well done is 175 degrees F.) (If the fire flares around the meat, remove the cover and spray the fire with water to prevent charring.) Remove from the grill, cover with a sheet of aluminum foil, and allow to rest for 5 to 10 minutes before carving.

NOTE: Marinade that has been in contact with raw meat may be used if the heat of the fire will have time to cook it along with the meat. That is why we do not advise basting again during the last half of grilling time.

Pollame

POULTRY

JOAN: My parents raised chickens, so we ate chicken often. My mother served it roasted, fried, stewed, and in soup. Later in life, my parents purchased a grill and Mom added that cooking technique to her chicken repertoire. Stan and I still eat a lot of chicken, and the recipes in this section represent the dishes I prepare most frequently. When I'm cooking I tend to improvise, depending on the ingredients I have on hand, how many people I'm serving, the time of year, whether the phone rings while I'm in the middle of cooking—anything can alter one of my recipes. The techniques for cooking chicken described in these recipes are specific, but many of the ingredients, such as the herbs and spices, may be changed to suit your own taste.

GIANNI: A very funny story comes to mind when I think about chickens. When we were in Italy, my wife, Laura, and I went to visit my sister Cati and brother-in-law Piero, who, among other things, raises chickens. When we got out of the car, I looked at the chickens and I thought, What is going on? All of the chickens looked as if they had sunglasses on. Piero told me that before he had devised these "sunglasses"—actually a small wire placed across each chicken's beak—the chickens had been pecking at one another, pulling out feathers and hurting one another. With these "sunglasses" on, they could see just fine to eat but couldn't aim to peck. It seemed very logical after Piero's explanation—much more logical than the idea of chickens wearing sunglasses.

STANLEY: Many years ago my sisters and I cooked a surprise meal for our mother's birthday, the main course being duck that was stuffed with sausages and apples. Though we were not experienced cooks, the meal was a success. That experience made me realize how versatile and relatively simple cooking poultry can be. This is especially true with chicken, which we eat in our house at least three times a week. The following recipes are fairly inexpensive, are easy to make, and can help you turn what is a rather ordinary meat into something new and elegant. Start with Gianni's chicken on a brick and then try my mother's *pollo alla cacciatora,* and you'll see what I mean.

COTOLETTE DI POLLO

Chicken Cutlets

MAKES 6 SERVINGS

JOAN: My mother prepared this recipe using veal cutlets. Today I prefer to use chicken cutlets because they are so easy to purchase and are a healthier choice. I serve it accompanied by *Risotto alla Milanese* (page 184) or Rice with Zucchini (page 181), sautéed broccoli di rape, or sautéed escarole. If you have any leftover chicken cutlets, they make a delicious sandwich on slices of country bread.

6 boneless, skinless chicken breast halves
2 large eggs
1 tablespoon water
1 cup plain dried bread crumbs
1 tablespoon freshly grated Parmesan cheese (optional)
Kosher salt
¼ cup olive oil, plus more as needed
1 lemon, cut into 6 wedges

Remove the white tendons from the chicken breasts and discard. Cut off the tender chicken pieces (the fillets) that are not part of the whole breasts and set them aside. Pound each piece of chicken breast between sheets of waxed paper or plastic wrap until it is uniformly ¼ inch thick. Pound the fillet pieces as well.

In a shallow bowl, beat together the eggs and water. In another shallow bowl, toss together the bread crumbs, cheese, and salt to taste. Dip the individual chicken pieces into the egg mixture, letting the excess drip off, and then into the bread crumb mixture. Coat the chicken thoroughly with the bread crumbs. Place the coated pieces of chicken on a cookie sheet and set aside for at least 5 minutes to allow the bread crumbs to dry and adhere.

In a large sauté pan, heat the olive oil over medium-high heat. When the oil is hot but not smoking, add as many pieces of chicken as will fit comfortably in the pan. Cook, turning once, until the breasts are no longer pink in the center but still tender, about 6 minutes per side. (Reduce the heat if the bread crumbs begin to brown too quickly.) Remove to a platter lined with paper towels to drain. Add more oil to the pan as needed to cook the remaining chicken pieces. Serve immediately, garnished with the lemon wedges.

VARIATION: Veal or chicken prepared this way may be used for a Parmigiana casserole. This dish is, I believe, is a purely American creation. Although the ingredients would suggest southern

Italian origins, I've never seen it served in Italy. I'm especially confused by the Parmesan cheese called for in several of the recipes I've seen, since southern Italians mostly use pecorino Romano. This has become a classic dish that is easy to prepare in advance and then bake just before serving. Arrange the cooked cutlets in a casserole, slightly overlapping. Spoon about 2 cups Joan's Basic Tomato Sauce (page 124) over the cutlets. Sprinkle 1 cup grated mozzarella cheese and ¼ cup grated pecorino Romano on top. Bake in a preheated oven at 350 degrees F to warm the cutlets through and melt the cheese, about 20 minutes. Serve with a salad and bread.

The Tropiano family minus young Vincent—back row, from left: *Pop, Mom, me, and Joe.* Front row, from left: *Angie, Gracie, and Natalie (Joe's wife).*

ALETTE DI POLLO AL FORNO

Baked Chicken Wings

MAKES 4 SERVINGS

JOAN: The creation of this dish is a good example of how I typically cook. I had some chicken wings and no recipe. I just began to mix together a little of this and a little of that, relying on ingredients I felt confident using, such as garlic, olive oil, and rosemary—my favorite herb. At the last moment I decided to add some white wine and tomato sauce. (I have since tried this recipe without the sauce and the dish was not as good.) Serve these wings for dinner, preceded by a pasta, such as Ditale with Beans (page 143), or a soup and accompanied by sautéed broccoli di rape or escarole. They are also nice as part of a buffet.

16 chicken wings, rinsed, patted dry, and wing tips removed
3 tablespoons olive oil
Kosher salt and freshly ground black pepper
6 cloves garlic, cut in half
1 small shallot, chopped
1 medium-size onion, quartered and separated into layers
Two 5-inch sprigs fresh rosemary
4 large fresh sage leaves
1 teaspoon dried thyme
1 teaspoon dried oregano
½ cup dry white wine
½ cup Salsa Marinara *or Basic Tomato Sauce (page 125, 123, or 124) or your own favorite tomato sauce*

Preheat the oven to 375 degrees F.

Split the wings into two pieces at the joint. Place the split wings in a roasting or baking dish large enough to hold them in a single layer. Drizzle the olive oil on top and season with salt and pepper. Add the garlic, shallot, onion, rosemary, sage, thyme, and oregano, and toss to coat evenly. Bake, stirring once or twice, until lightly browned, about 15 minutes. Stir in the wine and bake about 5 minutes.

Stir in the tomato sauce and bake, stirring once or twice, until the wings are browned and cooked through, about another 10 minutes. Serve immediately.

POLLO AL ROSMARINO

Chicken with Rosemary

MAKES 4 SERVINGS

JOAN: Our desire to eat foods that are lower in fat and cholesterol prompted me to create this tasty chicken dish. I sauté tender chicken breasts and flavor them with lemon, lime, and rosemary. Serve this with a crisp, dry white wine, a tossed salad, and some warm Italian bread. This healthful meal can be prepared in less than thirty minutes.

4 boneless, skinless chicken breast halves
¼ cup olive oil
2 cloves garlic, thinly sliced
1 cup dry white wine
1 tablespoon chopped fresh rosemary leaves
Kosher salt and freshly ground black pepper
3 tablespoons freshly squeezed lemon juice
2 tablespoons freshly squeezed lime juice
2 tablespoons butter or margarine (optional)

Preheat the oven to 300 degrees F. Place a serving platter in the oven.

Remove the white tendons from the chicken meat and discard. Remove the tender chicken pieces (the fillets) that are not part of the whole breast, and freeze them to bread and cook with chicken cutlets (page 224).

Place each piece of chicken between two sheets of waxed paper or plastic wrap. Lightly pound the breasts until they are uniformly about ¼ inch thick. Set aside.

Warm the olive oil in a large sauté pan set over medium heat. Add the garlic and cook until it is slightly colored, about 2 minutes. Remove the garlic and set aside.

Place the chicken breasts in the pan and brown them, about 3 minutes per side. Remove the cooked chicken to the warmed platter in the oven. Drain off any oil in the sauté pan. Reduce the heat to medium-low and add the wine, stirring and scraping the bottom of the pan. Add the rosemary and return the garlic to the pan. Cook, stirring frequently, to flavor the wine, about 1 minute. Season with salt and pepper. Return the chicken to the pan, along with any juices that have accumulated on the platter. Add the lemon and lime juices and cook to flavor the chicken, turning frequently, about 1 minute. Transfer the chicken back to the warm platter.

Increase the heat to high and add the butter to the pan. Briskly stir the butter to emulsify the sauce. Spoon the sauce over the chicken and serve immediately.

VARIATION: ½ pound any variety of mushroom may be thinly sliced and cooked in 2 tablespoons olive oil before preparing the chicken. Set aside and add to the pan with the butter to warm through before spooning over the chicken.

ROLLATINA DI POLLO CON MOZZARELLA AFFUMICATA, SPINACI, E PROSCIUTTO

Chicken Rolled and Stuffed with Smoked Mozzarella, Spinach, and Prosciutto

MAKES 6 TO 8 SERVINGS

GIANNI: My aunt Angela ran the Scappin family trattoria in Mason Vicentino. She never married and lived with my family. My father did most of the cooking for the trattoria, so during the week it was her responsibility to feed me and my four hungry siblings. She used this practical recipe to make a satisfying meal for all of us out of only one whole chicken breast.

I have created a stuffing that uses smoked mozzarella, although any cheese of a similar tender consistency may be substituted. The breasts may be stuffed, rolled in aluminum foil, and refrigerated for several hours before baking, making this a quick and simple dish to serve.

1 pound spinach, washed well and tough stems removed
8 thin slices prosciutto, cut into short ½-inch-wide strips
¼ pound smoked mozzarella, cut into small dice
Kosher salt and freshly ground black pepper
4 whole boneless, skinless chicken breasts
4 teaspoons olive oil
4 teaspoons mixed chopped fresh herbs, such as parsley, rosemary, and/or sage
3 tablespoons butter
1 tablespoon shallots
1 cup Marsala wine
1 cup dry white wine

Preheat the oven to 400 degrees F.

Place the spinach in a medium-size saucepan over medium-high heat with a small amount of water. Cover and cook to wilt, about 5 minutes. Drain the spinach and squeeze out all of the water. Roughly chop and place in a small bowl. Add the prosciutto and mozzarella, season with salt and pepper, and toss to combine. Set aside.

Trim off any fat on the chicken breasts. Remove the white tendon and discard. Spread one whole breast flat on a sheet of waxed paper or plastic wrap, slightly overlapping the halves of the breast in the center. Cover with another sheet of waxed paper or plastic wrap, and pound the breast to flatten into a circular shape that is about doubled in size.

Spread one quarter of the spinach filling on one half of the breast. Fold the other half on top, sandwich style. Firmly roll the chicken into a sausage shape. Brush the top lightly with 1 teaspoon of the olive oil. Sprinkle 1 teaspoon of the fresh herbs over the chicken. Wrap snugly in a single layer of aluminum foil. Repeat this procedure with the remaining three whole breasts.

Place the wrapped rolls in a baking dish and bake until cooked through, about 30 minutes. Remove from the oven and allow to rest for 5 minutes before unwrapping.

While the chicken is resting, melt 1 tablespoon of the butter in a medium-size sauté pan set over medium-high heat. Add the shallots and cook until softened, about 2 minutes. Increase the heat to high and add the wines. Cook, stirring occasionally, until the liquid is reduced to ½ cup. Whisk the remaining 2 tablespoons butter into the sauce to thicken it slightly. Remove from the heat and set aside.

Slice each cooked breast on the diagonal into 6 to 8 pieces. Arrange several slices in a fan shape on each plate. Spoon some of the sauce on top, and serve immediately.

VARIATIONS: Several different stuffings may be used to prepare this dish:

- In a small sauté pan, warm 1 tablespoon olive oil over medium heat. Add ½ cup each diced artichoke hearts, potatoes, and onions and cook until softened, about 10 minutes. Season with 1 teaspoon chopped fresh mint or parsley leaves. Stuff the breasts with equal portions of this mixture, topping with fresh chopped herbs.
- Crumble ½ cup goat's cheese into a bowl. Toss with ¼ cup diced sun-dried tomatoes, ¼ cup roughly chopped pine nuts, and 2 tablespoons plain dried bread crumbs. Stuff the breasts with equal portions of this mixture, topping with fresh chopped herbs.
- In a small sauté pan, warm 1 tablespoon olive oil over medium heat. Add ½ cup thinly sliced onions, 1 finely diced clove garlic, and ½ cup thinly sliced mushrooms. Cook, stirring, until softened, about 10 minutes. Transfer to a bowl and allow to cool. Add ½ cup finely diced Asiago or Fontina cheese, 1 tablespoon chopped fresh parsley leaves, and 2 tablespoons plain dried bread crumbs. Toss to combine. Stuff the breasts with equal portions of this mixture, topping with fresh chopped herbs.

PETTO DI POLLO SEMPLICE ALLA SALVIA

Simple Chicken Breast with Sage

MAKES 2 SERVINGS

GIANNI: I recommended this recipe to a food journalist who visited my family's trattoria. He asked me why sautéed chicken tends to be dry and bland. After briefly explaining this recipe, I tucked a few sage leaves into his pocket and wished him luck. In his review of our restaurant he mentioned that it was the easiest and tastiest chicken breast he had ever prepared. The secret to its success is to control the heat so that the chicken breast does not brown too quickly and the meat remains tender and moist. I serve this dish with a tossed green salad, sautéed broccoli di rape, roasted vegetables, or a simple carrot salad.

2 boneless, skinless chicken breast halves
Kosher salt and freshly ground black pepper
1 tablespoon butter, cut into thirds
2 teaspoons canola or olive oil
4 fresh sage leaves
¼ cup dry white wine

Remove the white tendons from the chicken meat and discard. The chicken breasts should be evenly thick, about 1 inch. If necessary, place each breast between two sheets of waxed paper or plastic wrap and pound slightly to achieve an even thickness.

Season the chicken breasts on both sides with salt and pepper. In a large skillet set over medium-low heat, warm two thirds of the butter with the oil. Add the sage to the pan. When the butter begins to foam, add the chicken breasts, smooth side down.

Cook slowly, lightly browning the breasts, about 6 minutes. Turn the breasts and continue cooking to lightly brown the other side, about 6 minutes. Add the wine and the remaining butter to the pan. Increase the heat to medium-high and reduce the liquid until slightly thickened, about 1 minute. Transfer the chicken to a plate, pour the sauce over the top, and serve immediately.

VARIATIONS: One of the following ingredients may be added to the sauce along with the wine:

- 2 tablespoons freshly squeezed lemon juice
- 3 tablespoons freshly squeezed orange juice
- 2 tablespoons Marsala wine

SPEZZATO DI POLLO "SCAPPINELLO"

Chicken with Sausage and Peppers

MAKES 8 TO 10 SERVINGS

GIANNI: When my father-in-law, Philip, was visiting us in my hometown of Mason Vicentino, he greatly enjoyed the northern Italian cooking style. However, he still longed for the garlic and spices of his Sicilian heritage. So I created this simple, hearty dish for him. I recommend serving it with a good Prosecco, a sparkling white wine from northern Italy.

I like to serve a soup, such as minestrone, or a traditional *antipasti* platter of cheeses, olives, and salami before this meal. Transfer the roasted meats and vegetables to a large serving platter, place in the center of the table along with a loaf of country bread, and allow everyone to serve themselves. The chicken, sausages, onions, and peppers may be prepared several hours in advance. Toss with the potatoes and herbs just before baking.

½ cup canola or peanut oil
One 4-pound free-range chicken, cut into 16 serving pieces (reserve the back and gizzards for broth)
Kosher salt and freshly ground black pepper
1 pound sweet or hot sausage, cut into ½-inch-thick slices
2 medium-size onions, each cut into 6 wedges
1 large green bell pepper, seeded and cut into 8 to 10 pieces
10 cloves garlic, cut in half
3 large Idaho or all-purpose potatoes, peeled, quartered lengthwise, and cut into ½-inch dice
Six 5-inch sprigs fresh rosemary
8 fresh sage leaves
1 teaspoon red pepper flakes or ½ fresh jalapeño pepper, seeded and diced

Preheat the oven to 450 degrees F.

Heat the oil in a large skillet set over medium-high heat. Add the chicken, skin side down, in a single layer (cook the chicken in batches if necessary). Season with salt and pepper and brown well on one side, about 5 minutes. Turn and brown lightly on the other side, about 3 minutes. Transfer to a roasting pan that will hold all of the ingredients in a single layer.

Drain off all but 1 tablespoon of the fat in the skillet. Add the sausages, onions, bell pepper, and garlic to the skillet. Cook, stirring frequently, until the sausage is lightly browned, about 3 minutes. Transfer to the roasting pan. Stir the potatoes, rosemary, sage, and red pepper flakes into the roasting pan. Toss well and bake, stirring occasionally, until the chicken is cooked through and the potatoes are browned, about 35 minutes. Remove from the oven and serve immediately.

POLLO ALLA CACCIATORA

Chicken Cacciatore

MAKES 4 SERVINGS

JOAN: My family raised chickens, keeping the young chicks under heat lamps in the basement until they were big enough to be moved to the chicken coop behind the garage. We gathered the eggs for baking and for frittatas and used the chickens to prepare dishes such as this one.

STAN: This recipe from Joan's family is very similar to my family's version. The only difference is that we didn't add tomatoes or marinara sauce.

¼ cup olive oil
2 red or green bell peppers, seeded and cut into 1-inch-wide strips
½ pound mushrooms, cut into ¼-inch-thick slices
One 3-pound free-range chicken, cut into serving-size pieces
Kosher salt and freshly ground black pepper
½ cup dry white wine
2 cloves garlic, roughly chopped
2½ cups roughly chopped onions (about 2 medium-size onions)
1 cup canned whole plum tomatoes, Salsa Marinara *(page 125), or your own favorite tomato sauce*

Warm the olive oil in a large sauté pan set over medium-high heat. Stir in the peppers and cook, stirring, until slightly softened, about 10 minutes. Remove from the pan and set aside.

Stir the mushrooms into the pan and cook, stirring, until slightly softened, about 8 minutes. Remove from the pan and set aside.

Season the chicken with salt and pepper. Add to the pan and brown lightly on both sides, about 15 minutes in all. Remove the chicken from the pan to a platter and set aside. Pour the wine into the pan and stir to incorporate any cooking juices. Add the garlic and onions and cook until the onions are slightly softened, about 3 minutes. Stir in the tomatoes, crushing them with your hand or the back of a slotted spoon as you add them to the pan. Return the chicken to the pan, along with any juices that have accumulated on the plate. Bring to a boil, then reduce the heat to a simmer. Cover and cook, stirring occasionally, until the chicken is cooked through, about 30 minutes.

Stir the peppers and mushrooms into the chicken. Return to a simmer, cover, and cook to blend in the flavor of these ingredients, about 10 minutes. The stew may be set aside at this point for several hours before reheating and serving with bread to dip into the sauce.

VARIATION: Rabbit cut into serving portions may be substituted for the chicken. Omit the peppers. Quarter rather than slice the mushrooms. To the basic recipe add 2 all-purpose potatoes, peeled, halved, and each half quartered. Stir these into the stew at the same time the rabbit is returned to the pot. Stir 6 Kalamata olives (optional) into the stew along with the mushrooms during the last 10 minutes of cooking.

POLLO AL MATTONE CON LIMONE E ROSMARINO

Chicken on a Brick with Lemon and Rosemary

MAKES 4 SERVINGS

GIANNI: My uncle Bortolo shared this simple recipe with me. He was a popular member of our family, loved for his good humor and for his poultry farm in Piovene, Italy. With every chicken he made a gift of a secret mixture of herbs he grew. This was the ingredient, he claimed, that made his chickens taste so good.

In Italy it is customary for kitchens to include an indoor grill, where poultry and meat are prepared. To cook a whole chicken easily, it is butterflied and held down on the grill by a brick or a heavy pot. In this way the chicken cooks quickly and the meat stays tender and juicy. To butterfly a chicken, follow the simple directions provided here—or ask the butcher to butterfly it for you.

To accompany the chicken, I recommend serving roasted potatoes or roasted vegetables and sautéed broccoli di rape or escarole.

One 3-pound free-range chicken, washed and patted dry, giblets discarded
1 tablespoon very thinly sliced lemon zest
1 cup white wine
3 tablespoons olive oil
1 tablespoon red wine vinegar
Kosher salt and freshly ground black pepper
1 tablespoon chopped fresh sage leaves
2 tablespoons chopped fresh rosemary leaves
1 clove garlic, finely chopped
¼ teaspoon red pepper flakes

To butterfly the chicken, trim the wings at the second joint (reserve for making stock). Place the chicken, breast side down, on a cutting board. Use a sharp knife or poultry shears to cut along either side of the backbone. Remove the bone and reserve it for making stock.

With scissors or kitchen shears, cut away and discard any small, sharp protruding bones. Use both hands to press down, breaking the ribs and flattening the chicken. Turn the chicken skin side up. Make a small incision just below the breast near the leg, where the meat thins out. Insert the bone end of the drumstick into the incision. Make a small incision in the thickest part of each chicken leg.

Place the chicken between two pieces of plastic wrap. Pound until the chicken is uniformly ½ inch thick. The chicken is now ready to cook.

In a large casserole or baking dish, whisk together the lemon zest, wine, olive oil, and vinegar. Add the chicken, skin side down. Season with salt and pepper. Sprinkle with the sage, rosemary, garlic, and red pepper flakes. Turn the chicken over and season with salt and pepper. Turn the chicken several times in the casserole to coat it evenly with the marinade. Cover and marinate in the refrigerator for at least 1 hour or for up to 24 hours. (Note: If you are going to marinate the chicken overnight, do not add any salt until just before cooking. The salt will cure the chicken and make the meat tough.)

Prepare a charcoal or gas grill. Wrap a brick or heavy rock in aluminum foil and set aside.

Remove the chicken from the marinade, reserving the marinade. Place the chicken, skin side down, on the grill. Sear the skin for about 5 minutes, and then rotate the chicken on the grill to make cross-hatched grill marks. Continue searing for another 5 minutes.

Turn the chicken over and baste with some of the reserved marinade. Place the brick on top of the chicken. Cover the grill and cook the chicken, basting from time to time with the marinade, until golden brown, about 30 minutes.

Remove from the heat, cover with aluminum foil, and allow to rest for 5 minutes before serving.

NOTE: Do not baste with the marinade during the last 5 minutes of cooking. Because it was in contact with the raw chicken, any unused marinade should be discarded and not served.

VARIATIONS:

- This chicken is equally delicious baked in a preheated oven at 375 degrees F. Heat 2 tablespoons olive oil in a wide cast-iron pan. Remove the marinade from the chicken and reserve. Sear the chicken, skin side down, placing a heavy pan or aluminum-foil-covered brick on top to hold it firmly in the pan. Cook until golden brown, about 7 minutes. Turn the chicken over. Pour the marinade into the pan. Place the brick on top and bake in the oven, uncovered, basting occasionally during the first 35 minutes of cooking time. Bake until the chicken is golden brown and cooked through, a total of about 45 minutes.
- Individual Cornish game hens may be prepared in this same way. Bake or grill for about 20 minutes.

ANITRA ARROSTA CON FICHI FRESCHI

Roast Duck with Fresh Figs

MAKES 4 SERVINGS

GIANNI: The choice of figs and port in this recipe was a happy accident. My mother has a good friend who always brings us seasonal fruit that she has grown on her land. Figs were in abundance when I created this dish, and so the sauce was born.

To balance the sweetness of the figs, I recommend serving a mixed salad of bitter greens, such as arugula, topped with thin slices of fennel bulb and tossed with a simple vinaigrette.

One 4-pound duck
Two 5-inch sprigs fresh rosemary
6 fresh sage leaves
4 cloves garlic, crushed
½ medium-size onion, peeled
2 tablespoons olive oil
Kosher salt and freshly ground black pepper
½ cup coarsely chopped onions
½ cup coarsely chopped carrots
½ cup coarsely chopped celery
3 cloves garlic, cut in half
One 5-inch sprig fresh thyme
⅓ cup honey
1 tablespoon butter
6 large fresh figs, quartered
1 cup port

Preheat the oven to 400 degrees F.

Wash the duck inside and out, reserving the giblets. Pat dry. If there is a long flap of neck skin, cut it off and discard it. Cut the wing tips at the joints and place in a large roasting pan along with the giblets. Set aside. Fill the duck cavity with 1 of the rosemary sprigs, the sage, and the crushed garlic. Add the onion half, positioning it so that it holds the herbs inside the duck.

Warm the olive oil in a large sauté pan set over medium-high heat. Add the duck and sear it, browning it evenly on all sides, 6 to 8 minutes. Remove from the pan and season all over with salt and pepper. Place the duck, breast side down, in the roasting pan. Roast, turning once, to render the fat, about 30 minutes.

Add the chopped onions, carrots, celery, and halved garlic to the roasting pan, distributing them evenly around the duck. Cook to soften the vegetables, about 15 minutes. Add the remaining 1 rosemary sprig and the thyme sprig. Continue cooking to begin to brown the vegetables, about 15 minutes.

Reduce the oven heat to 350 degrees F. Brush one third of the honey over the duck. Continue roasting until the duck is golden brown and cooked through, about 30 minutes. During this time, brush the duck twice with additional honey and stir the vegetables.

Remove the duck from the oven. Place it on a cutting board and cover with aluminum foil. Set aside.

Remove the giblets and wing tips from the vegetables and discard. Discard the sprigs of herbs. Drain off the fat, reserving about ½ cup of the cooking juices. Place the reserved cooking juices and the vegetables in a blender, puree until smooth, and set aside.

Melt the butter in a sauté pan set over medium-high heat. Stir in the figs and cook until softened and lightly browned, about 5 minutes. Pour in the port. Allow to simmer until reduced by half, about 8 minutes. Stir in the pureed vegetables and simmer gently to warm through, about 2 minutes. Cut the duck into portions and serve, topping each portion with some of the sauce.

VARIATIONS:

- Plums, quartered and pitted, may be substituted for the figs and cooked in the same way.
- 4 Granny Smith apples or 4 firm, ripe pears may be substituted for the figs. Peel, core, and coarsely chop 2 of the apples or pears. Cook these with the vegetables around the duck. Peel and core the other 2 apples or pears. Cut into ½-inch-thick slices and cook in the butter until softened and lightly browned before adding the port and pureed vegetables.

POLLO ARROSTO

Roasted Chicken with Vegetables

MAKES 4 SERVINGS

JOAN: Every fall my father made wine. There was no science to his method, and whatever didn't work one year would be changed the next. If the wine wasn't drinkable, we had lots of vinegar. Stan claims that the year my father made his best batch of wine was the year we became engaged. On Sundays my mother often liked to serve this one-dish meal, accompanied by a glass of homemade wine. To her basic recipe I have added rosemary. Serve it with a crisp salad, Italian bread, and in place of my father's wine, a glass of Pinot Grigio or Chianti.

One 3-pound free-range chicken, giblets removed
Kosher salt and freshly ground black pepper
1 cup roughly chopped onions (about 1 medium-size onion)
Four 5-inch sprigs fresh rosemary
Four 5-inch sprigs fresh thyme
⅓ cup plus 1 tablespoon olive oil
2 large carrots, cut into 2-inch pieces
3 medium-size red or Yukon Gold potatoes, peeled and quartered
3 cloves garlic, peeled
½ cup dry white wine

Preheat the oven to 350 degrees F.

Rinse the chicken and pat it dry. Salt and pepper the inside of the cavity, and fill it with half the chopped onions, 2 sprigs of the rosemary, and 2 sprigs of the thyme. Truss the chicken and rub it all over with 1 tablespoon of the olive oil. Place in a roasting pan or large baking dish.

In a bowl, toss together the remaining 2 sprigs each rosemary and thyme, the remaining onions, and the carrots, potatoes, garlic, and ⅓ cup olive oil. Season with salt and pepper. Surround the chicken with the vegetables. Pour the wine over the vegetables and bake, stirring the vegetables occasionally, until the chicken juices run clear and the vegetables are roasted, about 1¼ hours.

Remove the chicken from the oven and transfer it to a cutting board. Allow to rest for 5 minutes before carving and arranging on a platter. Remove the vegetables from the roasting pan with a slotted spoon and arrange around the chicken. Serve immediately, with the pan juices.

Pesce

FISH AND SHELLFISH

JOAN: The Hudson River flows right by my hometown of Verplanck, New York. When I was growing up, it was fairly unpolluted and local residents caught a wide variety of fish from the nearby docks or from small boats. The catch of the day was sold door-to-door. My mother frequently purchased whole fish this way, cleaning and gutting them herself before baking them. She would slice certain varieties of fish into fillets to flour and pan-fry.

Fishing was a part of our lives, along with crabbing. My brothers, sisters, and our friends would go crabbing, using homemade box nets. We would feast on them under Pop's grape arbor, cracking them open on newspapers spread out on a picnic table. We still get together, along with a dear friend, Josey, to go crabbing on Cape Cod. Stan and I are both very fond of fish and eat it quite often—usually grilled, baked, or broiled.

GIANNI: My favorite family fish story is one my father told us as children as a kind of morality tale. My father grew up in a very poor family and fish was considered a luxury. On rare occasions his father would bring home a whole small salted fish called *renga,* an oily, strongly flavored herring that has been salted and soaked in brine. It was hung above the dining table, and when a circle of hot polenta or foccacia was placed underneath, steam would rise, causing the fish to release its salty oil, which would drip down onto the polenta or foccacia. When the family gathered for dinner, the children were allowed to break off pieces of polenta or bread and touch them to the fish to absorb some of its flavor. But only the father, who needed to be strong for work, was allowed to eat the fish meat. Today I know of only one shop that that still sells *renga* prepared this way. It is located near an old bridge in Bassano del Grappa and has been selling all types of fish from that spot for over 250 years.

STANLEY: In the 1940s journalist Joseph Mitchell wrote a story that appeared in *The New Yorker* about a man who called himself a seafoodatarian. He was lean and healthy and looked much younger than his ninety-some years. His strictly fish diet seemed unusual at that time but these days we all know the benefits of eating fish. Here you will discover how to prepare the *frutti di mare* in healthy, simple, and extraordinary ways, all of which are unforgettable. Two of my favorites are Gianni's baked whole fish and my mother's bluefish. When you make them, you will see why.

PESCE AL FORNO INTERO

Baked Whole Fish

MAKES 4 SERVINGS

GIANNI: This was one of the most popular dishes I prepared when I was working in various New York City restaurants. I baked whole red snapper, sea bass, striped bass, pompano, and salmon, and on some evenings we served as many as forty fish. It was not a complicated dish to prepare, but it put the waiters "in the weeds," meaning it overwhelmed them with work. Serving this dish required them to perform in front of the customers, boning and plating the fish at the table. This took more time than just bringing a dish from the kitchen, and the waiters worried that their other customers were being neglected. So there was a lot of rushing around on the nights this dish was on the menu.

One 3-pound fish, gutted and scaled (head and tail left on)
Kosher salt and freshly ground black pepper
4 cloves garlic, crushed
Five 5-inch sprigs fresh rosemary
One 5-inch sprig fresh thyme
5 fresh parsley stems
2 tablespoons chopped fresh fennel leaves
½ lemon, cut into wedges
4 celery stalks
4 tablespoons extra virgin olive oil
1 cup dry white wine
¼ cup water
2 tablespoons freshly squeezed lemon juice

Preheat the oven broiler.

Season the cavity of the fish with salt and pepper. Tuck the garlic, rosemary, thyme, parsley, fennel, and lemon wedges into the cavity of the fish. Place the celery stalks on the bottom of a roasting pan large enough to hold the fish, and lay the fish on top. Brush 2 tablespoons of the olive oil over the fish. Broil the fish about 3 inches below the heat source until the skin colors slightly, about 3 minutes. Remove from the oven and reduce the oven temperature to 375 degrees F. Roast the fish until the flesh is firm and flakes away when a small knife is inserted near the spine, about 35 minutes. Remove from the oven. Transfer the fish to a warm serving platter, cover with aluminum foil, and set aside.

Remove the celery from the pan and discard it. Place the pan over medium heat and add the wine, water, and lemon juice. Whisk in the remaining 2 tablespoons olive oil and simmer to thicken slightly, about 1 minute. Pour the sauce over the fish and serve immediately.

VARIATION: Carrots may be used instead of celery under the fish.

PESCE AL SALE AROMATIZZATO

Baked Whole Fish in an Aromatic Salt Crust

MAKES 4 TO 6 SERVINGS

GIANNI: If you want to impress your guests, this is the dish to prepare. It's perfect for large parties, makes an unforgettable centerpiece for a buffet, and is always tender and moist. I would use red snapper, striped bass, or sea bass. Garnish it with lemon slices, and sprinkle with olive oil or drizzle some Balsamic Herb Oil (page 324) over each portion. Simple vegetables, such as roasted potatoes and sautéed spinach, make good side dishes.

5 pounds sea or kosher salt
2 large egg whites
2 cups water
One 4-pound fish, gutted and scaled, fins removed (head and tail left on)
Kosher salt and freshly ground black pepper
4 tablespoons chopped fresh fennel leaves
1 lemon, cut into 6 wedges
Eight 5-inch sprigs fresh rosemary
2 bay leaves
5 fresh parsley stems
4 cloves garlic, crushed
1 tablespoon finely chopped fresh sage leaves
1 lemon, thinly sliced

Preheat the oven to 400 degrees F.

In a large bowl, combine the salt, egg whites, and water. The salt should be moist but not wet. Set aside.

Line a large roasting or baking pan with two layers of aluminum foil. Fold up the edges of the foil to make a boat shape. Spread one quarter of the salt mixture on top of the foil. Place the whole fish on top of the salt. Season the cavity of the fish with salt and pepper. Place 2 tablespoons of the fennel leaves, the lemon wedges, 4 of the rosemary sprigs, and the bay leaves, parsley stems, and crushed garlic in the cavity. Place the remaining 4 rosemary sprigs, the chopped sage, and the remaining 2 tablespoons fennel leaves on top of the fish. Arrange the thinly sliced lemon down the center of the fish.

Cover the fish with the remaining salt mixture, patting it into place to completely enclose the fish. (If the head and tail protrude from the baking dish, wrap them in aluminum foil.) Bake until the fish reaches an internal temperature of 145 degrees F (use an instant-read thermometer to check this), about 45 minutes. Remove from the oven and set aside to rest for 20 minutes. When ready to serve, crack the salt shell with a hammer. (If you want to impress your family and friends, do this at the table.) Lift the solid salt away from the fish. Discard the lemon and herbs and gently separate the skin of the fish from the meat. Transfer portions of the fish to each dinner plate, and serve immediately.

FILETTI DI PESCE IN GUAZZETTO DI POMODORO E BASILICO CON CROSTINI

Fillets of Fish in a Basil Tomato Sauce with Crostini

MAKES 4 SERVINGS

GIANNI: My mother, Maria-Bertilla, never traveled more than one kilometer from our home in Mason Vicentino to purchase food. Every Friday she relied on the arrival of a fishmonger who drove his small truck to the village from Chioggia, a town near Venice that is famous for its fish. My mother would select the freshest whitefish—fish similar to halibut, grouper, snapper, and sea bass—and slice it into fillets. She would sauté fresh herbs, tomatoes, potatoes, and onions in a casserole, and then lay the fillets on top. When the family was gathered for dinner, she would bake the fish in the short time it took to set the table and open some wine. The simple preparation of this dish makes an elegant meal that is perfect for family and company alike.

5 tablespoons olive oil
1 small onion or 2 shallots, thinly sliced
5 fresh or canned whole plum tomatoes, peeled and diced
8 large fresh basil leaves, chopped
½ cup dry white wine
3 tablespoons water
2 cloves garlic, thinly sliced
Kosher salt and freshly ground black pepper
4 fish fillets about 1 inch thick (7 ounces each)
4 large red potatoes, left unpeeled
4 to 8 slices day-old country-style bread
1 clove garlic, peeled and cut in half
1 tablespoon chopped fresh parsley leaves

Preheat the oven to 375 degrees F.

In a large ovenproof sauté pan, heat 3 tablespoons of the olive oil over medium-low heat. Add the onion or shallots and cook, stirring, until softened and translucent, about 6 minutes. Add the tomatoes, basil, wine, water, and the 2 sliced garlic cloves. Season with salt and pepper and stir to combine. Add the fish, and spoon some of the tomato mixture on top. Cover and place in the oven. Bake for 10 to 15 minutes for thin fillets (snapper or sea bass) and 20 to 25 minutes for thicker fillets (halibut or cod). The fish is done when it is firm and flakes away when tested with a fork.

Meanwhile, bring a large saucepan filled with salted water to a boil. Add the potatoes and cook until tender when pierced with a fork, 15 to 20 minutes. Cut each potato into ½-inch-thick slices. Set aside and keep warm.

During the last 5 minutes of cooking time for the fish, toast the bread slices until lightly browned. Rub each slice with the garlic clove, then brush each slice with some of the remaining 2 tablespoons olive oil.

In the center of four deep plates or shallow soup bowls, arrange equal portions of the sliced potatoes. Top each portion with a fish fillet, and spoon some of the onion-and-tomato sauce over the fish. Garnish with the parsley and serve immediately with the toasted bread.

VARIATIONS:

- 1 teaspoon capers, rinsed and patted dry, and a dozen pitted Niçoise or Calabrese olives may be added to the sauce as a garnish with the parsley.
- Polenta makes an excellent side dish in place of the potatoes.

PESCE AZZURRO ALLA GRIGLIA

Broiled Bluefish

MAKES 6 SERVINGS

STAN: As a child I was frightened of fish bones and stayed away from eating fish. But this preparation always appealed to me, and I recall one or two of our children learning to eat fish by sampling this dish. Part of what makes this fish dish enticing is the topping—it is outstanding.

STANLEY: Like most kids, I found it exhausting to eat around the bones in fish. However, this recipe for bluefish was so tasty it was impossible to resist.

JOAN: In this recipe the bluefish is butterflied—meaning it is left whole, sliced in half lengthwise, and opened up flat on the baking or broiler pan. This way the fish cooks quickly and does not require turning to brown evenly. I serve a pasta, such as *Marinara con Funghi* (page 129) or *Spaghetti con Pomodoro e Tonno* (page 153), before the bluefish. Sautéed mushrooms and a crisp salad make excellent side dishes for this main course.

One 3-pound bluefish, cleaned, head and tail removed, and butterflied
2 tablespoons freshly squeezed lemon juice
½ cup plain dried bread crumbs
3 cloves garlic, finely chopped
2 tablespoons finely chopped fresh parsley leaves
½ cup olive oil
1 lemon, cut into ¼-inch-thick slices
Lemon wedges for garnish (optional)

Preheat the oven to 350 degrees F.

Line a broiling pan with aluminum foil. Place the fish on the foil and sprinkle with the lemon juice. In a small bowl, mix together the bread crumbs, garlic, and parsley. Gradually add the olive oil, stirring with a fork, until the ingredients stick together. Evenly sprinkle the bread crumb mixture over the fish. Arrange the lemon slices in a slightly overlapping line down the middle of the bluefish, on top of the bread crumb mixture. Bake until the fish flakes away from the bone, about 30 minutes.

Remove from the oven. Set the oven on broil and return the fish to the oven. Broil until the bread crumbs are lightly toasted, about 4 minutes. Remove from the oven and serve immediately, garnished with lemon wedges if you like.

VARIATION: Sea trout or sea bass is also delicious prepared this way.

PESCE SPADA ALLA GRIGLIA

Grilled Swordfish

MAKES 4 SERVINGS

JOAN: I think of fish as a summertime meal. Stan and I enjoy preparing this swordfish dish on our gas grill. It may also be cooked on a charcoal barbecue, or baked and then finished under the broiler. Serve it with grilled vegetables and a tomato salad.

¼ cup olive oil
6 tablespoons freshly squeezed lemon juice (from about 2 lemons)
Two 3¼-inch-thick swordfish steaks (about 2 pounds in all)
1 lemon, cut into quarters

Stir the olive oil and 3 tablespoons of the lemon juice together in a glass baking dish. Add the swordfish and marinate for 10 minutes, turning the steaks over once. Place the fish on a lightly oiled cooking rack, or oil the rack of the grill. Grill the fish on one side to sear and warm through, about 5 minutes. Turn, and drizzle the remaining 3 tablespoons lemon juice on the swordfish. Grill until the fish is cooked through and easily breaks into sections, about 5 minutes more. Serve immediately, garnished with the lemon quarters.

PESCE SPADA IN AGRODOLCE FACILE

Sweet-and-Sour Swordfish

MAKES 6 SERVINGS

GIANNI: Though I hate to admit it to Joan, this recipe is based on southern Italian cooking. The type of capers makes a big difference in the flavor. I prefer salt-packed capers, rinsing them several times in cold water before adding them to the pan. They have a sweet taste and will not overwhelm the sauce. I look for capers grown on the island of Pantelleria, which is in the Mediterranean southwest of Sicily and is famous for producing the highest-quality capers. Capers packed in brine may also be used; drain and rinse them very well before adding to the sauce.

Six 1-inch-thick swordfish steaks (about 6 ounces each)
Kosher salt and freshly ground black pepper
½ cup plus ½ teaspoon all-purpose flour
¼ cup vegetable oil
2 teaspoons olive oil
1 cup dry white wine
½ cup balsamic vinegar
3 tablespoons salted capers, well rinsed, drained, and patted dry
1 tablespoon chopped fresh parsley leaves

Slice off and discard any dark skin along the edges of the swordfish steaks. Pat the steaks dry with paper towels, and season with salt and pepper. Dredge lightly in the ½ cup flour, shaking off any excess.

Heat the vegetable oil in a large nonstick pan over medium-high heat. When the oil is hot but not smoking, add the fish. Cook until browned, about 5 minutes, and then turn. Continue to cook until the fish is firm and browned, about another 5 minutes. Transfer the fish to a warm platter and set aside.

Discard any oil left in the pan and wipe it clean. Add the olive oil and warm over medium-high heat. Add the remaining ½ teaspoon flour and stir, allowing the flour to brown. Add the wine and vinegar and bring to a boil. Continue cooking, shaking the pan and stirring occasionally, until the sauce thickens into a light syrup, about 6 minutes. Stir in the capers and parsley. Remove from the heat. Arrange each swordfish steak on a plate, and spoon some sauce over each portion. Serve immediately.

SALMONE ALLA GRIGLIA

Grilled Salmon

MAKES 6 SERVINGS

JOAN: We were taught this simple recipe by our nephew Jeff Ratte and his wife, Sarah, who live in Seattle. While visiting them, we took a trip to that city's famous Pike Place Market, where the fishmongers shout orders at each other and throw large whole fish from man to man with perfect accuracy.

At home we usually prepare this in the summer on our gas grill. I ask Marcel or Sal, my local fish purveyors, to butterfly the salmon. They always do a perfect job, slicing the salmon in half lengthwise so it can be opened up flat but stays in one piece. It may also be baked in the oven and finished under the broiler. I serve pesto or *Spaghetti alla Crudaiola* (Spaghetti with Fresh Tomatoes, page 135) before the salmon. Grilled vegetables make a nice side dish.

One 3-pound salmon, cleaned, head and tail removed, and butterflied
¼ cup olive oil
2 tablespoons freshly squeezed lime juice (from about 1 lime)

Place the butterflied salmon on a large sheet of aluminum foil. Brush the salmon with the olive oil and drizzle with the lime juice. Place the fish, still on the foil, on the grill. Close the grill's cover and cook until the fish is firm and pale pink, about 25 minutes.

VARIATION: Salmon steaks may also be prepared this way. They do not need to be placed on aluminum foil.

TONNO ALLA GRIGLIA

Grilled Tuna

MAKES 4 SERVINGS

JOAN: I think tuna is best served rare to medium-rare for maximum flavor. This is delicious when served with grilled zucchini and portobello mushrooms.

Four 1-inch-thick tuna steaks (about 7 ounces each)
¼ cup olive oil
3 tablespoons freshly squeezed lime juice (from about 2 limes)
1 tablespoon balsamic vinegar

Prepare a charcoal or gas grill. When the fire is ready, brush each tuna steak with the olive oil and lime juice. Grill the tuna for 5 minutes, turning once. Remove from the grill, sprinkle with the vinegar, and serve.

TONNO TIEPIDO ALLA CHIANTI CUCINA

Tuna Tiepido in the Chianti Cucina Style

MAKES 4 SERVINGS

STANLEY: My wife, Kate, and I like our tuna pan-seared and served on a bed of arugula. Here is our recipe, which is in homage to the *tonno tiepido* served at the restaurant Chianti Cucina in Los Angeles.

1 tablespoon balsamic vinegar
1 tablespoon extra virgin olive oil
5 tablespoons olive oil
Kosher salt and freshly ground black pepper
2 bunches arugula, stemmed and washed
Four 1-inch-thick tuna steaks (about 7 ounces each)
16 long shavings Parmesan cheese (about 3 ounces)

In a small bowl, whisk together the vinegar, extra virgin olive oil, 3 tablespoons of the olive oil, and salt and pepper to taste. Pour this dressing over the arugula and toss to distribute evenly. Arrange the arugula on a serving platter and set aside.

Season the tuna steaks with salt and pepper. Heat the remaining 2 tablespoons olive oil in a large cast-iron or heavy-bottomed skillet set over medium-high heat. When the oil is hot but not smoking, add the tuna and cook to sear each side, about 1 minute per side. Remove to a cutting board and cut the tuna on the bias into ½-inch-thick slices. Arrange the tuna slices on top of the arugula. Lay the Parmesan shavings on top, and serve immediately.

TONNO ALLA PIASTRA CON INSALATA DI POMODORO E PANE

Seared Tuna with Tomato Bread Salad

MAKES 4 SERVINGS

GIANNI: I love shopping at the open-air markets in Italy, where the fish is so fresh and so beautifully displayed. I go planning to buy one or two things and somehow always end up with two full bags. Then, of course, when I get it home it's a nightmare—scaling and cleaning them all, to say nothing of deciding how best to cook the different varieties. Occasionally in the summer I will find a market stand that is selling tuna caught off the coast of Sicily. I like to prepare it this way, in a simple marinade, accompanied by a salad full of Italy's exceptionally flavorful and juicy tomatoes.

3 tablespoons freshly squeezed lemon juice (from about 1 lemon)
1 sprig fresh thyme
2 sprigs fresh rosemary, broken in half
1 clove garlic, crushed
¼ cup plus 1 teaspoon olive oil
2 tablespoons sherry vinegar or mild white vinegar
Freshly ground black pepper
Four 1-inch-thick tuna steaks (about 7 ounces each)

FOR THE TOMATO BREAD SALAD:

Three ½-inch-thick slices country bread, cut into ¼-inch cubes
2 cups ½-inch wedges ripe tomato (about 3 large tomatoes)
1 cup peeled, seeded, and cubed cucumbers
Kosher salt and freshly ground black pepper
2 tablespoons chopped fresh basil leaves
¼ teaspoon chopped fresh oregano leaves
2 tablespoons extra virgin olive oil
½ red onion, diced
2 tablespoons balsamic vinegar
12 Gaeta or Kalamata olives, pitted

In a shallow dish large enough to hold all the tuna steaks in a single layer, mix together the lemon juice, thyme, rosemary, garlic, ¼ cup of the olive oil, vinegar, and pepper to taste. Add the tuna and coat with the marinade on both sides. Marinate the tuna at room temperature for at least 30 minutes but not more than 2 hours.

To make the salad, preheat the oven to 300 degrees F. Place the bread cubes on a baking sheet and bake, stirring occasionally, until dry, about 8 minutes. Do not brown. Set aside.

In a large bowl, stir together the tomato wedges, cucumbers, and salt and pepper to taste, basil, oregano, extra virgin olive oil, and onion. Set aside for 30 minutes.

Wipe a large cast-iron or nonstick skillet with the remaining 1 teaspoon olive oil and set over medium-high heat. When the skillet is hot, add the tuna and sear on both sides, about 1 minute per side for rare or 2 minutes per side for medium-rare.

Add the bread cubes, vinegar, and olives to the tomato salad. Toss, and serve immediately with the tuna.

VARIATIONS:

- This recipe may be prepared with swordfish.
- The remaining half of the red onion may be cut into ½-inch-thick slices. Warm 2 tablespoons olive oil in a small skillet set over medium-high heat. Add the onion slices and cook, stirring frequently, until browned, about 8 minutes. Serve on top of the bread salad.
- Here is a recipe for a marinade that is less traditionally Italian but is also very good with tuna or swordfish: Serve with the bread salad if desired, or it may be accompanied by an arugula and tomato salad, Caponata (page 34), or Potato Salad (page 290).

½ tablespoon peeled and chopped fresh ginger
2 medium-size cloves garlic, crushed or sliced
3 tablespoons teriyaki sauce
1 teaspoon coarsely ground black pepper
2 sprigs fresh rosemary, broken in half
2 tablespoons canola oil
Kosher salt to taste

Whisk all of the ingredients together in a shallow dish. Add the tuna and turn to coat with marinade on both sides. Cover and set aside to marinate at room temperature for at least 30 minutes but not more than 2 hours. Cook following the instructions for the basic tuna recipe.

FAGIOLI E PESCE IN CASSERUOLA

Shellfish and Bean Casserole

MAKES 4 SERVINGS

GIANNI: I love the combination of hearty beans and fish. Lots of other people must too, because I notice that dishes similar to this one are finding their way onto more and more American restaurant menus. This recipe is tasty and economical—with inexpensive beans adding flavor and volume to the other more costly main ingredients, shrimp and squid.

This dish may be served for lunch or as a light supper. I allow guests to help themselves from the casserole, which I place in the center of the table along with a basket filled with toasted country bread that has been rubbed with garlic. It is also terrific served as an appetizer in shallow soup bowls with extra virgin olive oil drizzled on top, or tossed with cooked fettuccine as a pasta course.

3 tablespoons extra virgin olive oil
2 large cloves garlic, thinly sliced
¼ teaspoon red pepper flakes or ½ jalapeño pepper, seeded and diced
½ pound medium-size shrimp, shelled and deveined
¾ pound cleaned baby squid, sliced ½ inch thick
Kosher salt and freshly ground black pepper
2 tablespoons chopped fresh parsley leaves
½ cup dry white wine
3 cups drained cooked white beans (such as cannellini or navy)
½ cup bean cooking liquid
2 cups peeled and diced fresh or canned whole plum tomatoes (about 4 tomatoes)
½ cup chicken or vegetable broth
6 fresh basil leaves

Warm the olive oil in a flameproof casserole set over high heat. Stir in the garlic. When the garlic begins to color, stir in the red pepper flakes, shrimp, squid, salt and pepper to taste, and 1 tablespoon of the parsley. Cook, stirring occasionally, until the shrimp turns light pink, about 2 minutes. Add the wine and continue cooking until it evaporates, about 1 minute.

Stir in the beans along with the bean cooking liquid. Add the tomatoes and broth, and season with salt. Bring the mixture to a boil and cook to slightly thicken the sauce, about 1 minute. Remove from the heat and stir in the remaining 1 tablespoon parsley and the basil. Serve immediately.

VARIATIONS:

- Canned beans that have been drained and rinsed may be used in place of cooked beans. Add ½ cup more broth to the recipe instead of the bean cooking liquid, and proceed with the recipe as written.
- ½ pound sea or bay scallops may be used in place of the shrimp. Quarter large scallops before cooking.
- ¾ pound red snapper or striped bass fillet may be used in place of the squid. Cut into four chunks before cooking.

COZZE IN BIANCO

Mussels with White Wine

MAKES 4 SERVINGS

JOAN: Stan and I first prepared this recipe during one of our many visits to Cape Cod with my sister Grace and her husband, Tony. We went to a protected cove on the ocean side of the Cape. As the tide went out, thousands of mussels appeared, clinging to the rocks in the shallow water. We gathered up a bucketful of the shiny black mollusks, scrubbed them clean, and steamed them in a delicate wine sauce with delicious results.

On a recent visit to Florence, we shopped at a local fish market and discovered some tiny clams, or cockles, packed in nets. They are a delicious substitute for the mussels in this recipe. When we returned home, we found these same cockles at Randazzo's Fish Market on Arthur Avenue in the Bronx. They also carry Australian cockles, which are very good.

I recommend serving this dish as a main course at lunch or as an appetizer before a special meal. Be sure to have focaccia or bread on hand to soak up the sauce.

This dish may also be served over cooked linguine.

¼ cup olive oil
2 cloves garlic, chopped
½ cup dry white wine
2 pounds mussels, scrubbed and debearded
2 tablespoons chopped fresh parsley leaves

Warm the olive oil and garlic together in a large pot set over medium heat. Add the wine and mussels. Cover and cook until the mussels open, about 5 minutes. Stir once or twice during the cooking time, bringing the mussels on the bottom of the pan up to the top. Add the parsley halfway through the cooking time. Spoon the cooked mussels into four soup bowls, discarding any unopened ones. Distribute the sauce among the bowls and serve immediately.

VARIATIONS:

- My sister Grace cooks mussels in beer. In a large saucepan, combine 1 tablespoon olive oil, 2 cloves garlic, chopped, 4 sprigs fresh parsley, and 1 can beer. Add the cleaned 2 pounds of mussels and toss. Cover the pot and bring to a boil. Simmer until the mussels open, about 5 minutes. Serve immediately as a first course, discarding any unopened mussels.
- Mussels cooked in marinara are excellent served over linguine. Follow Grace's recipe above, substituting 1 cup *Salsa Marinara* (page 125) for the beer.

Vegetali e Contorni

VEGETABLES AND SIDE DISHES

JOAN: Gardening and raising animals were a way of life for my parents, and a form of relaxation as well. At our house on the Point they cultivated a wide variety of fresh fruits and vegetables. Everyone helped in the garden, turning the soil and planting in the spring, harvesting and canning in the fall. In fact, I have pictures of Stanley as a baby helping Pop in the garden.

The garden came right up to the edge of the house, and there was something growing year-round. A wide variety of summer vegetables were enjoyed at their peak—pole beans, cucumbers, peppers, zucchini, eggplant, and more. A portion of the harvest would be canned and preserved for the winter—especially the tomatoes. Garlic and onions were used throughout the year. They were stored in the root cellar along with potatoes and celery. Pop had a cold frame in which he started seeds in the early spring for summer planting, and in the winter he grew parsley in it. He covered hardy vegetables, such as escarole, to protect them from frost so that we could enjoy them deep into the colder winter months. Thanks to all this hard work and planning, I think my parents hardly ever ate a vegetable they hadn't grown.

GIANNI: Although my parents didn't keep a huge vegetable garden, we had several neighbors who shared their harvest with us every year. My father had a friend named Guido Mascarello, who took his produce to different open-air markets around the Veneto. At the end of the day he would come by the house and let my father pick out whatever he wanted from the vegetables that had not sold.

My mother cooked vegetables all the way through. As a kid I liked these soft vegetables and ate them spread on slices of bread. Now I prefer to cook vegetables quickly so they have a little crunch and retain their healthy properties.

STANLEY: Vegetables. Children hate them, some adults pretend to like them, some people live on them exclusively. The following recipes are for all of the above. For a young boy to look forward to eggplant sandwiches is a rare thing. I did. For children to beg for more stuffed mushrooms seems an impossibility, but it's not. It may happen to people you know if you follow these recipes. You will find these dishes to be more than something that "goes with." Instead, you may end up looking for dishes to "go with" them. Enjoy.

PURÉ DI FAGIOLI, ROSMARINO, E AGLIO

Puree of White Beans, Rosemary, and Garlic

MAKES 8 SERVINGS

GIANNI: These pureed beans are made especially flavorful by the addition of olive oil that has been infused with rosemary. To create a pungent oil, it must be heated with the rosemary for at least twenty minutes. Simply warming the oil on top of the stove is not as effective as the method I devised for this recipe: Placing the oil and rosemary in a jar that is then set in the pot along with the simmering beans. This is an efficient way of preparing the small amount of oil called for—or you may use some of the *Olio all'Aglio e Rosmarino* (Garlic Rosemary Oil) found on page 325.

You do not need to presoak the dried cannellini beans called for in this recipe. Canned beans may be substituted for dried in this recipe. They don't need to be cooked, so you can begin the recipe at the point where they are processed with the olive oil. (Reserve 3 tablespoons of the canned bean liquid to use in place of the cooking water called for.) Serve this as a side dish with lamb or seafood, or spread it on top of bruschetta.

1 cup dried cannellini beans, picked over and rinsed
½ medium-size onion, peeled
1 teaspoon kosher salt, plus more as needed
6 tablespoons extra virgin olive oil
Four 5-inch sprigs fresh rosemary
6 cloves roasted garlic (page 321) or 3 cloves fresh garlic, peeled
¼ teaspoon ground cumin
2 tablespoons freshly squeezed lemon juice
1 teaspoon chopped fresh parsley leaves
Freshly ground black pepper

Place the beans in a large pot. Fill the pot with water to a level 2 inches above the beans. Add the onion and 1 teaspoon salt, and bring to a boil. Cover, reduce the heat to a simmer, and cook until the beans are tender, about 1½ hours.

Meanwhile, place the olive oil in a heat-resistant jar (such as a canning jar). Strip the rosemary leaves from the sprigs and add to the oil. When the beans have cooked for 1 hour and 10 minutes, place the jar in the pot of simmering beans and let it heat for the last 20 minutes of cooking time. This will infuse the oil with the flavor of the rosemary. (If using canned beans, place the jar in a pot of boiling water and simmer for 20 minutes.)

Remove the oil-filled jar from the beans and set it aside. Discard the onion and drain the beans, reserving 3 tablespoons of the cooking water. Place the beans in a food processor or blender along with the reserved cooking water, garlic, cumin, and lemon juice. Strain the olive oil, discarding the rosemary leaves, and add the oil to the beans. Process until all of the ingredients are blended and the beans are smooth. Stir in the parsley, and season with salt and pepper.

VARIATION: Shrimp may be served with these beans to make a delicious appetizer. Shell and devein 8 jumbo shrimp. Warm 2 tablespoons olive oil and 1 clove garlic, chopped, in a small sauté pan set over medium-high heat. When the oil is hot but not smoking, add the shrimp and cook until pink and cooked through, about 7 minutes. Distribute equal portions of the bean puree onto eight small plates. Top each plate with 1 of the cooked shrimp. In a small bowl, whisk together 1 tablespoon balsamic vinegar and 1 tablespoon extra virgin olive oil. Drizzle some of this dressing over each plate and serve.

FAGIOLI STUFATI ALL'UCCELLETTO

Stewed Beans Tuscan-Style

MAKES 6 TO 8 SERVINGS

GIANNI: Every Italian household prepares a version of this bean dish, in the same way that all Americans are familiar with pork and beans. I serve these as a side dish with pork, stewed meat, lamb, or grilled fish. They are also delicious pureed and served on bruschetta for lunch or as an appetizer. The advantage of using great Northern beans is that they do not require any presoaking. If you choose to use other dried beans, such as cannellini, they may be cooked, drained, and set aside several hours before you add them to the sautéed vegetables.

1 pound dried great Northern or navy beans
8 cups water
2 cloves garlic, lightly crushed
6 large fresh sage leaves
Two 5-inch sprigs fresh rosemary
5 tablespoons olive oil
⅓ cup diced pancetta or bacon (optional)
1 cup chopped onions
¾ cup diced carrots
¾ cup diced celery
5 fresh or canned whole plum tomatoes, peeled, seeded, and chopped
2 tablespoons chopped fresh parsley leaves
Kosher salt and freshly ground black pepper

Rinse the beans, removing any oddly colored ones or stones. Place the beans in a large flameproof casserole set over low heat. Add the water and bring to a gentle simmer. Add the garlic, 3 of the sage leaves, 1 sprig of the rosemary, and 1 tablespoon of the olive oil. Simmer until the beans are tender but not mushy, about 45 minutes. Strain, discarding the garlic and sage, and set aside.

Add the remaining 4 tablespoons olive oil to a sauté pan set over medium-high heat. When the oil is hot but not smoking, add the pancetta or bacon, stirring briskly. Stir in the onions, carrots, and celery and cook, stirring, to soften slightly, about 5 minutes. Chop the remaining 3 sage leaves and the leaves from the remaining rosemary sprig, and add to the vegetables along with the tomatoes and parsley. Then season with salt and pepper. Cook to warm the tomatoes, about 5 minutes more. Stir in the beans and reduce the heat to medium. Cook to warm the beans and to flavor them with the tomatoes, about 10 minutes. Season with additional salt and pepper if desired, and serve.

VARIATIONS:

- Thyme or marjoram may be substituted for or added to the sage and rosemary.
- A terrific way to use any leftover beans is to puree them in a blender or food processor until smooth. Add a small amount of olive oil (or a small quantity of the water the beans cooked in) and process until the beans reach a spreadable consistency. Serve at room temperature on toasted bread or crackers as an appetizer or as a lunch dish. Pureed beans may be stored in the refrigerator for up to 3 days or frozen in an airtight container for up to 1 month.

Laura and I on a trip to Quebec, Canada.

LENTICCHIE BRASATE

Braised Lentils

MAKES 6 SERVINGS

GIANNI: One day at Le Madri, a very well-dressed elderly woman named Georgette came to the restaurant and ordered this dish. When it was served, she asked the waiter if she could speak with me. Georgette explained that she was originally from Morocco, where lentils are a staple. She suggested that the next time I cooked this dish I should add a little fennel at the last moment. I followed her advice and the flavor was amazing. I have prepared it this way ever since. Serve these lentils as a side dish with grilled fish or lamb or as a topping for bruschetta.

1½ cups dried green lentils, picked over and rinsed
¼ cup extra virgin olive oil
⅓ cup finely chopped shallots
⅓ cup finely chopped carrots
⅓ cup finely chopped celery
¼ cup chopped fresh parsley leaves
1 bay leaf
¼ cup peeled and crushed tomatoes (about 2 fresh or canned)
4 cups chicken broth
Kosher salt and freshly ground black pepper
½ bulb fresh fennel, very finely chopped or thinly sliced

Place the lentils in a medium-size saucepan and cover with water to a level 1 inch above the lentils. Bring to a boil and cook to parboil the lentils, about 5 minutes. Drain, rinse in cold water to cool, and set aside.

Warm the olive oil in a medium-size saucepan set over medium heat. Add the shallots, carrots, and celery and cook, stirring occasionally, until the vegetables are golden, about 8 minutes. Stir in the parsley, bay leaf, and lentils and cook to flavor with the vegetables, about 2 minutes. Stir in the tomatoes, then pour in 3 cups of the chicken broth. Season with salt and pepper. Bring to a boil, then reduce the heat to a simmer. Cook until the lentils are tender, adding more broth as necessary to keep the liquid just above the lentils, about 15 minutes. Stir in the fennel and cook to flavor the broth, about 5 minutes. Remove from the heat and allow to rest at least 10 minutes before removing the bay leaf and serving.

VARIATIONS:

- 2 strips bacon, diced, may be cooked with the shallots, carrots, and celery to add a smoky taste to the basic lentil recipe.
- 2 tablespoons freshly squeezed lemon juice may be stirred into the lentils just before serving.
- This recipe may be used to make a delicious lentil soup. Follow the basic recipe, adding 1 peeled and cubed all-purpose or Idaho potato when you add the tomatoes. Increase the broth by 2 cups (for a total of 6 cups). Proceed with recipe as written.

FAGIOLINI AL POMODORO

String Beans with Tomatoes

MAKES 4 SERVINGS

JOAN: My father grew wide, flat Italian pole beans in his garden. Some days he would pick a basket of beans, a few tomatoes, and a small zucchini. My mother would cook them all together to create a light dish for lunch or dinner, followed by chicken or meat.

1 cup water
1 pound string beans, ends trimmed
1 small zucchini, cut in quarters lengthwise and chopped into ½-inch-wide chunks
1 medium-size all-purpose potato, peeled and quartered
½ cup chopped and seeded ripe tomatoes or canned whole plum tomatoes, crushed
2 tablespoons olive oil
Kosher salt and freshly ground black pepper
1 clove garlic, cut in half

Place the water in a medium-size pot set over medium-high heat. Add the string beans, zucchini, potato, and tomatoes. Stir in the olive oil and season with salt and pepper. Add the garlic, bring to a boil, then cover, reduce the heat to medium-low, and simmer until the vegetables are tender, about 25 minutes. Remove the vegetables to a serving dish with a slotted spoon. Spoon some of the sauce on top and serve immediately.

ASPARAGI

Asparagus—Hot or with Vinaigrette

MAKES 4 SERVINGS

JOAN: In the spring my father would take us for walks on the roads beside the Hudson River. He knew just where to go to find the wild asparagus that grew there. My mother used asparagus only in frittatas, but I like it hot as a side dish with roasted lamb or chicken. I also like it served at room temperature as a salad or as part of an *antipasto*. Here are two of my favorite ways to prepare asparagus.

HOT ASPARAGUS

2 pounds asparagus, tough bottoms snapped off
2 tablespoons extra virgin or regular olive oil
1 clove garlic, minced
Kosher salt and freshly ground black pepper

Fill a large skillet halfway with cold salted water. Bring to a boil. Add the asparagus, cover, and simmer until tender when pierced with a fork at the stem end, about 5 minutes. Remove with a slotted spoon to a serving dish. Add the olive oil and garlic and toss. Season with salt and pepper, and serve immediately.

• • •

ASPARAGUS VINAIGRETTE

2 pounds asparagus, tough bottoms snapped off
1 recipe Basic Vinaigrette (page 322)

Fill a large skillet halfway with cold salted water. Bring to a boil. Add the asparagus, cover, and simmer until tender when pierced with a fork at the stem end, about 5 minutes. Remove with a slotted spoon to a serving dish. Allow to cool completely before tossing with the vinaigrette.

CARCIOFI ALLA CONCETTA

Concetta's Stuffed Artichokes

MAKES 4 SERVINGS

JOAN: I had begun to work on this book project before my mother passed away at the age of eighty-seven, and I was very excited about preserving so many of her recipes. One day I went to visit her in the hospital. I told her that I didn't have her recipe for stuffed artichokes and I wanted to include it in the book. Without hesitation she began to tell me how she prepared them. The nurse who was attending her said, "Only an Italian could come out of surgery and start discussing food."

But the telling of a recipe is very different from the actual process of making a dish with its creator, and unfortunately I never had a chance to cook these with my mother. So this recipe, which I have named for her, is based on my memories of my mother's stuffed artichokes. She did not overstuff them, using just a teaspoon or less of the stuffing between the leaves to complement the artichoke's naturally rich flavor. The irony is that during all the years my mother made stuffed artichokes, Stan never ate them. In the course of testing different stuffings for this recipe, he ate quite a few and now he loves them.

4 medium-size or 2 extra-large artichokes, stems and top ¼ inch sliced off and discarded, sharp outer leaf points snipped off and discarded
2 teaspoons chopped fresh parsley leaves
5 teaspoons finely grated pecorino Romano cheese
2 large cloves garlic, minced
1 cup roughly grated day-old bread or 1 cup plain dried bread crumbs, or a combination of both
4 tablespoons olive oil

Preheat the oven to 350 degrees F.

Snugly fit the artichokes in a small saucepan and add water to a depth ¼ inch below the tops of the artichokes. Cover, bring to a boil, and simmer until an outside leaf pulls away easily, about 20 minutes. Do not overcook or the artichokes will fall apart. Remove from the water, turn upside down to drain, and set aside to cool.

In a small bowl, mix together the parsley, cheese, garlic, and bread crumbs. Sprinkle teaspoons of the filling between the leaves, working from the outer leaves toward the center of the artichoke, spreading the inner leaves slightly if necessary. Place the artichokes in a glass baking pan. Drizzle 1 tablespoon of the olive oil over each artichoke (2 tablespoons if using extra-large ones). Fill the pan with water to a depth of 1 inch. Cover with aluminum foil and bake for 30 minutes. Remove the foil, add more water to the pan if necessary, and continue baking until the artichokes are tender and lightly browned, about 15 minutes more. Serve hot or at room temperature.

VARIATIONS:

- When serving steamed or boiled artichokes that have not been stuffed, I like to whisk together 1 teaspoon freshly squeezed lemon juice and ¼ cup melted butter to dip the tender leaves into before eating.
- 1 steamed artichoke may be served as part of an *antipasto* with drinks before dinner. Separate the leaves and arrange on a platter. Serve along with a small dish of Basic Vinaigrette (page 322).

PEPERONI IN PADELLA

Pan-Fried Peppers

MAKES 4 SERVINGS

STAN: My family grew a year's worth of vegetables and herbs every summer in three different gardens, and it was inevitable that I would be asked to help tend them. One day, when I was twelve or thirteen years old, my father asked me to hold up my hand. He placed his hand against mine and said, "Your hands are as big as mine. In Italy that means you go to work." That summer I was placed in charge of tending the gardens. When I complained about the amount of work, my father would laugh and respond, *"La terra e troppa bassa per te."* That means "The earth is too low for you." I not only understood his humor but agreed with him.

My gardening chores took up most of the day, so my father would pack sandwiches filled with these sweet, slowly cooked peppers for my lunch. This quickly became my favorite midday meal and a kind of reward for all the hard work.

JOAN: For a colorful presentation I like to use a combination of red, green, and yellow peppers when I prepare this recipe.

¼ cup olive oil
4 bell peppers, seeded, and cut into ½-inch-wide strips
Kosher salt and freshly ground black pepper

Warm the olive oil in a small sauté pan set over medium-high heat. Add the peppers and stir. Cover and cook, stirring occasionally, until the peppers become soft and begin to lose their shape. Remove cover and saute 20 to 25 minutes. Season with salt and pepper, and serve warm or at room temperature. The peppers may be stored in the refrigerator for up to 4 days.

BROCCOLI DI RAPE ALLA TUCCI

Broccoli Rabe Tucci-Style

MAKES 4 SERVINGS

JOAN: On page 268 you will find the Tropiano recipe for broccoli rabe. I grew up with that recipe, and when I married Stan I learned how to cook broccoli rabe this way. The basic difference is that the Tuccis sauté their rabe and the Tropianos boil theirs. Both families serve it as a side dish with meat, chicken, or fish. It also may be served between slices of Italian bread as a sandwich or as a topping on pizza or focaccia.

2 pounds broccoli rabe (about 2 bunches), washed
½ cup olive oil
3 cloves garlic, chopped
Kosher salt
¼ cup water
1 lemon (optional), quartered

Snap off the flowered stems and leaves of the broccoli rabe, discarding the tough stems. Roughly chop the remaining stems, leaving the buds whole, and set aside.

Warm the olive oil in a large sauté pan set over medium-high heat. Add the garlic and cook, stirring, until lightly colored, about 2 minutes. Add the broccoli rabe. Season with salt, add the water, and cover. Reduce the heat to a simmer and stir occasionally until tender, 8 to 10 minutes. (More water may be added, ¼ cup at a time, if the broccoli rabe begins to stick to the pan.) Serve with the lemon quarters.

BROCCOLI DI RAPE ALLA TROPIANO

Broccoli Rabe Tropiano-Style

MAKES 4 SERVINGS

JOAN: We have included two methods for cooking broccoli rabe because my mother's recipe is very different from the Tucci version. Rather than sautéing the broccoli rabe, my mother cooked hers in boiling water, which results in a less bitter flavor. I like it cooked either way.

Many of the recipes in this book call for reserving some of the cooking water before draining vegetables or pasta. This flavorful water is used in place of tap water to achieve the right consistency in a finished dish. If I refrigerate or freeze cooked broccoli rabe, I store it in a container filled with cooking water. This helps to preserve the taste, and in this way I am also sure to have cooking water on hand to add to any recipe.

2 pounds broccoli rabe (about 2 bunches), washed
¼ cup olive oil
1 clove garlic, cut in half

Snap off the flowered stems and leaves of the broccoli rabe, discarding the tough stems. Roughly chop the remaining stems, leaving the buds whole, and set aside.

Bring a large pot of salted water to a boil. Add the broccoli rabe and cook until tender, about 5 minutes. Remove to a bowl with a slotted spoon. Add ½ cup of the cooking water to the broccoli rabe and set aside. (This may be done several hours in advance.)

Warm the olive oil in a sauté pan set over medium-high heat. Add the garlic and cook to flavor the oil but do not brown the garlic, about 2 minutes. Add the broccoli rabe along with 2 tablespoons of the cooking water. (More water may be added, 2 tablespoons at a time, if the broccoli rabe begins to stick to the pan.) Cover and simmer to flavor the broccoli rabe with the garlic and oil, about 3 minutes.

VARIATION:

- Stir 1 cup of drained and rinsed canned cannellini beans into the broccoli rabe along with the water. Serve drizzled with extra virgin olive oil.

SCAROLA

Escarole

MAKES 4 SERVINGS

JOAN: My father grew escarole in his garden every year. It was very hardy and, if the winter was mild, could survive into late November or early December. He would cover the plants with a bushel basket at night to protect them from frost. Because escarole was handy and homegrown, my mother used it in many of her recipes and often served it as a side dish. We like escarole prepared this way on top of pizza. It freezes well in small batches, packed in containers filled with some of the cooking water.

1 pound escarole (about 1 large head), washed, stems removed, and leaves roughly chopped
3 tablespoons olive oil
2 cloves garlic, cut in half

Bring a large pot of salted water to a rapid boil. Add the escarole and cook until tender but firm, about 5 minutes after the water returns to the boil. Remove the escarole with a slotted spoon, place in a bowl, and set aside. Reserve ½ cup of the cooking water. Set aside. (The escarole may be parboiled and set aside several hours before proceeding with the recipe.)

Warm the olive oil in a large sauté pan set over medium heat. Add the garlic and cook to flavor the oil but do not let it brown, about 2 minutes. Add the escarole and the reserved cooking water. Cook, stirring occasionally, to warm through and bring the flavor of the garlic and escarole together, about 4 minutes. Serve immediately.

VARIATIONS:

- Kale, Swiss chard, and mustard greens may also be prepared this way. They may need to be sautéed for an additional 5 minutes to soften and absorb the garlic flavor.
- Cannellini or other white beans make a delicious addition to this recipe. Warm one 19-ounce can cannellini beans, drained and rinsed, with the reserved cooking water. Add the beans and water to the escarole as it warms through with the garlic and oil.
- Cannellini beans may also be warmed in ¾ cup Joan's Basic Tomato Sauce (page 124). Stir the tomato-bean mixture into the escarole in place of the cooking water as it warms with the garlic and oil.

FUNGHI SALTATI

Sautéed Mushrooms

MAKES 4 SERVINGS

STAN: The Tucci family used to gather wild mushrooms during their spring and fall visits to Vermont. My sister-in-law, Teddy, is very knowledgeable about mushrooms and continues to pick them in the vicinity of her home. My father, Stanislao, favored the "woody" flavored mushrooms that grow on trees. He said they tasted better than a good steak.

JOAN: Today there are so many varieties of mushrooms available in stores that I prepare this dish using a mixture of white, cremini, and portobello.

¼ cup olive oil
1 clove garlic, chopped
10 ounces mushrooms, cut into ¼-inch-thick slices
1 tablespoon chopped fresh parsley leaves
Kosher salt and freshly ground black pepper

Warm the olive oil in a medium-size saucepan set over medium-high heat. Add the garlic and cook until slightly softened but not browned, about 1 minute. Add the mushrooms and cook, stirring occasionally, until softened and browned, about 12 minutes. Sprinkle with the parsley, season with salt and pepper, and serve immediately.

VARIATION: This mixture of mushrooms may be served over 1 pound cooked pasta that has been tossed with ¼ cup olive oil. Serve with extra virgin olive oil drizzled on top. Garnish with Parmesan cheese if you like.

PATATE ARROSTO

Roasted Potatoes with Rosemary

MAKES 4 SERVINGS

JOAN: My father stored the potatoes he grew over the summer in our cold, dry cellar along with the salami he was curing and the wine he was aging. This simple recipe for roasting potatoes with rosemary is very flavorful and has been popular with everyone I have served it to.

10 large Yukon Gold or baking potatoes, peeled and quartered, or red potatoes, left unpeeled and quartered
4 cloves garlic, cut in half
1 tablespoon chopped fresh rosemary leaves
2 teaspoons chopped fresh oregano leaves or ½ teaspoon dried
Kosher salt and freshly ground black pepper
¼ cup olive oil

Preheat the oven to 375 degrees F.

Place the potatoes in a large baking dish or casserole. Add the garlic, rosemary, and oregano and season with salt and pepper. Drizzle the olive oil over the potatoes and toss to coat evenly. Bake, stirring occasionally, until the potatoes are browned and cooked through, about 1½ hours. Serve immediately.

VARIATION: 2 medium-size carrots, cut into 2-inch pieces, may be roasted with the potatoes.

TIMBALLO DI CAVOLFIORE, ERBETTE FRESCHE, E ACCIUGA

Cauliflower, Herb, and Anchovy Timbale

MAKES 4 SERVINGS

GIANNI: My good friend and former sous chef, Franceso Blanco, taught me this recipe. He is a passionate cook and lives in Sicily. Whenever we cooked together, I was always impressed with the way he combined simple ingredients and gave them a well-balanced southern Italian flavor. In the north we would never think to put anchovies together with cauliflower. In this recipe they complement the cauliflower perfectly without giving the dish a fishy flavor. This vegetable dish, which is similar to a potato gratin, may be prepared ahead of time and reheated in the oven. It is very nice served as a side dish with roasted chicken, or it may be served as a lunch dish with crunchy bread and a tossed green salad.

When I boil cauliflower, I always add a little flour and lemon juice as I prepare the cooking water. This helps the cauliflower retain its white color. In this recipe I add a slice of onion to flavor the water. You may also add herbs, carrots, or celery to make a broth for the cauliflower to cook in. (I also follow this procedure when I cook artichokes.)

3 tablespoons butter
¼ cup plain dried bread crumbs
1 medium-size head cauliflower, rinsed and separated into florets
4 tablespoons all-purpose flour
2 tablespoons freshly squeezed lemon juice
One ½-inch-thick slice onion
2 tablespoons extra virgin olive oil
¾ cup diced onions
1 tablespoon chopped fresh parsley leaves
1 tablespoon chopped fresh marjoram leaves
⅛ teaspoon ground nutmeg
Kosher salt and freshly ground black pepper
1¼ cups milk
2 tablespoons chopped anchovy fillets
½ cup finely grated Parmesan cheese

Preheat the oven to 350 degrees F. Grease a 9-inch round casserole or baking pan with 1 tablespoon of the butter. Sprinkle the bread crumbs on the bottom and sides of the pan and set aside.

Bring a large pot of salted water to a rapid boil. Add the cauliflower florets, 1 tablespoon of the flour, the lemon juice, and the onion slice. Simmer until the florets are easily pierced with a fork, about 10 minutes. Drain, discarding the onion slice, and set aside.

Warm the olive oil in a large sauté pan set over medium-high heat. When the oil is hot but not smoking, add the chopped onions and drained cauliflower. Stir in the parsley, marjoram, and nutmeg and season with salt and pepper. Cook until the florets start sticking to the pan a bit, about

5 minutes. Reduce the heat to medium-low and roughly mash the cauliflower with the back of a wooden spoon or with a potato masher. Add the remaining 2 tablespoons butter. Sprinkle in the remaining 3 tablespoons flour. Mix well, then stir in the milk. Continue cooking and stirring until the mixture thickens and the milk has been absorbed, about 8 minutes.

Remove from the heat and stir in the anchovies. Stir in ¼ cup of the Parmesan cheese. Pour the mixture into the prepared baking pan. Sprinkle the remaining ¼ cup Parmesan on top. Bake until heated through and golden brown on top, about 25 minutes.

VARIATIONS:

- ¼-inch-thick slices fresh tomatoes may be arranged on top of the cauliflower after it has baked. Set aside for a few moments to allow the cauliflower to warm the tomatoes through before serving.
- For a rich version of this dish, heavy cream may be substituted for the milk.
- For a lighter version of this dish, olive oil may be substituted for the butter.
- 4 hard-boiled eggs may be sliced and arranged between layers of the cooked cauliflower before baking.
- Other cheeses, such as Fontina, Gruyère, or Asiago, may be substituted for the Parmesan.
- This cauliflower mixture is terrific served over cooked penne. Eliminate the baking dish and follow the basic recipe. After adding the milk to the cauliflower, cook 1 pound of penne in rapidly boiling salted water until *al dente,* following the package instructions. Complete the cauliflower recipe, reserving the final ¼ cup Parmesan cheese. Add the cooked drained penne to the pan with the cauliflower mixture and toss. Serve immediately, garnished with the remaining ¼ cup Parmesan.

PURÉ DI PATATE AI CARCIOFINI

Mashed Potatoes and Artichokes

MAKES 4 SERVINGS

GIANNI: Fresh artichokes are very popular in Italy, and when they are in season they may be purchased at every local farmer's market. There are many recipes that call for only the rich artichoke heart, or bottom, which is hidden beneath all the spiky leaves. That is why at many of the farm stands you will see older women working quickly to peel half a dozen artichokes down to their hearts. The hearts are then rubbed with lemon juice, packed into small bags, and sold to customers who are happy to go home with half their work already done for them.

I have rarely seen freshly peeled artichoke bottoms for sale in the United States, so you may need to purchase whole artichokes for this recipe and peel them down to the heart yourself. Reserve some of the tender leaves to use as a garnish. Canned artichoke bottoms or frozen artichoke hearts may be substituted for fresh. The artichokes may be prepared several hours ahead and mixed into the mashed potatoes just before serving.

2 tablespoons olive oil
½ cup chopped shallots
1 clove garlic, chopped
1 tablespoon chopped fresh parsley leaves
½ pound artichoke bottoms or hearts, cut into ½-inch pieces
½ teaspoon chopped fresh thyme leaves
Kosher salt and freshly ground black pepper
2 cups water
2½ pounds Idaho potatoes, peeled
1 clove garlic, peeled
¾ cup milk, warmed
6 tablespoons (¾ stick) butter, softened

Warm the olive oil in a small sauté pan set over medium-high heat. Add the shallots, chopped garlic, and parsley and cook, stirring, until the shallots soften, about 5 minutes. Stir in the artichokes and thyme, then season with salt and pepper. Add the water and bring to a boil. Reduce the heat to medium-low and simmer until all of the liquid has been absorbed and the artichokes are tender, about 12 minutes. Remove from the heat and set aside.

Place the potatoes in a large pot of salted water. Add the whole garlic clove and bring to a boil. Reduce the heat to medium and simmer the potatoes until tender when pierced with a fork, about 20 minutes. Drain the potatoes, discard the garlic, and return the potatoes to the pot. Heat over low heat to remove any excess moisture, about 1 minute. Remove from the heat and add the milk and butter. Use a potato masher or electric mixer set on low to incorporate all of the ingredients, leaving the mixture slightly chunky. Stir in the artichokes. Season with salt and pepper and serve.

PATATE E PEPERONI

Potatoes and Peppers

MAKES 4 SERVINGS

JOAN: This simple vegetable mixture is a delicious side dish. It may be prepared several hours ahead of time and reheated just before serving. I sometimes serve it as a lunch dish, accompanied by a crusty bread.

2 long, green Italian frying peppers
2 medium-size all-purpose or red potatoes
¼ cup olive oil
1 small ripe plum tomato (optional), roughly chopped
Kosher salt and freshly ground black pepper

Cut the pepper lengthwise into ¼-inch-wide strips, discarding the seeds and stems. Peel the all-purpose potatoes or scrub the red potatoes. Cut them in half and then into ¼-inch-thick slices.

Warm the olive oil in a medium-size nonstick frying pan set over medium-low heat. When the oil is hot but not smoking, add the potato slices and cook, stirring frequently, until they just begin to color, about 5 minutes. Add the pepper slices and continue cooking until both vegetables are soft, about 15 minutes. Add the tomato and season with salt and pepper. Toss the vegetable mixture to combine well, and continue cooking until the tomato has softened slightly, about 5 minutes. Serve immediately.

CASSERUOLA DI MELANZANE CON PATATE

Eggplant and Zucchini Casserole with Potatoes

MAKES 8 SERVINGS

JOAN: We refer to this casserole as Nonno's dish. *Nonno* means "grandfather" in Italian, and it was Stan's father who originally prepared this recipe. It is an excellent complement to meat or chicken. I remember enjoying this casserole on a cold, rainy day when we were camping in upstate New York. Stan's sister Rosalinda lived about half an hour away from our campsite, so she and her husband, Lee, came over for lunch. They brought Nonno's dish, still warm from the oven, and it was just what we needed to cheer up an otherwise dreary day. This casserole may be assembled one day in advance, refrigerated overnight, and baked the next day. Or it may be assembled and frozen for up to one month. Allow the casserole to defrost before baking, or bake the frozen casserole for an additional thirty minutes.

1 medium-size eggplant, cut into ½-inch-thick slices
½ cup olive oil
2 medium-size zucchini, cut into ½-inch-thick slices
2 medium-size all-purpose potatoes, peeled and cut into ¼-inch-thick slices
1 red bell pepper, seeded and cut into ½-inch-thick slices
2 cups Salsa Marinara *(page 125) or your own favorite tomato sauce*
½ cup finely grated pecorino Romano cheese

Preheat the oven broiler.

Lightly brush both sides of the eggplant slices with some of the olive oil, and place on a baking sheet. Place under the broiler and brown lightly on each side, about 2 minutes per side. Remove from the oven and set aside. Reduce the oven temperature to 350 degrees F.

Place about one third of the remaining olive oil in a large sauté pan set over medium-high heat. Cook the zucchini in the oil until the white of the zucchini has turned yellow but is still firm, about 2 minutes per side. Remove to a plate and set aside. Repeat this process with the potatoes, then the bell pepper, adding more oil as necessary and cooking each vegetable until slightly cooked but still firm, about 3 minutes on each side.

Cover the bottom of a large shallow casserole with about ½ cup of the marinara sauce. Arrange a layer of eggplant slices on top of the sauce. Top the eggplant with a thin layer of marinara sauce and a sprinkling of the Romano cheese. Layer the zucchini on top of the eggplant, followed by a layer of potato, and finally a layer of bell pepper. Top with the remaining marinara sauce and Romano cheese.

Cover and bake until the mixture is bubbling and the vegetables are tender, about 40 minutes. Remove the cover and continue baking until the vegetables are soft when pierced with a fork, about another 10 minutes. Allow the casserole to stand for 10 minutes before serving.

VARIATIONS:

- To make a great cold sandwich, place a leftover portion of this casserole between slices of Italian bread.
- Some of the recommended alternate ingredients for this dish include substituting a green or yellow bell pepper for the red pepper and substituting yellow squash for the zucchini.
- A smaller, deeper casserole may be substituted for the large shallow one called for here. Arrange alternating layers of the vegetables as you would when preparing lasagna, and proceed with the recipe as written.

FUNGHI E PATATE AL FORNO

Mushroom and Potato Casserole

MAKES 8 SERVINGS

GIANNI: When we were collecting recipes for this book I remembered this dish, which I regularly prepared at a restaurant in Washington, D.C. The trouble was, I had never written the recipe down. I wrote one version, which Mimi and Joan tested, but it didn't come out well at all. So, with everyone standing around the Tucci kitchen, I tried to remember the real recipe. Talk about pressure! But we all worked at it and finally arrived at this version, which is even better than I remember. So the moral of the story is to trust your instincts and don't be afraid to try things. Serve it as a side dish with simply prepared fish, meat, or chicken.

1 pound porcini, portobello, or cremini mushrooms, stems removed and reserved and caps cut into ¼-inch-thick slices
1 cup finely chopped onions
2 cloves garlic, minced
1 teaspoon finely chopped fresh oregano leaves
2 tablespoons chopped fresh parsley leaves
4 tablespoons extra virgin olive oil
3 large baking potatoes, peeled, halved, and cut into ½-inch-thick slices
2½ teaspoons kosher salt
Freshly ground black pepper
1 cup chicken broth

Preheat the oven to 375 degrees F.

Roughly chop the mushroom stems. Set aside.

In a small bowl, toss together the onions, garlic, oregano, and parsley. Set aside.

Drizzle 1 tablespoon of the olive oil over the bottom of a small casserole, about 9 × 11 inches. Sprinkle 1 tablespoon of the onion mixture over the bottom of the casserole. Arrange the potato slices on top of the onion mixture, overlapping them to form a single dense layer. Season with the salt and grindings of pepper, and top with ⅓ cup of the onion mixture. Sprinkle the chopped mushroom stems on top. Season with salt and pepper. Sprinkle ⅓ cup of the onion mixture on top. Top the casserole with a dense, single overlapping layer of mushroom slices. Distribute the remaining ⅓ cup onion mixture over the top. Season with salt and pepper. Drizzle the remaining 3 tablespoons olive oil on top. Pour the chicken broth into the casserole, cover, and bake until the potatoes are tender and the mushrooms have softened, about 50 minutes. Serve immediately.

PARMIGIANA DI MELANZANE

Vegetable Casserole

MAKES 6 SERVINGS

JOAN: My father grew only a few eggplants in his garden, so when they were in season my mother would purchase a bushel of them. Some of them she would pickle and some she would use in recipes similar to this one.

In this dish the vegetables are sautéed individually before being baked together in a casserole. This is done to maintain the distinct flavor of each vegetable.

½ cup plus 2 tablespoons olive oil
1 medium-size eggplant, roughly chopped
1 medium-size zucchini, roughly chopped
½ pound cremini or white mushrooms, stems discarded and caps roughly chopped
½ cup roughly chopped onions
Kosher salt and freshly ground black pepper
1 cup Salsa Marinara *(page 125) or your own favorite tomato sauce*
¼ cup freshly grated Parmesan or pecorino Romano cheese

Preheat the oven to 350 degrees F.

Warm ¼ cup of the olive oil in a medium-size sauté pan set over medium heat. Add the eggplant and cook, stirring, until softened, about 5 minutes. Use a slotted spoon to transfer the eggplant to a medium-size casserole dish and set aside. Add 2 more tablespoons of the olive oil and the zucchini to the sauté pan and cook until the center is softened and the rind is still firm, about 3 minutes. Transfer the zucchini to the casserole with a slotted spoon and set aside. Add 2 more tablespoons of the olive oil and the mushrooms to the sauté pan and cook until softened, about 3 minutes. Transfer the mushrooms to the casserole with a slotted spoon and set aside. Finally, add the remaining 2 tablespoons olive oil and the onions to the sauté pan and cook until softened, about 3 minutes. Transfer to the casserole with a slotted spoon.

Season the vegetables with salt and pepper. Add the marinara sauce and toss to distribute the sauce evenly among the vegetables. Sprinkle with the cheese. Bake until the vegetables are cooked through, about 25 minutes. Serve immediately.

VEGETALI ARROSTITO

Roasted Vegetables

MAKES 8 SERVINGS

JOAN: My mother loved vegetables and cooked them every day, usually following the popular method of boiling them in lots of salted water. The only vegetable I remember her roasting is potatoes. A few years ago it seemed that every cooking show and magazine was featuring recipes for roasted vegetables. I decided to try my own version. I mixed together my favorite vegetables—potatoes, butternut squash, zucchini, carrots—and cooked the firm ones first, adding the softer ones later so that they retained their shapes and fresh flavors. The marinara sauce and balsamic vinegar nicely accent this dish.

1 tablespoon roughly chopped fresh basil leaves
1 tablespoon chopped fresh rosemary leaves
1 tablespoon chopped fresh parsley leaves
1 tablespoon chopped fresh thyme leaves
2 large Yukon Gold or Red Bliss potatoes, peeled, cut in half, and then into 2-inch pieces
2 large carrots, peeled, cut in half, and then into 1-inch pieces
4 cloves garlic, cut in half
Kosher salt and freshly ground black pepper
3 tablespoons Salsa Marinara *(page 125) or your own favorite tomato sauce (optional)*
½ cup olive oil
1 large yellow or green zucchini, cut in half, and then into 1-inch pieces
1 large sweet potato, peeled, cut in half, and then into 1-inch pieces
1 medium-size butternut squash, peeled, cut in half, and then into 1-inch pieces
1 tablespoon balsamic vinegar
1 tablespoon extra virgin olive oil

Preheat the oven to 350 degrees F.

In a small bowl, combine the chopped herbs. Set aside.

In a large casserole or baking dish, toss the potatoes and carrots with half of the herb mixture. Stir in the garlic and season with salt and pepper. Stir in the tomato sauce and ¼ cup of the olive oil. Bake, stirring occasionally, until the potatoes begin to brown and soften, about 30 minutes.

Add the zucchini, sweet potato, butternut squash, and the remaining herbs and ¼ cup olive oil. Toss to coat evenly. Continue baking, stirring occasionally, until all of the vegetables are browned but firm and cooked through, about 1 hour. Drizzle the vinegar and extra virgin olive oil over the vegetables and toss. Serve immediately.

VARIATIONS:

- Turnips may be added to this casserole and cooked along with the potatoes.
- Different fresh herbs, such as marjoram, sage, and oregano, may be substituted for the rosemary and thyme.

Circa 1963, Stanley (right) with his second cousins Thomas Michael and Eileen Stinson at the Bear Mountain Zoo.

VEGETALI ALLA GRIGLIA

Grilled Vegetables

MAKES 4 TO 6 SERVINGS

JOAN: We serve grilled fresh vegetables in the summer to accompany grilled fish. This recipe is for two of our favorites, zucchini and mushrooms. Small heads of radicchio cut into quarters are also very good prepared this way. Eggplant, cut into ½-inch-thick slices, may be grilled as directed here.

3 medium-size zucchini, cut lengthwise into ¼-inch-thick slices
3 portobello mushroom caps, cut into ¼-inch-thick slices
1 cup olive oil
¼ cup extra virgin olive oil
¼ cup balsamic vinegar
Kosher salt and freshly ground black pepper

Brush one side of the zucchini and mushroom slices with some of the olive oil. Place, oiled side down, on a prepared grill. Brush the tops of the zucchini and mushroom slices with olive oil. Grill, turning once or twice and brushing occasionally with oil, until golden brown and cooked through, about 6 minutes.

Place on a serving platter. Drizzle with the extra virgin olive oil and vinegar, and season with salt and pepper. Serve immediately or at room temperature.

VARIATION:

GIANNI: My recipe for grilled vegetables is very similar to Joan's. In addition to the vegetables she recommends, I like to grill asparagus, endive, tomatoes, and onions. Sometimes I will cook whole carrots, potatoes, artichokes, or sweet potatoes in boiling water until just tender when pierced with a knife. I then halve or quarter these vegetables lengthwise and proceed with the basic grilling recipe. (Remember to remove any of the fine choke from the center of the artichokes before grilling.)

PALLINE DI RICOTTA

Ricotta Balls

MAKES 6 SERVINGS

JOAN: Stan's sister Dora remembers their mother preparing these delicate ricotta balls as a side dish to serve with chicken or veal in place of potatoes or rice. She served them plain. If you would like a light sauce, I recommend warming 3 tablespoons butter with 6 fresh sage leaves over low heat. Spoon this simple sauce over the cooked ricotta balls just before serving.

- *1 cup ricotta cheese (about ½ pound)*
- *1 large egg, lightly beaten*
- *1 tablespoon finely chopped fresh parsley leaves*
- *1 cup plain dried bread crumbs*
- *Kosher salt and freshly ground black pepper*
- *1 tablespoon butter, cut into thirds*

Mix together the cheese, egg, parsley, bread crumbs, and salt and pepper to taste to form a soft dough that holds together, adding a small amount of additional bread crumbs if necessary. Set aside.

Grease a large sauté pan with one piece of the butter. Fill the sauté pan with water to a depth of 1½ inches. Add the remaining butter and bring to a simmer.

Scoop out tablespoons of the dough and shape into compact balls. Add the balls to the simmering water and cook to warm through, about 3 minutes. Remove from the water with a slotted spoon and serve immediately.

INSALATA DI POMODORO

Fresh Tomato Salad

MAKES 4 SERVINGS

JOAN: My father grew wonderful tomatoes in his garden, and when they were in season we ate this salad almost every day. My mother, however, didn't eat raw tomatoes. Instead, she would use a piece of fresh or grilled bread (*biscotto,* as we called it) to soak up the juice and the dressing.

3 large ripe tomatoes
¼ cup extra virgin olive oil
3 fresh basil leaves, torn in half
1 clove garlic, quartered
Kosher salt and freshly ground black pepper

Cut the tomatoes in half and then into ½-inch-wide wedges. Cut these wedges in half to create chunks. Place in a medium-size serving bowl and toss with the olive oil, basil, and garlic. Season with salt and pepper just before serving.

VARIATIONS:

- For an excellent luncheon salad, add a 6-ounce can Italian tuna, drained and flaked apart with a fork, and substitute ¼ cup thinly sliced red onions for the garlic.
- Another way to vary the basic recipe is to add a cucumber that has been peeled, cut in half lengthwise, and then cut into ¼-inch-thick slices. Toss with 1 tablespoon red wine vinegar and a pinch of chopped fresh oregano leaves in addition to the ingredients in the basic recipe.

INSALATA DI SEDANO

Celery Salad

MAKES 4 SERVINGS

STAN: My brother, Frank, was fourteen years older than me. As a kid I remember him preparing this simple salad. He deftly chopped the celery with a knife that was too sharp for me to handle and topped it with lots of freshly ground black pepper.

JOAN: When preparing this salad, use the large, tender inner stalks of the celery. (I reserve the tough outer stalks for making soup.) This salad is a delicious accompaniment to any lunch or dinner.

4 cups ¼-inch-thick slices celery (about 6 stalks)
¼ cup extra virgin olive oil
Freshly ground black pepper and kosher salt

Toss the sliced celery in a medium-size serving bowl with the olive oil and generous grindings of pepper. Do not add the salt until just before serving.

VARIATION:

GIANNI: My celery salad recipe is very similar to this one. However, I like to add the following ingredients: 1 Granny Smith apple, peeled, cored, and julienned, and ½ cup crumbled goat's or Gorgonzola cheese.

INSALATA DI FAGIOLINI

String Bean Salad

MAKES 4 SERVINGS

JOAN: This is another recipe I learned from Stan's family. I like to prepare this dish when tender white or pale yellow beans are available in the market. It is a wonderful salad that is delicious served cold or at room temperature to accompany grilled meats or fish. The beans may be cooked, then cooled and refrigerated one day in advance. Refrigerate in an airtight container overnight. Return to room temperature before proceeding with the recipe.

1 pound string, waxed, or haricot vert beans, ends trimmed
1 clove garlic, chopped
Kosher salt and freshly ground black pepper
2 tablespoons red wine vinegar
¼ cup olive oil

Bring a large pot of salted water to a boil. Add the beans and cook until *al dente,* about 7 minutes (haricot vert beans will cook in about 4 minutes). Remove the beans to a serving plate and allow to cool. In a small bowl, mix together the garlic, salt and pepper to taste, and the vinegar. Gradually whisk in the olive oil. Pour over the cooled beans and toss.

INSALATA DI BARBABIETOLE ROSSE

Beet Salad

MAKES 4 SERVINGS

JOAN: Stan's family prepared this recipe in the summer and fall using fresh beets from their large garden. In the winter they would substitute canned whole beets. Fresh beets may be cooked one day ahead of time. Leave whole, cover, and store in the refrigerator. Return to room temperature before slicing, dressing, and serving. I serve this salad as part of a summer buffet.

6 medium-size beets, tops removed
1 teaspoon chopped fresh oregano leaves or ½ teaspoon dried
2 tablespoons red wine vinegar
1 clove garlic, chopped
2 tablespoons olive oil

Trim each beet to remove any roots and the tougher skin on the top and bottom. Place in a pot and cover with cold water. Bring to a boil and cook until the beets are tender when pierced with a knife, about 20 minutes. Drain and set aside to cool slightly. Peel the beets while they are still warm to the touch, and cut into ¼-inch-thick slices. Toss with the oregano, vinegar, garlic, and olive oil. Serve at room temperature.

VARIATIONS:

- Beet greens may be cooked and served as a side dish. Follow the recipe for escarole on page 269.

GIANNI: My recipe for beet salad is very similar to Joan's. I substitute balsamic vinegar for the red wine vinegar and add ½ cup thinly sliced red onions, 1 tablespoon finely grated orange zest, 2 teaspoons chopped fresh chives, and 2 teaspoons chopped fresh parsley leaves to her basic recipe.

INSALATA DI CAROTE

Carrot Salad

MAKES 4 SERVINGS

JOAN: During the year that we were living in Italy, Stan and I enjoyed eating out at local trattorias. We liked to frequent neighborhood spots that we could easily walk to from our apartment. One restaurant had a long table set up near the entrance where they displayed an array of colorful salads, among which was a simple carrot salad. I ordered it and loved its taste and texture. I decided to try it at home, and this recipe has been part of my repertoire ever since.

Dress this salad just before serving so the flavor and texture stay crisp. I often serve this dish at lunch, and sometimes when I'm serving it with dinner I will add ¼ cup soft, plump raisins.

2 large carrots, peeled
¼ cup extra virgin olive oil
1 tablespoon freshly squeezed lemon juice
Kosher salt and freshly ground black pepper

Use a vegetable peeler to cut the carrots into long thin strips. There should be about 2½ cups of carrot strips. Place in a bowl and toss with the olive oil and lemon juice. Season with salt and pepper and serve.

VARIATION:

GIANNI: To this traditional recipe I like to add the following ingredients to create a colorful, refreshing salad: 1 peeled, cored, and grated Granny Smith apple, 1 cup thinly sliced radicchio, 1 cup thinly sliced endive, and 2 cups thinly sliced tender cabbage.

INSALATA DI CAVOLI

Italian Cole Slaw

MAKES 4 SERVINGS

STAN: My mother made this salad often. It's great at lunch with a sandwich or served as a salad after spareribs or other meats. The trick is to cut the cabbage as thin as possible and to toss the salad just before serving to achieve a crisp, fresh flavor.

JOAN: Cole slaw is a classic summer salad that is usually prepared using mayonnaise. I find this version to be less filling and more refreshing.

1 teaspoon kosher salt
Freshly ground black pepper
2 tablespoons red wine vinegar
¼ cup olive oil
½ head tender cabbage, trimmed, cored, and thinly sliced

In a large serving bowl, whisk together the salt, generous grindings of pepper, the vinegar, and the olive oil. Just before serving add the cabbage and toss well.

INSALATA DI PATATE

Potato Salad

MAKES 4 SERVINGS

JOAN: Potatoes prepared this way make a great lunch dish served along with roasted peppers, a green salad, and an assortment of olives and cheeses. I also serve this salad with grilled meat or as part of a buffet. Serve it warm, at room temperature, or chilled.

6 large all-purpose, red, or Yukon Gold potatoes (about 2 pounds), scrubbed
1 clove garlic, crushed in a press
1 teaspoon Dijon mustard
2 tablespoons red wine vinegar
Kosher salt and freshly ground black pepper
¼ cup olive oil
1 tablespoon chopped fresh parsley leaves
2 tablespoons chopped onions or shallots

Place the potatoes in a large pot. Cover with water to about 1 inch above the potatoes. Add salt and bring to a boil. Continue to boil until tender when pierced with a knife, about 15 minutes. Drain, run under cold water to cool, and cut into 2-inch pieces. (If using all-purpose potatoes, peel and discard the skins.) Place in a large serving bowl.

In a small bowl, whisk together the garlic, mustard, vinegar, and salt and pepper to taste. Gradually whisk in the olive oil. Pour over the potatoes and toss to coat evenly. Add the parsley and onions, toss gently, and serve.

INSALATA DI LENTICCHIE ALLA MEDITERRANEA

Mediterranean Lentil Salad

MAKES 8 SERVINGS

GIANNI: Lentils are traditionally eaten in Italy at the end of the year because people say, "Eat lentils and it will bring you money in the New Year." I don't know how or where this expression came from, and even though it hasn't worked yet, I don't want to tempt fate so I continue to eat lentils. This salad may be served to accompany fish, meat, or chicken and is also delicious served for lunch.

1 pound dried green lentils, picked over
1 bay leaf
1 cup diced red onions
1 clove garlic, chopped
1 tablespoon chopped fresh parsley leaves
⅛ teaspoon ground cumin
1 teaspoon chopped fresh mint leaves
3 tablespoons freshly squeezed lemon juice (from about 1 lemon)
2 tablespoons red or sherry wine vinegar
3 tablespoons extra virgin olive oil
Kosher salt and freshly ground black pepper

Place the lentils in a large pot and add water to a level 2 inches above them. Add the bay leaf and set over medium-high heat. Bring to a boil, then simmer gently over medium-low heat until the lentils are tender, about 1 hour. Drain the lentils and allow to cool.

In a large serving bowl, toss the lentils with the onions, garlic, parsley, cumin, and mint. In a separate bowl, whisk together the lemon juice, vinegar, olive oil, and salt and pepper to taste. Pour the dressing over the lentils and toss to coat evenly. Serve immediately.

VARIATIONS:

- Any good-quality lentil may be substituted for the green lentils called for in this recipe.
- Chickpeas, borlotti (pinto or cranberry), or cannellini beans may be substituted for the lentils. Dried beans should be soaked overnight before proceeding with the basic recipe. Canned beans that have been drained and rinsed may be tossed with this dressing.
- ½ red bell pepper and 1 tender stalk celery, both cut into small dice, may be added to the salad.
- I recently tried a lentil salad that included 1 tablespoon coconut oil. Although not an Italian ingredient, it was very good.

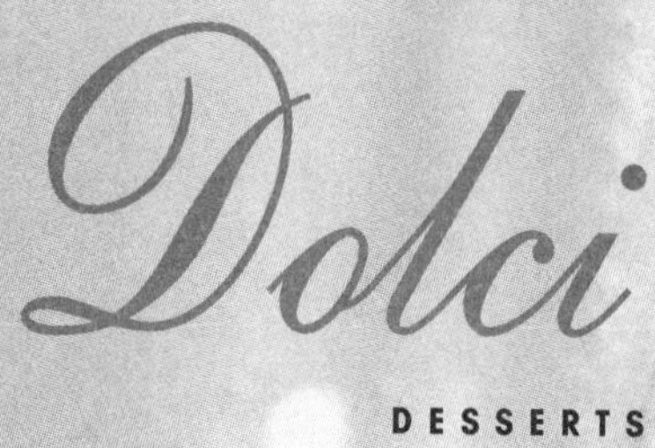

Dolci

DESSERTS

JOAN: *Biscotti* are really the only sweet I bake on a regular basis. They keep well, and Stan enjoys them with espresso after lunch or dinner. My mother, who shared her recipe with me, loved to bake *biscotti* in many shapes—braiding, and making them in a circle. She baked quite a bit, and Sunday dinners were not complete without a slice of her terrific apple pie. My brother Vince remembers our mother baking sour cream cakes—because she was always in a hurry, it wasn't unusual to find a few eggshells in the cake.

My sister Angie and her husband, Joe, have carried on this baking tradition, preparing desserts professionally and for family gatherings. Every year Angie, along with my sister Grace and sisters-in-law, Marilyn and Natalie, would bake an incredible assortment of outstanding treats for the Feast of Our Lady of Mt. Carmel. They cooked for several days to satisfy close to forty people who assembled under the grape arbor in my parents' backyard. As a result, our family has pretty high standards for baked goods.

Other than for holiday and birthday parties, our family doesn't eat a lot of desserts today. Traditionally our meals end with a dish of seasonal fresh fruits, dried figs, and nuts in their shells. This type of dessert is as good for conversation as it is for the digestion. I think this family custom goes back to my childhood. Toward the end of the evening or after a Sunday afternoon supper, we would hear the whistle of the peanut man. It was a treat for us children to be able to run outside and purchase our individual bags of hot roasted peanuts. My father would eat his while finishing a glass of homemade wine. Along with my brothers, Joe and Vince, I still like to have wine and peanuts after dinner.

GIANNI: No holiday meal is complete without dessert. For me, Christmas equals *panettone* and Easter equals *colomba,* a cake that is baked in the shape of a dove and signifies peace. Classic *panettone* is made with raisins and candied fruit, although it may also be baked with chocolate or cream inside. Fresh *panettone* is always served with a bottle of Spumante, a sweeter, less expensive version of Champagne. Leftover *panettone* is eaten over the next few mornings with *caffè latte.* We purchased our *panettone* from the Ponticello bakery and they were always light, sweet, and the best I've ever had. I have begged them for their family recipe but they will not part with it. They did, however, give me the recipe for their exceptional orange cookies, which I have included in this section.

The week before Christmas, my father and I would visit all the good customers who had supported my mother's small grocery store throughout the year. We made our rounds in our little Cinque Cento Fiat Familiara to wish them a merry Christmas and to present them with a *panettone.* Of course, the size of the *panettone* signified just how good a customer they had been. That was the most prosperous week of the year for me because for every door I knocked on, there were always a few lire stuffed into my pockets. The pleasant exception was when people wanted me to taste their fritters or drink a hot chocolate or, in some cases, wine. As I was too young for wine, I preferred the hot chocolate, which warmed me up after my many trips in and out of the car.

Celebrating birthdays was a big thing in my family. There were so many of us that we had a party almost every month. On Sundays we indulged in some of the little *pastine,* or small pastries, from the local pastry shop, often eating them while they were still warm. This shop is now run by my neighbor and friend Francesco Pigato, and I have included his recipe for *ciambella Veneta,* a typical sweet bread from our region. Whenever I return to Italy, I try to convince Francesco to bring his outstanding pastries to America. But he is very content with his life the way it is, so between visits I must bake my own favorite desserts, many of which are included here.

STANLEY: I believe dessert exists so we might stave off the inevitable depression that follows a great meal. A rush of sugar will do this, at least for a time. It is also the one part of the meal, as we tried to show in *Big Night,* that has no real time constraints. It can drift into the night, or right into breakfast. The *dolci* that follow are perfect for this most relaxing part of a fine repast.

BISCOTTI CASARECCI DEL PONTICELLO

Ponticello's Orange Cookies

MAKES ABOUT 48 COOKIES

GIANNI: In my town there is a bakery called Ponticello, which means "little bridge." It has been run by one family for four generations and is now operated by Daniela, who is a terrific and dedicated baker. Her day begins at 4 A.M. with the preparation of the first of four batches of bread. The bread is so good that people line up to purchase it, knowing that the warm loaves will be ready for sale at 6, 8, 10, and 12 o'clock each day. When I was running my family's restaurant, Ponticello supplied all of the bread we served. On the days that I went to pick up our order, the bread's aroma filled my car and I had to remember to purchase an extra loaf so I could eat it on the ride home.

When I returned to the United States, I wrote to thank Daniela for all the wonderful bread Ponticello had baked for us. She wrote back and sent me this cookie recipe, which has been handed down from generation to generation in her family. They were originally cooked in the bakery's coal oven, just as the embers were dying. Serve them with coffee after dinner, for a sweet at breakfast, or use in place of the ladyfingers in tiramisù.

4 cups all-purpose flour
2 tablespoons baking powder
Pinch of kosher salt
2 large eggs
1 cup sugar
½ cup (1 stick) butter, softened
1 teaspoon pure orange extract
½ cup milk

Preheat the oven to 350 degrees F. Line several baking sheets with parchment paper and set aside.

In a medium-size bowl, whisk together the flour, baking powder, and salt. Set aside.

In a large bowl, beat together the eggs and sugar with an electric mixer. Add the butter and beat just to combine. Gradually beat the flour mixture into the egg mixture. Pour the orange extract into the milk, and with the mixer running, gradually add the milk to the batter. The dough will come together to form a ball.

Turn the dough out onto a work surface. Flatten it into a disk shape and cut into quarters. Roll each quarter into a log about 1 inch in diameter. Cut each log into ½-inch-thick slices, and place them 1 inch apart on the prepared baking sheets. Bake until lightly golden brown, about 18 minutes. Remove to a rack to cool completely. Store in an airtight container for up to 2 weeks.

BISCOTTI TROPIANO

Tropiano Biscotti with Anisette Flavoring

MAKES ABOUT 36 COOKIES

JOAN: My mother taught me how to bake these *biscotti,* which are wonderful with coffee or dipped in red wine.

2½ cups all-purpose flour
2 teaspoons baking powder
¼ teaspoon kosher salt
2 tablespoons anise seeds
4 large eggs
1 cup sugar
¼ cup (½ stick) butter, melted and cooled
3 tablespoons pure anise extract or anisette liqueur

Preheat the oven to 350 degrees F. Grease and flour two baking sheets or line them with parchment paper, and set aside.

In a medium-size bowl, sift together the flour, baking powder, and salt. Stir in the anise seeds. Set aside.

Place the eggs in a large bowl and beat with an electric mixer on high speed until foamy. Add the sugar and beat until smooth, about 1 minute. Beat in the melted butter and anise extract. Reduce the speed to low and beat in the dry ingredients until just incorporated.

With a rubber spatula, scoop one quarter of the dough out onto one of the prepared baking sheets. Use the spatula to shape the dough into a log about 10 inches long × 2 inches wide × ¾ inch thick. Repeat this procedure with the other three quarters of the dough. Place two logs 2 inches apart on each prepared baking sheet.

Bake until the logs are light golden brown and firm to the touch, about 25 minutes. Remove from the oven and allow the logs to cool slightly on the baking sheets.

Reduce the oven temperature to 325 degrees F.

Lift each log off the baking sheet and transfer to a cutting board. Use a serrated knife to cut each log on the bias at 1-inch intervals. Lay the cookies, cut side down, on the baking sheets.

Return the *biscotti* to the oven and bake until lightly browned and dry, about 5 minutes. Turn them over and continue baking to dry and lightly brown the other side, another 5 minutes. Transfer to a wire rack to cool completely. Store in an airtight container for up to 1 week or in the freezer for up to 1 month.

VARIATION:

- ½ cup coarsely chopped almonds may be stirred into the batter along with the dry ingredients.

CANTUCCI TOSCANI

Tuscan Biscotti

MAKES ABOUT 36 COOKIES

GIANNI: After *biscotti* became the rage at cafés and bars in America a few years ago, I decided to experiment with some recipes. I wanted to produce a cookie with a wonderful anise-nut flavor and with a less tooth-breaking bite than I usually found. This recipe produces a cookie that is crisp and not too sweet. I like to serve it with after-dessert wines.

My first choice would be Torcolato di Maculan, a dessert wine made near my home in Italy. It is great to drink cold, makes a nice addition to sorbet and granita recipes that call for wine, and can also be used to prepare a warm vinaigrette salad dressing. Sauternes, Moscato, and Vin Santo are other very good dessert wines that pair well with this cookie. Of course, *biscotti* are also very good to eat in the morning with coffee or milk.

3¼ cups all-purpose flour
2½ teaspoons baking powder
½ teaspoon kosher salt
½ cup (1 stick) butter, softened
1¼ cups sugar
2 large eggs
2 large egg yolks
¼ cup honey
½ teaspoon pure vanilla extract
¼t teaspoon pure almond extract
¼ teaspoon pure anise extract
1 cup unblanched whole almonds

In a medium-size bowl, mix together the flour, baking powder, and salt. Set aside.

In a large bowl, with an electric mixer on high speed, cream the butter and sugar together until light and fluffy, about 5 minutes. Add the whole eggs and yolks, one at a time, beating after each addition. Beat in the honey. Add the extracts and mix well. Reduce the speed to low and gradually beat in the dry ingredients. Stir in the almonds, mixing until they are well dispersed.

Turn the dough out onto a sheet of plastic wrap. Form the dough into a ball and flatten it slightly. Wrap and refrigerate until firm, about 30 minutes.

Preheat the oven to 350 degrees F. Grease two baking sheets or line them with parchment paper, and set aside.

Remove the dough from the plastic wrap and divide it in half. On a lightly floured work surface, roll half the dough into a baguette-shaped log about 2 inches wide × 13 inches long, and transfer it to one of the prepared baking sheets. Repeat with the other half of the dough, transferring it to the other prepared baking sheet. Bake until firm and golden, about 30 minutes. Remove from the oven and allow to cool for 15 minutes.

Reduce the oven temperature to 250 degrees F.

Transfer the cooled logs to a cutting board. Using a serrated knife, slice each log on the bias at ½-inch intervals. Place the slices on the baking sheets, cut side down. Bake until dry and lightly browned, about 10 minutes on each side. Transfer the *biscotti* to a wire rack and allow to cool completely. Store in an airtight container for up to 1 week.

REGINA

Fried Cookies

SERVES 12

JOAN: *Regina* means "queen" in Italian and these cookies are crownlike in shape—thus the name. People would ask my mother to prepare them for special occasions such as weddings and christenings, and she was always happy to oblige.

I cooked my first batch of these cookies as a young married woman to bring to a gathering at Stan's family's house, hoping to impress them. I watched with anticipation as the cookies were tasted and was surprised when no one said anything. When I sampled one myself, I realized why. I must have substituted salt for the sugar—the cookies tasted awful.

3 large eggs, at room temperature
¼ cup granulated sugar
4½ teaspoons solid vegetable shortening, melted
3 tablespoons milk
1 tablespoon whiskey
½ teaspoon kosher salt
3½ cups all-purpose flour
4 cups corn oil for frying
1 cup confectioners' sugar

In a large bowl, beat the eggs with an electric mixer until foamy. Add the granulated sugar and blend thoroughly. Beat in the melted shortening, milk, whiskey, and salt. Gradually add 2½ cups of the flour, ½ cup at a time, beating to form a firm dough. Turn the dough out onto a floured work surface. Knead, adding more flour, ¼ cup at a time, until the dough is no longer sticky. Test the center of the dough by breaking it in half. The center should be almost as dry as the surface of the dough. If it is still sticky, add more flour and continue to knead. Set the dough aside to rest under a dish towel for 5 minutes.

Cut off one third of the dough, leaving the rest under the dish towel. On a lightly floured work surface, roll the dough out into a large, evenly thin circle (the dough should be paper-thin). Use a pastry wheel to cut the dough into long strips about ¾ inch wide. Separate three of the strips. Pinch the strips together at one end and then loosely braid them. Pinch the ends of the braided strips together. Pinch the top and bottom of the braid together to form a crown. Set it aside on a clean dish towel and continue to braid the remaining dough strips. Any scraps may be reserved and fried along with the crowns.

When the first third of the dough is finished, repeat the procedure with the remaining dough, one third at a time, braiding it into crowns.

Pour the corn oil into a small frying pan to a depth of 1 inch. (Reserve any remaining oil to add to the pan as needed. If you add oil to the pan, be sure to let it reheat before adding any dough.)

Warm the oil over medium heat until it is hot but not smoking. Add one small scrap of rolled dough to the oil. If the oil bubbles and the dough rises to the surface, the oil is hot enough for cooking.

Line two baking sheets with paper towels. Set aside. Place ¼ cup of the confectioners' sugar in a fine-mesh sieve and set aside.

Add two braided crowns to the pan. Use a fork to lightly fluff each cookie so that the braids open slightly as they begin to cook. Fry the cookies until lightly browned on both sides, about 3 minutes. Remove from the oil to one of the paper-towel-lined baking sheets. Drain and transfer to the other paper-towel-lined baking sheet. Repeat with the remaining crowns, adding more oil to the pan as needed.

Shake the sieve with the confectioners' sugar over the warm cookies to lightly dust them, adding more confectioners' sugar to the sieve as necessary. When they have cooled, transfer the cookies to a serving dish. The cookies may be dusted with additional confectioners' sugar just before serving.

CASTAGNOLE O FRITTOLE DELLA MAMMA BERTILLA

Mamma's Little Fritters

MAKES 6 TO 8 SERVINGS

GIANNI: The season of Lent is preceded by carnivals and festivals in Italy as in many other countries. My mother prepared these fritters for us only during that time of the year, and whenever I prepare them, it brings back great memories of the sights, flavors, and excitement of this festival. *Castagnole* are fried in batches and are similar to a doughnut without the hole. They cook best in a cast-iron pan.

1¼ cups all-purpose flour
2 teaspoons cornstarch or potato starch
½ teaspoon baking soda
¼ teaspoon kosher salt
¼ cup raisins (optional)
1 tablespoon rum or grappa
¼ cup (½ stick) butter, softened
3 tablespoons plus 2 teaspoons granulated sugar
1 large egg
2 teaspoons grated lemon zest
¼ cup plus 1 tablespoon milk
½ teaspoon pure vanilla extract
Corn or canola oil for frying
Confectioners' sugar for dusting

Sift together the flour, cornstarch, baking soda, and salt in a large bowl. Set aside. (If you are using the raisins, soak them in the rum for 5 minutes.)

In a small bowl, cream together the butter and sugar until light and fluffy. Add the egg and beat until combined. Add the lemon zest, milk, vanilla, and rum. (Stir in the raisins if using.) Add to the dry ingredients and mix well to create a batter that is slightly thicker than pancake batter and can be pushed off the spoon with your finger. If it is too thin, stir in a small amount of additional sifted flour. Set aside.

Line a large plate with paper towels and set aside.

Fill a medium-size sauté pan with corn oil to a depth of 1 inch. Heat until almost smoking (about 425 degrees F). Scoop out a generous tablespoon of batter and add it to the oil. It should bubble and float in the oil. Slowly add more batter, a generous tablespoon at a time. Cook in small batches, turning in the oil, until the *castagnole* are dark brown and cooked through, about 3 minutes. Remove from the oil with a slotted spoon, and drain on the paper-towel-lined plate. Allow to cool slightly, then transfer to a serving dish. Place the confectioners' sugar in a fine-mesh sieve and shake over the *castagnole* to lightly dust. Serve immediately.

CREMA CANNOLI

Cream-Filled Cannoli

MAKES 48 SMALL SHELLS

JOAN: This recipe for cream-filled cannoli, a classic Italian dessert, comes from Stan's sister Dora. She prepares them during the Christmas holidays, making the cream several hours ahead of time and filling the cannoli shells just before serving. Dora prefers to use small shells, which may be purchased at Italian bakeries and gourmet stores. The cinnamon flavoring may be purchased at bakeries, drugstores, or specialty food shops.

3 pounds ricotta cheese
½ pound confectioners' sugar, plus more for dusting
2 drops liquid cinnamon flavoring
⅛ teaspoon pure vanilla extract
48 cannoli shells

Thoroughly mix together the ricotta, sugar, cinnamon flavoring, and vanilla. Store in the refrigerator until ready to fill the shells. Stir briskly, and then, using a small spoon, fill each shell with the cream. Arrange on a serving platter. Place some confectioners' sugar in a fine-mesh sieve and shake over the filled shells to lightly dust. Serve immediately.

STRUDEL

Strudel Filled with Apples, Pears, and Walnuts

MAKES 6 SERVINGS

GIANNI: The Veneto area, where I grew up, is very close to the Austrian border. This proximity has influenced the local cooking for centuries and explains why apple strudel can be found in most of the local bars and cafes. The *pasta matta,* or crazy dough, used in this recipe is lower in fat than traditional puff pastry and is very flavorful.

FOR THE PASTRY:

1¼ cups cake flour
2 teaspoons granulated sugar
½ teaspoon kosher salt
1 large egg, at room temperature
1 teaspoon white or cider vinegar
2 tablespoons butter, melted
2½ tablespoons warm water

FOR THE FILLING:

¼ cup raisins
2 tablespoons dark rum (such as Myers's)
2 tablespoons butter
2 cups peeled, cored, and diced apples (about 2 large apples)
2 cups peeled, cored, and diced firm ripe pears (about 2 large pears)
2 tablespoons freshly squeezed lemon juice
½ cup plus 2 teaspoons granulated sugar
¼ cup pine nuts or roughly chopped walnuts
¾ cup finely crushed cookie crumbs (such as amaretti or graham crackers) or plain dried bread crumbs

1 large egg
2 tablespoons water
2 tablespoons confectioners' sugar

To prepare the pastry, sift together the flour, sugar, and salt in a medium-size bowl. In a small bowl, whisk together the egg, vinegar, melted butter, and warm water. Using a fork, slowly work the liquid ingredients into the flour. When the dough comes together, turn it out onto a lightly floured work surface and knead it into a compact circular shape. Wrap in plastic wrap and refrigerate for at least 30 minutes. (The dough may also be made in a food processor fitted with a steel blade.)

To prepare the filling, soak the raisins in the rum to soften, about 5 minutes. Melt the butter in a large skillet set over medium-high heat. Add the apples and pears and cook, tossing frequently, until warmed through, about 3 minutes. Stir in the lemon juice, ½ cup of the sugar, the rum-raisin mixture, and the pine nuts. Cook to flavor the fruit with these ingredients, about 2 minutes. Strain the fruit in a fine-mesh sieve, reserving the liquid. Set the fruit aside to cool. Return the liquid to the skillet and increase the heat to high. Reduce the liquid to a thickened, caramel-colored syrup,

8 to 10 minutes. Stir this syrup into the fruit mixture and allow to cool to room temperature. Stir in the crushed cookies. The filling should be dry and sticky.

Preheat the oven to 400 degrees F. Line a baking sheet with parchment paper and set aside. In a small bowl, whisk together the egg and water to make an egg wash. Set aside.

On a lightly floured surface, roll the dough out into a ⅛-inch-thick rectangle measuring about 10 × 17 inches. Trim the rolled dough to a rectangle measuring about 15 × 8½ inches, with the long edge facing you. Brush the dough with some of the egg wash. Use a fork to randomly prick the dough.

Distribute the filling evenly over the dough 2 inches up from the long edge of the dough and 1 inch in from either end. Pull the long edge of the pastry gently upward and tightly fold it over the filling. Roll the strudel into a neat log. Place the filled strudel, seam side down, on the prepared baking sheet.

Tuck the ends of the pastry neatly under the strudel. Arrange thin strips of the cut-away dough in a decorative pattern of crosses or X's on top of the filled strudel. Brush the top and sides with the remaining egg wash, and randomly prick the top with a fork. Sprinkle with the remaining 2 teaspoons sugar. Bake until the pastry is cooked and golden brown, 25 to 30 minutes.

Just before serving, place the confectioners' sugar in a fine-mesh sieve. Sprinkle over the top of the strudel to dust, and serve warm or at room temperature, cutting slices on the bias.

VARIATIONS:

- ¼ teaspoon grated orange zest may be added to the filling.
- Chopped dried figs or chopped pitted dates may be used in place of the raisins.
- All pears or all apples may be substituted for the mix of apples and pears.

CREMA PASTICCERA

Italian Cream

MAKES ENOUGH FILLING FOR 48 SMALL OR 28 LARGE CREAM PUFFS

JOAN: Stan's family prepared cream puffs for dessert during the Christmas and Easter holidays, and when special company was invited to dinner. Over the years they used different recipes for cream puffs from a variety of cookbooks, but the recipe for the cream filling always remained the same. A good general cookbook will have a classic recipe for cream puffs that may be filled with this light cream. The filling may be prepared two days in advance. Cover and refrigerate. Return to room temperature and stir briskly before filling the cream puffs. The filling may also be frozen for up to three months.

4 large eggs, lightly beaten
1½ cups granulated sugar
1½ cups cake flour (not self-rising)
4 cups milk
2 tablespoons finely grated lemon zest (from about 3 lemons)
1 teaspoon pure vanilla extract
1 cup (2 sticks) unsalted butter, softened
48 small or 28 large cream puffs
Confectioners' sugar for dusting

Place the eggs, granulated sugar, cake flour, milk, lemon zest, and vanilla in a large saucepan and beat together with an electric mixer until smooth. Place the saucepan over low heat and cook, stirring, until thickened, about 5 minutes. Remove from the heat and set aside to cool slightly.

Stir the butter into the cream until it has melted completely.

Cut a ¾-inch-thick slice off the top of each cream puff and set aside. Remove any soft dough from inside the puff and discard. Generously fill each puff, capping them with the reserved tops. Arrange on a serving platter. Place a few tablespoons of confectioners' sugar in a fine-mesh sieve. Shake over the filled cream puffs to dust lightly, and serve.

VARIATION: Dora, Stan's sister, created another wonderful use for this filling. She would purchase a round sponge cake from a local bakery and slice it into four equal layers. She brushed each layer with a tablespoon or two of dark rum, such as Myers's, and then spread a thick layer of the cream filling between the layers and on the top of the final layer. She dusted the middle layers with unsweetened cocoa powder, shaking a few tablespoons through a fine-mesh sieve to evenly coat the cream.

CIAMBELLA VENETA DI PIGATO

Veneto Sweet Bread

SERVES 8 TO 10

GIANNI: My friend and neighbor Francesco shared this family recipe with me. Francesco is a third-generation baker. His grandfather opened their original shop in 1919. It was the first commercial oven in our area, and he began by baking breads. He passed his recipes on to his son, who continued to bake breads and began to bake pastries. Francesco has carried on with many of the traditional recipes while adding some of his own. His pastries are some of the finest I have ever tasted. This recipe is a variation on a cake that is very popular and available all over Italy. Delicious with coffee after dinner or for breakfast, it has just a hint of lemon flavor. This cake keeps well for one or two days, stored in an airtight container. Serve it plain or, in the summer, with assorted sliced fruit and fresh berries.

½ cup milk
½ cup (1 stick) butter, melted
½ cup plus 1 tablespoon sugar
1 large egg
1 teaspoon pure vanilla extract
2½ cups all-purpose flour
½ teaspoon kosher salt
2 teaspoons baking powder
2 teaspoons grated lemon zest (from about 1 lemon)
1 large egg yolk
1 tablespoon water

Preheat the oven to 350 degrees F. Lightly grease a baking sheet or line with parchment paper and set aside.

Place the milk and butter in a small saucepan set over medium heat. Melt the butter and warm the milk through but do not boil. Remove from the heat and stir in ½ cup of the sugar. Set aside to cool to room temperature. Whisk in the egg and vanilla. Set aside.

Sift 2¼ cups of the flour, the salt, and the baking powder together in a large bowl. Add the zest and stir to combine. With an electric mixer set on low, gradually add the butter mixture. Mix just to combine.

Dust a work surface with the remaining ¼ cup flour. Turn the dough out onto the work surface and knead, working in just enough of the flour to make a smooth, soft dough. Roll the dough into a log shape about 1 inch thick and 18 inches long. Bring the ends of the log together to form a circle, pinching to seal the joint. Place on the baking sheet.

Whisk together the egg yolk and water. Brush this egg wash on the top and sides of the dough. Dust the dough with the remaining 1 tablespoon sugar. Bake until the bread is golden brown and a knife inserted in the center comes out clean, about 30 minutes. Let cool completely on a wire rack before serving.

DOLCE DI PERA DELLA ZIA ANGELA

Angela's Pear Cake

MAKES 1 CAKE; ABOUT 12 SERVINGS

GIANNI: When I was growing up, my aunt Angela was like a second mother to me, and every afternoon she baked a different cake. Because I have always loved pear desserts, this one stands out in my memory. It may also be prepared using thin slices of apple.

½ cup chopped walnuts or almonds
1 teaspoon ground cinnamon
1½ cups sugar
2 cups all-purpose flour
1 teaspoon baking powder
1 teaspoon baking soda
Pinch of kosher salt
1 cup (2 sticks) butter, softened
2 large eggs
1 teaspoon pure vanilla extract
1 cup heavy cream
1 cup peeled, cored, and thinly sliced pear (about 1 large pear)

Preheat the oven to 375 degrees F. Grease and flour a tube pan, tapping out any excess flour, and set aside.

In a small bowl, toss together the nuts, cinnamon, and ½ cup of the sugar. Set aside.

Sift together the flour, baking powder, baking soda, and salt in a medium-size bowl. Set aside.

In a large bowl, beat together the butter and remaining 1 cup sugar with an electric mixer until creamy, about 5 minutes. Scrape down the sides of the bowl with a rubber spatula. Add the eggs, one at a time, beating after each addition. Mix in the vanilla and heavy cream. Scrape down the sides of the bowl and stir in the flour mixture. Mix until just combined.

Spoon half of the batter into the prepared pan, spreading it evenly with a rubber spatula. Arrange the pear slices in a single even layer over the batter. Sprinkle half of the nut mixture on top of the pears. Evenly spread the remaining batter on top. Sprinkle the remaining nut mixture on top of the batter. Bake until golden brown and slightly firm to the touch, 40 to 45 minutes. (A skewer inserted in the center may not come out clean because of the cooked pears.) Allow to cool before serving. Store in an airtight container for up to 2 days.

DOLCE DI PRUGNE E POLENTA

Plum and Polenta Cake

MAKES 8 SERVINGS

GIANNI: Ground cornmeal is a primary ingredient in the cooking of the Veneto region of Italy, where I grew up. Many baking recipes using cornmeal were created during the Second World War, when ingredients from outside our region were in short supply. My aunt Angela created this cake and it is a family favorite.

⅓ cup plus 2 tablespoons finely ground cornmeal or semolina flour
1 cup all-purpose flour
1½ teaspoons baking powder
Pinch of kosher salt
13 tablespoons butter, softened
¾ cup granulated sugar
4 large egg yolks
2 large eggs
1 teaspoon grated lemon zest
1 teaspoon pure vanilla extract
4 plums, cut in half and pitted
2 tablespoons packed light brown sugar

Preheat the oven to 350 degrees F. Grease and lightly flour an 8 × 2-inch round cake pan or an 8-inch springform pan, tapping out any excess flour. Set aside.

In a small bowl, toss together the cornmeal, all-purpose flour, baking powder, and salt. Set aside.

In a large bowl, beat the butter and granulated sugar together with an electric mixer, until pale yellow and creamy, about 5 minutes. Scrape down the sides of the bowl with a rubber spatula and add the egg yolks, one at a time, beating after each addition. Scrape down the sides of the bowl and add the whole eggs, one at a time, beating after each addition. Mix in the lemon zest and vanilla. Add the dry ingredients and blend until just combined.

Spread the batter in the prepared pan. Place the plum halves, skin side down, at even intervals on top of the batter. Sprinkle the brown sugar on top of the fruit and batter. Bake until the cake is golden brown on top and a toothpick inserted in the center comes out clean, about 45 minutes.

VARIATION: Quartered figs (about 6) or pitted sweet cherries (about ½ cup) may be used in place of the plums.

TORTA SABBIOSA CON SALSA AL MASCARPONE

Traditional Flaky Cake with Mascarpone Sauce

MAKES 8 TO 10 SERVINGS

GIANNI: For many years I worked with a wonderful chef, Marta Pullini, and we came to be good friends. Marta has always been interested in adapting recipes from the Emilia Romagna region of Italy, where she is from, and I noticed that many of her dishes were similar to ones I had grown up with. Marta inspired me to revisit many of the family recipes I took for granted. I thought this cake was too old-fashioned to bring back, but then I remembered its delicate texture and great flavor and decided, "Why not?" This is a very flaky, light-tasting cake. Potato starch is available in health food stores and in some supermarkets. This cake may be stored in an airtight container for up to three days.

14 tablespoons (1¾ sticks) butter, softened
¾ cup plus 2 tablespoons granulated sugar
1 teaspoon pure vanilla extract
1½ cups potato starch
½ teaspoon kosher salt
3 large eggs
1 tablespoon baking powder
1 tablespoon cognac or dark rum

FOR THE MASCARPONE SAUCE:
8 ounces mascarpone cheese, at room temperature
2 tablespoons confectioners' sugar
1 tablespoon Grand Marnier, brandy, or grappa

Preheat the oven to 300 degrees F. Grease the bottom and sides of a loaf pan with butter or cooking spray. Line the bottom and sides of the pan with parchment paper. Lightly grease the parchment paper with butter or cooking spray, and set aside.

In a large bowl, with an electric mixer, cream the butter with the granulated sugar and vanilla until very creamy, about 5 minutes. Mix in the potato starch and salt. Add the eggs, one at a time, beating after each addition. In a small bowl, whisk together the baking powder and cognac. Beat this mixture into the cake batter.

Pour the batter into the prepared loaf pan. Bake until it is lightly browned and a cake tester comes out clean, about 1 hour. (Do not open the oven during the first 40 minutes of baking or the cake may fall.) Remove the cake from the oven and allow it to cool in the pan. When it has cooled, gently remove it from the pan and peel away the parchment paper.

When ready to serve, whisk together the mascarpone cheese, confectioners' sugar, and Grand Marnier. Cut the cake into 1-inch-thick slices and top with a dollop of mascarpone sauce.

VARIATIONS:

- Whipped cream or the zabaglione recipe on page 316 may be served in place of the mascarpone sauce.

- This cake may also be served with assorted fresh summer berries.

TORTA FREGOLOTTA

Crumbly Cake

MAKES 8 SERVINGS

GIANNI: In the Veneto region there are many beautiful towns, such as Treviso and Asolo. Among these hill towns, which are dotted with vineyards, are the famous Renaissance villas of Palladio. This simple traditional recipe may be as old as some of those villas. My very good friend Guiotto Sergio shared this recipe with me. The very dry, loose batter may look strange, but don't worry, it will come together in the heat of the oven and turn out just fine.

Fregolotta, or crumbly cake, is typically served in the autumn during the first pressing of the grapes. The cake is placed in the center of the table and each person is poured a glass of Novello, or new wine, which is comparable to the French Beaujolais. Small pieces of *fregolotta* are broken off and neatly dipped into the wine before eating. You may serve this dessert with any sweet wine or with a steaming cup of espresso.

½ cup plus 2 tablespoons finely ground blanched almonds
½ cup finely ground cornmeal
½ cup plus 2 tablespoons sugar
2 cups plus 2 tablespoons cake flour (not self-rising)
2 large egg yolks
1 teaspoon pure vanilla extract
1 teaspoon grated lemon zest
1 teaspoon grated orange zest
10 tablespoons (1¼ sticks) butter, softened

Preheat the oven to 375 degrees F. Grease a 9 × 15-inch baking sheet and set aside.

In a large bowl, toss together the almonds, cornmeal, sugar, and cake flour. Make a well in the center of these dry ingredients and add the egg yolks, vanilla, and lemon and orange zests. Use a fork to incorporate the wet ingredients into the dry ingredients. With your hands, rub the butter into the dry mixture to form a crumbly dough.

Shake the dough out onto the prepared baking sheet, spreading to distribute it evenly. Pat it down. Bake until golden brown and firm, about 25 minutes. Allow to cool, and serve. Or break into small pieces and store in an airtight container for up to 1 week.

DOLCE DI RICOTTA SEMPLICE

Simple Ricotta Cake

MAKES ONE 8-INCH CAKE; 8 SERVINGS

GIANNI: This cake is best made one day before you plan to serve it. The cake is very moist and tender, so be very careful when removing it from the pan. If you like, it may be served with the sauce described in the recipe for *Cremino di Ricotta con Frutta Stagionale* on page 318, using either raspberries or strawberries for the sauce.

2 cups ricotta cheese
1½ tablespoons butter, softened
5 large eggs
3 tablespoons all-purpose flour
1¼ cups confectioners' sugar
2 tablespoons pure vanilla extract
1 tablespoon dark rum, such as Myers's (optional)
2 cups heavy cream
½ teaspoon grated lemon or orange zest

If the ricotta cheese is very wet, place it in a fine-mesh sieve lined with cheesecloth. Place the sieve over a bowl, refrigerate, and drain the ricotta for 2 hours.

Preheat the oven to 325 degrees F.

Completely line an 8-inch springform pan with two overlapping layers of aluminum foil. Grease the foil with the softened butter and dust lightly with flour. Set aside.

Place the eggs in a large bowl. With an electric mixer set on high speed, beat the eggs just to combine, about 10 seconds. Add the ricotta, flour, confectioners' sugar, vanilla, and rum and beat just to combine. Reduce the mixer speed to low and gradually add the heavy cream. Stir in the zest.

Pour the mixture into the prepared springform pan, and bake until the edges of the cake are firm and the top is golden brown, about 1 hour. (If the top begins to brown too quickly, cover the pan with aluminum foil and continue to bake.) Remove the pan from the oven, set it on a wire rack, and allow to cool for 3 to 4 hours. Remove the outer ring of the pan and cut away the foil. Cover and refrigerate the cake for at least 3 hours before serving.

TORTINE DI CIOCCOLATO CALDO

Warm Individual Chocolate Tortes

MAKES 8 SERVINGS

GIANNI: These individual chocolate tortes, or soufflés, were a favorite among the patrons of Le Madri. One good customer, Glenn Dopf, liked them so much that he asked me if there was any way he could have some to serve at home. I devised this recipe so that the soufflés could be prepared in advance and frozen. Whenever Glenn had company coming for dinner, he would drop by the restaurant to pick up several frozen soufflés. He would pop them in the oven twenty minutes before he wanted to serve dessert, sit back, and enjoy the praise of his guests for the wonderful dessert he had made. Glenn and I became very good friends, and he has done much for me since I came to the United States. He is also my son's godfather. Until now I never revealed his soufflé secret!

It is important that the chocolate used to prepare these soufflés contain a high percentage of cocoa butter—at least 52 percent. I recommend bittersweet chocolate produced by Lindt, Valrhona, Callebaut, or Ghirardelli, all widely available in grocery stores.

10 ounces bittersweet chocolate
1½ cups (3 sticks) butter
7 large eggs, separated
1 teaspoon pure vanilla extract
1 teaspoon sifted all-purpose flour
3 tablespoons sugar

Grease 8 individual disposable aluminum tart pans (about 4 inches in diameter, 1⅜ inches deep, capable of holding 1 cup of liquid) with vegetable oil. Set aside.

Fill the bottom of a double boiler with water to a depth just below but not touching the bottom of the insert. Bring the water to a boil over medium-high heat. Place the chocolate in the top of the double boiler and fit the top into the bottom of the pot. Melt the chocolate, stirring frequently. Add the butter, stirring it into the chocolate as it melts. Remove from the heat and transfer to a large bowl. Allow to cool almost to room temperature, about 15 minutes.

Preheat the oven to 400 degrees F.

Whisk the egg yolks, one at a time, into the chocolate mixture. Whisk in the vanilla, then the flour. Set aside.

In a large bowl, beat the egg whites with an electric mixer on high speed until stiff peaks form. With the mixer set on low, gradually blend in the sugar, 1 tablespoon at a time.

Use a rubber spatula to fold half of the egg white mixture into the chocolate mixture. When they are fully incorporated, fold in the remaining egg whites.

Divide the batter evenly among the prepared aluminum pans, filling each one to within ¼ inch of the top. Bake immediately, until a slight crack appears in the top of each soufflé, 10 to 12 minutes.

After a small crack has appeared on top, remove one soufflé from the oven. Gently run a thin, sharp knife around the edge of the soufflé. Turn the soufflé upside down over a plate. A fully cooked soufflé will come out easily. If the soufflé does not come out easily, return it to the oven and let them bake for an additional 2 minutes. Allow the soufflés to rest for 1 minute before serving.

NOTE: To freeze the soufflés for baking at a later time, place the unbaked soufflé-filled tart pans on a baking sheet. Freeze until firm, about 1 hour. Cover the firm soufflés in plastic wrap and transfer to an airtight container and store in the freezer for up to 1 month. When ready to bake, preheat the oven to 350 degrees F. Bake until a slight crack appears in the top of each soufflé, 20 to 25 minutes, and unmold as described above.

VARIATIONS:

- Greasing the tart pans with walnut oil (or any nut oil of your choice) before baking or freezing will subtly change the flavor of the soufflés.
- Chocolate soufflés are delicious served alone, accompanied by a dollop of whipped cream or a small portion of raspberry or strawberry sorbet. In summer, decorate each plate with a few fresh berries and a sprig of mint.

TIRAMISÙ DELLA LIVIA

Livia's Tiramisù

MAKES 10 TO 12 SERVINGS

GIANNI: I prefer my sister Livia's recipe for tiramisù to all others I've tried, and have always received raves when I've included it on a menu. Having tasted her fair share of tiramisù at the homes of friends and relatives, Livia took the elements that she liked best about each recipe (not too sweet, not too heavy, etc.) and incorporated them into a recipe of her own. The most important tip she learned is that the secret to a good tiramisù is a well-beaten egg-and-sugar mixture, which seems to minimize the "eggy" flavor. Livia also suggests that the recipe can be extended to provide more servings by folding whipped cream into the mascarpone along with the egg whites. This recipe is best if made the day before so that the tiramisù has ample time to set. It also freezes well.

The width and length of ladyfinger cookies varies from brand to brand, so the total number of cookies needed to fill a particular baking dish will also vary. Generally one 7-ounce package will fill the rectangular dish recommended here.

4 large eggs, separated
8 tablespoons granulated sugar
1 pound mascarpone cheese
1 cup crushed amaretti cookies (optional)
2 cups brewed espresso coffee
1 tablespoon dark rum, Grand Marnier, or Cointreau
One 7-ounce package ladyfinger cookies
2 tablespoons unsweetened cocoa powder

In a medium-size bowl, beat the egg yolks with 6 tablespoons of the sugar until foamy and pale. Beat in the mascarpone until smooth. Set aside.

In a large bowl, whip the egg whites with an electric mixer. When they are frothy, add the remaining 2 tablespoons sugar. Continue beating until they hold stiff peaks. Fold the egg whites into the mascarpone mixture, then fold in the crushed amaretti cookies. Set aside.

Mix the espresso with the rum in a shallow bowl. Soak each ladyfinger, one at a time, in this mixture until it has softened slightly and absorbed some of the liquid. (The cookies should not be mushy but your fingers should be able to make a light indentation in them.) Arrange the cookies in an 11 × 7 × 2-inch baking dish to form a tightly packed single layer. Use pieces of broken cookies to fill in any gaps. (If the cookies seem dry, a small amount of the coffee mixture may be spooned on top.)

Spread the mascarpone cream mixture evenly over the cookies. Shake the cocoa through a fine-mesh sieve to evenly coat the top. Refrigerate to set for at least 2 hours before serving.

VARIATIONS:

- Instant espresso coffee may be used in place of brewed.
- Decaffeinated espresso may be used.
- *Biscotti Casarecci del Ponticello* (page 294) may be substituted for the ladyfingers.

PERE AL VINO ROSSO CON ZABAGLIONE AL MOSCATO

Poached Pears in Red Wine with Muscat Sabayon

MAKES 4 SERVINGS

GIANNI: When I was growing up, my father and mother worked most nights at our family's trattoria and bar. My aunt Angela needed to keep the children occupied, especially in the winter when it was dark early in the evening and we couldn't play outside. To keep us at the dinner table a little longer, Aunt Angela would poach pears or apples on the wood-burning stove. For a special treat she would whip up a zabaglione because she knew we loved this sweet sauce almost more than the fruit.

These pears may be poached one day in advance. Cool, cover, and refrigerate in their poaching liquid. Return the pears to room temperature and reduce the sauce just before serving.

4 firm, ripe Bosc pears, peeled, stems left intact
¾ cup sugar
3 cups fruity red wine, such as Beaujolais, Merlot, or Dolcetto d'Alba
2 cloves
One 2-inch cinnamon stick
1 loosely packed tablespoon long thin strips lemon zest (from about ½ lemon)

FOR THE ZABAGLIONE:

2 large egg yolks
2 tablespoons plus 1 teaspoon sugar
¼ cup Moscato wine or other sparkling wine
2 tablespoons Marsala wine

Trim the base of the pears so that they will stand upright on a plate. Place the pears in a small saucepan; they should fit snugly. Sprinkle the sugar over the pears, then pour the wine over to cover (water may be added if necessary). Add the cloves, cinnamon stick, and lemon zest. Bring to a boil over medium-high heat. Cover, and reduce the heat to a low simmer. Cook until the pears are still firm but tender when pierced with a knife, about 10 minutes. Remove from the heat and allow the pears to cool in the wine mixture.

Use a slotted spoon to transfer the pears to a plate and set aside, reserving the wine in the saucepan. Over high heat, boil the wine, reducing the liquid to a thick syrup measuring about ¾ cup, 6 to 8 minutes. Strain through a fine-mesh sieve and set aside.

Fill the bottom of a double boiler with water to a depth just below but not touching the bottom of the insert. Bring the water to a boil over medium-high heat. In the top of the double boiler, whisk together the egg yolks, sugar, sparkling wine, and Marsala wine. Reduce the heat to medium to simmer the water. Fit the top of the double boiler into the bottom of the pot and cook the mixture, whisking constantly, until it thickens and becomes frothy and light, about 2 minutes. Remove from the heat immediately. Distribute the zabaglione equally among four dessert plates or shallow bowls. Brush each pear with some of the syrup and place in the center of the zabaglione. Extra syrup may be drizzled on the rim of the plates or bowls. Serve immediately.

VARIATION: This zabaglione may be served as a dessert on its own, garnished with fresh berries or topped with sweet chocolate shavings. Prepare the zabaglione sauce as described in the recipe. Remove from the heat and cool by placing the pan in a large bowl filled with ice and water. With an electric mixer, whip 1 cup heavy cream until stiff peaks form. Fold the whipped cream into the chilled zabaglione. Pour into individual glasses or bowls and refrigerate for at least 1 hour before serving, or prepare one day in advance.

CREMINO DI RICOTTA CON FRUTTA STAGIONALE

Ricotta Cheese with Fresh Fruit

MAKES 6 SERVINGS

GIANNI: This type of dessert was served to us children as a treat. It is similar to ice cream and may be prepared without using a machine. It is delicious topped with any type of fresh berry or sliced soft fruits such as peaches and nectarines.

2 pints fresh raspberries
1⅓ cups sugar
1 tablespoon freshly squeezed lemon juice
1 vanilla bean or 1 teaspoon pure vanilla extract
¾ cup milk
2½ cups ricotta cheese (cow or sheep's milk)

Place the raspberries in a blender or food processor. Add ⅓ cup of the sugar and the lemon juice, and process until smooth. Pass the mixture through a fine-mesh sieve and discard the seeds. Set aside.

Soak the vanilla bean in the milk for 1 hour, or stir the extract into the milk. Place the ricotta in a medium-size bowl. Stir in the milk and remaining 1 cup sugar. Mix until the ingredients are fully combined and smooth. Divide equally among six serving plates. Top with the raspberry sauce, and serve.

VARIATION: This dessert may also be topped with chocolate sauce, chopped nuts, or semisweet chocolate chips.

PESCHE AL VINO

Peaches and Wine

MAKES 4 SERVINGS

JOAN: This is a simple and wonderful summer dessert. I like to serve the peaches in glass goblets with *biscotti* on the side.

Serving this dessert reminds me of Compare Pullano, who was a neighbor and good friend as well as my godfather. He and my dad had an ongoing competition over who could raise the best chickens or make the finest wine. They also loved to show off to each other with examples of their successful gardening, although neither of them would ever admit the success of the other.

One afternoon Compare arrived with a beautiful peach from his garden. Although the peach was bigger than any my father had grown, he was only willing to admit that it was okay. They decided to have a glass of wine and share this peach. My father cut it into several slices and they soaked the slices in their wine for several minutes before eating them. It is an exceptional dessert.

8 medium-size ripe peaches
3 cups dry red wine
1 tablespoon plus 1 teaspoon sugar

Peel the peaches, pit them, and slice into bite-size wedges (you should have about 4 cups). Place in a large bowl and cover with the wine. Sprinkle the sugar on top and gently stir. Cover and leave at room temperature for 3 to 4 hour hours before serving.

Basics

JOAN AND GIANNI: You may already know how to prepare some of the recipes in this section, but we hope you will find these "basics" helpful. We find improvising to be a fun and gratifying part of cooking; any changes on your part will not hurt these unpretentious recipes.

AGLIO ARROSTITO

Roasted Garlic

MAKES 1 HEAD ROASTED GARLIC

GIANNI: Use this roasted garlic in the Puree of White Beans, Rosemary, and Garlic on page 256. You can also spread roasted garlic on toasted bread that has been drizzled with extra virgin olive oil and serve it as an appetizer.

1 large head fresh garlic
1 tablespoon olive oil
¼ teaspoon kosher salt

Preheat the oven to 350 degrees F.

Cut off and discard the top of the head of garlic, slicing through about ¼ inch of the central cloves. Rub the garlic with the olive oil and sprinkle with the salt. Place in a small baking dish and cook until aromatic and lightly browned, about 1½ hours.

VINAIGRETTE ALL'ITALIANA

Basic Vinaigrette

MAKES ½ CUP

JOAN: I prepare this basic dressing almost every day to serve over a simple green salad. Stan and I maintain the Italian tradition of eating salad at the end of the meal. I think salad eaten at this point makes you feel less full, especially when tossed with a light dressing such as this one. I prepare the dressing in the bowl I plan to toss the salad in. Just before serving I give the dressing a fresh whisk and then toss it with the greens. This recipe makes enough dressing for about ½ pound of salad greens.

This is also a delicious dressing for a salad my mother-in-law prepared. In the early spring when the family went for car rides, she would stop at different fields to hunt for dandelion greens. She would select only those greens that were still tender and had not yet flowered, cutting them out of the ground with a knife and stashing them in a bag. At home the dandelions were trimmed to remove any flower buds or roots, and then they were soaked in very cold tap water before being patted dry. One or two sliced hard-boiled eggs were added to the greens. This salad was a treat because the fresh tart greens were available for only a few weeks of the year.

My mother also gathered fresh dandelion greens. She would cook them in salted boiling water, drain them, and then dress them with freshly sautéed sliced garlic and olive oil. I like them prepared either way, and in the early spring I can often find dandelions at greenmarkets or at vegetable stands along Arthur Avenue in the Bronx.

½ small clove garlic, peeled
2 teaspoons kosher salt
Freshly ground black pepper
½ teaspoon dry mustard
2 tablespoons red wine vinegar
¼ cup extra virgin olive oil

Place the garlic and salt in the bottom of a salad bowl. Crush the garlic with the flat side of a knife blade and mash it into the salt to release its flavor. Whisk in pepper to taste, the mustard, and the vinegar. Then gradually whisk in the olive oil. Set aside for a few minutes before adding the salad greens. Toss to evenly coat with the dressing. Serve immediately.

VARIATIONS:

- The dry ingredients may be combined in the salad bowl several hours before serving. Whisk in the vinegar and oil just before adding the greens.
- 1 tablespoon balsamic vinegar may be substituted for 1 tablespoon of the red wine vinegar, or all balsamic vinegar may be used instead of the red wine vinegar.

VINAIGRETTE ALLO SCALOGNO

Sherry Shallot Vinaigrette

MAKES 1 CUP

GIANNI: In the summertime when tender fresh herbs are readily available, I like to select a few and add them to a salad composed of mixed lettuces. The herbs' colors blend into the salad but their flavors provide little surprises for your taste buds. Select several leaves of basil, tarragon, chives, Italian parsley, and sage. You may want to begin with individual herbs to see which you like best and then experiment with different combinations and quantities. Slice the herbs into long, thin strips and add them to the salad just before tossing with the dressing. Garnish with edible flowers such as nasturtiums, calendulas, or marigolds.

This dressing is appropriate for any simple green salad, and I also like to use it on the Arugula with Prosciutto, Pears, and Parmesan salad on page 62. It may be stored for up to two weeks in the refrigerator. However, the shallots should be removed after one day; this may be done by straining the dressing through a fine-mesh sieve. Allow the dressing to return to room temperature before whisking briskly and serving over tossed greens.

1 shallot, diced
1 tablespoon Dijon mustard
¼ cup sherry vinegar
½ teaspoon kosher salt
Freshly ground black pepper
¼ cup canola oil
3 tablespoons extra virgin olive oil
1 tablespoon hot water

In a small bowl or widemouthed jar, whisk together the shallot, mustard, vinegar, salt, and pepper. Slowly add the canola oil, olive oil, and finally the hot water, whisking to make a smooth, emulsified dressing. Set aside until needed.

OLIO AL BALSAMICO PER PESCE AL VAPORE O VEGETALI

Balsamic Herb Oil for Steamed Fish or Vegetables

MAKES ABOUT 1½ CUPS

GIANNI: This versatile sauce is wonderful on simple steamed, grilled, or broiled fish. Spoon some over grilled lamb or chicken breast, or toss with steamed vegetables or grilled or roasted mushrooms.

Be certain to use only fresh herbs when preparing this recipe. Allow the oil to marinate for at least one day at room temperature before serving. After three days, strain the dressing through a fine-mesh sieve and discard the herbs and garlic. The strained oil may be stored in a covered container in the refrigerator for up to three months. Return it to room temperature before serving.

½ cup balsamic vinegar
1 tablespoon freshly squeezed lemon juice
1 teaspoon kosher salt
¼ teaspoon freshly ground black pepper
1 cup extra virgin olive oil
Two 5-inch sprigs fresh chives
One 5-inch sprig fresh rosemary
One 5-inch sprig fresh thyme
One 5-inch sprig fresh oregano
1 bay leaf
3 stems fresh parsley
1 clove garlic, cut in half
1 teaspoon peeled and chopped fresh ginger (optional)

In a stainless steel bowl, whisk together the vinegar, lemon juice, salt, and pepper. While you continue to whisk, add the olive oil in a steady stream. Add the chives, rosemary, thyme, oregano, bay leaf, parsley, garlic, and ginger. Let steep at room temperature for 1 day after which store in the refrigerator for up to 3 days. After 3 days, strain through a fine-mesh sieve lined with cheesecloth to remove all the aromatics, discard them, and store the oil in a covered jar in the refrigerator. Return to room temperature and whisk before using.

OLIO ALL'AGLIO E ROSMARINO

Garlic Rosemary Oil

MAKES 2 CUPS

GIANNI: You may keep this oil in a bottle stored in the refrigerator for quite a long time. Serve it on grilled meat or fish. It is also delicious to dip pieces of fresh bread into this flavored oil.

12 cloves garlic, peeled
Two 5-inch sprigs fresh rosemary
2 cups olive oil or canola oil

Place all of the ingredients in a small saucepan set over medium-high heat. Clip a deep-fry thermometer onto the side of the pan, making sure that the end is in the oil but not resting on the bottom of the pan. Bring the oil to a boil and continue to boil until the thermometer registers between 220 and 250 degrees F.

Reduce the heat to maintain it between 220 and 250 degrees F for 10 minutes. The garlic will begin to color but it shouldn't brown. If the oil exceeds this temperature range, simply remove the saucepan from the heat and allow it to cool. Return the pan to the heat when the oil is closer to the mark of 220 degrees F. After 10 minutes, remove the oil from the heat and set it aside to cool. Strain the cooled oil through a fine-mesh sieve lined with cheesecloth. Discard the garlic and rosemary.

Store in an airtight container in the refrigerator for up to 3 months. Return to room temperature before serving.

OLIO AL POMODORO E BASILICO

Fresh Tomato Basil Oil

MAKES ABOUT 2½ CUPS

GIANNI: This oil tastes like pure summer in a bottle. Serve it over poached or grilled fish, or drizzle it over mozzarella or ricotta cheese. It is also delicious to dip pieces of fresh bread into this flavored oil. It may be stored in the refrigerator for up to three months.

1 pound ripe tomatoes, seeded and coarsely chopped
1 cup packed fresh basil leaves
1 teaspoon red pepper flakes
5 cloves garlic, peeled
3½ cups olive oil

Place all of the ingredients in a medium-size saucepan set over medium-high heat. Clip a deep-fry thermometer onto the side of the pan, making sure that the end is in the oil but not resting on the bottom of the pan. Bring the oil to a boil and continue to boil until the thermometer registers between 220 and 250 degrees F.

Reduce the heat to maintain it between 220 and 250 degrees F for 10 minutes. The garlic will begin to color but it should not brown. Stir occasionally to make sure none of the ingredients are sticking to the bottom of the pan. If the oil exceeds this temperature range, simply remove the saucepan from the heat and allow it to cool. Return the pan to the heat when the oil is closer to the mark of 220 degrees F. After 10 minutes, remove the oil from the heat and set it aside to cool. Strain the cooled oil through a fine-mesh sieve lined with cheesecloth. Discard the garlic, herbs, and tomatoes.

Store in an airtight container in the refrigerator for up to 3 months. Return to room temperature before serving.

SALSA PER BISTECCA

Steak Sauce

MAKES ABOUT 1 CUP; ENOUGH FOR 6 SERVINGS

STAN: The Tucci family often enjoyed grilled steaks topped with this homemade sauce at the Politi camp in Roxbury, Vermont. My aunt Maria Politi is credited with creating this recipe, which has become a family staple.

JOAN: I recommend preparing this sauce with a high-quality, flavorful red wine vinegar that is not too acidic. It may be prepared several hours in advance and set aside at room temperature. Or store it in the refrigerator for up to a week. Return it to room temperature before serving.

1 cup olive oil
1 tablespoon red wine vinegar
1 tablespoon chopped fresh parsley leaves
1 clove garlic, peeled and finely diced
1 teaspoon chopped fresh oregano leaves
Kosher salt and freshly ground black pepper

Place the olive oil, vinegar, parsley, garlic, and oregano in a 2-cup jar. Cover, and shake to mix well. Season with salt and pepper and shake again. Set aside until ready to serve, making sure to shake well before using.

SALSA PEVERADA

An Unusual and Tasty Salsa for Beans

MAKES 4 TO 6 SERVINGS

GIANNI: I mix about half a cup of this sauce into two cups of warm or room-temperature beans—such as black beans or kidney beans—and serve it as part of a luncheon or *antipasto* spread. It is also good spread on bruschetta and served with a drink before dinner. This sauce freezes well.

½ cup plus 3 tablespoons extra virgin olive oil
1 cup thinly sliced onions
2 tablespoons chopped fresh parsley leaves
2 teaspoons chopped fresh sage leaves
¼ pound chicken livers, trimmed of membranes and roughly chopped (about ½ cup)
1 cup roughly chopped soppressata or other hard salami (about ¼ pound)
2 tablespoons dry white wine
Kosher salt and freshly ground black pepper
2 tablespoons raisins, softened in hot water to cover for 5 minutes and drained
1 teaspoon grated lemon zest
¼ cup red wine vinegar

Warm 3 tablespoons of the olive oil in a sauté pan set over medium-high heat. Add the onions and cook, stirring, until softened, about 2 minutes. Stir in the parsley and sage, increase the heat to high, and add the chicken livers and salami. Cook, stirring constantly, until the livers are cooked and the salami is warmed through, about 3 minutes. Add the wine, and season with salt and pepper. When the wine has evaporated, stir in the raisins and warm through, about 2 minutes. Remove from the heat and stir in the lemon zest.

Spoon the sauce into a food processor or blender. With the machine running, add the vinegar and remaining ½ cup olive oil. Puree to create a thick sauce.

Index

Page numbers in *italics* refer to illustrations.